First and Last Things

First and Last Things

RICHARD
HOGGART

AURUM PRESS

First published in Great Britain
1999 by Aurum Press Ltd
25 Bedford Avenue, London WC1B 3AT

A catalogue record for this book is available from the British Library.

ISBN 1 85410 660 0

1 3 5 7 9 10 8 6 4 2
1999 2001 2003 2002 2000

Design by Roger Lightfoot
Printed in Great Britain by
MPG Books Ltd, Bodmin

Contents

Acknowledgements

The works of most authors quoted here are out of copyright. The quotations from modern authors are so small as to fall well within normally accepted limits for use in this type of book. I am, of course, very grateful to the authors (or their executors) and their publishers, who are:

Edward Arnold, Allen Lane, Basil Blackwell, Cambridge University Press, Jonathan Cape, Chapman and Hall, Chatto & Windus, Clarendon Press, Constable, Faber & Faber, the Fabian Society, George Allen and Unwin, Heinemann, Knopf, Little, Brown, Macmillan, Merlin, John Murray, Nelson, Norton, Oxford University Press, Penguin, Polity, Routledge, Secker and Warburg, Viking, Yale University Press.

Among translators, I am particularly indebted to Dr M. A. Screech for his monumental edition of Montaigne.

Many people have given help, large and small, over the years. I am much indebted to: Stefan Collini, Bernard Crick, Geoffrey Goodman, John Gordon, Alex Graham, Stephen Hearst, Douglas Johnson, Graham Martin, Muriel McNaughton, John Miller, Toby Mundy and Rob Watt; and to two friends now dead, Catharine Carver and John Wilson.

I owe special thanks to Piers Burnett, Karen Ings and all at Aurum; and to my agent Mike Shaw, who never wavered in his confidence in what would finally emerge.

As on other such occasions, my wife Mary and our three children have been constant and invaluable supports.

For Mary – as always

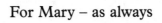

'The present life of men on earth [is] as if . . . you sit feasting . . . and a single sparrow should fly swiftly into the Hall, and coming in at one door, instantly fly out through another.'

BEDE

'The universe is transformation; our life is what our thoughts make it.'

MARCUS AURELIUS

'What can be said at all, can be said clearly.'

WITTGENSTEIN

Foreword

Origins

WHILST WRITING THIS book, I found myself wondering whether it ought to have a preliminary note, much like those Health Warnings on cigarette packets: 'WARNING – NOT TO BE READ BY ANYONE UNDER 55'. But perhaps not. More and more of us are now crossing that threshold into retirement. Others who are not there yet soon will be, and might be a little interested in these pages.

A possible minimum age for reading such a book, sadly but I hope mistakenly, recalls also that for many younger readers – from twenty to fifty-odd, say – the discussion of shared values or virtues might seem irredeemably old-fashioned, beside the point, not related to 'the real world' they believe they inhabit. 'Who are you to say that any one book is better than another, George Eliot better than the latest best-seller?', I am regularly asked after giving a talk about literature.

The book's origins are mixed. The main impulse was the attempt to find our mother's grave, which is described in the Prologue. That led to thinking about my recurrent interests over the years, and especially about the hold of the idea and the reality of family life.

Chesterton called all this the landscape of memory. For George Eliot it was the invisible network of the inner mind.

A casual remark by a friend gave another push. He remarked on my frequent use of quotations from all kinds of writers. That reinforced the search for a pattern of principal concerns, for it soon became clear that my favourite quotations mirrored and gave body to such a pattern.

Even at this late stage, I became increasingly impressed by the ways in which writers, and especially poets, have over the centuries caught our common experiences in what Auden briskly called 'memorable speech', and by the extent to which my own imagination is by now inextricably literary. Thought weaves all the time between the ideas themselves and literary expressions of them, most of which seem to me considerable and rightly to be remembered. They act as props of the imagination.

Graham Greene thought aphorisms almost always meaningless generalisations. It is true that even in the greatest writers they sometimes seem at first banal, though banality in unforgettable form. They express much of the banality, the ordinariness, of our lives. They say: 'Just remember; these are among the ground-rules.' Such truths, even the most apparently obvious, have to be rediscovered in each generation, even by those so generation-conscious that they often assume that no truths are carried over ('Of course, in our generation we no longer assume . . .'). Later, they may realise that some aphorisms still hit them hard. The main elements – stresses, sorrows, pleasures, challenges – in our lives do not greatly change; 'progress' is not in this vocabulary. As a result, those epigrams we find most engrossing become like well-rubbed pebbles in the pockets of the mind. Low down, but always there. Indelibly ours; not the result of casual cherry-picking.

Finally, I realised as I went along and as never before, the special power a handful of authors hold for me. Of these, Auden is pre-eminent. I can imagine some readers expostulating: 'What! Auden again.' I apologise for that. Still, Auden was a major poet of our time and a considerable intellect; not a common combination. He was the first poet I 'made my own' in late adolescence, and the one I have since lived with more than with any other modern author.

In what is likely to be a final gathering together of main themes, I have had to include some about which I have written earlier, but not many, and those almost always approached from new angles.

To assemble 'main interests' sounds slightly flaccid, as if it might list one's hobbies. I mean rather those interests, private or public, which have been steadily with me throughout life. In putting such things down and trying to set them in order one is always looking for a clearer sense of identity. So this architecture – well, shape – becomes more than usually important.

In the end, I decided to put first the most fundamental questions – though some of them I have relatively neglected until latterly – of belief, unbelief and morals. 'Living a moral life in a godless age', a friend called this. That became Part One.

From there, in Part Two, to the day-by-day social and political life. And so, in Part Three, to the more sensuous, the earthy aspects, of living; some of which we often prefer not to mention.

On reading the typescript, a colleague said that the book is a mixture of Memoir, Manifesto and Meditation (Reflection, I would prefer to say, choosing a more secular word). In that perspective the first three parts are a mixture of reflection and manifesto. Parts Four and Five mix memoir and reflection; they ask, with T. S. Eliot: 'What are the roots that clutch?' That, in general, is how the shape has turned out.

Richard Hoggart
Farnham, 1995–9

First and Last Things

Prologue

Looking for the Grave

THE DEATH CERTIFICATE, when we finally acquired one a year or so ago, said that Adelaide (an error; her name was 'Adeline') Emma Hoggart had died at the age of forty-six, and was buried on 17 February 1927. The cause of death, translated, was tuberculosis; she seems to have died on the fifteenth; the address given as her 'abode' was '123 Beckett Street', which was and is the enormous St James' Infirmary in a grim part of North Leeds; a delicate touch.

Two days from death to burial in the local churchyard; a rapid procedure. Especially in comparison with ours; sixty-seven years had passed before one of us even thought of enquiring. Tom, the oldest of the three, was by then recently dead. He was the only one who remembered the funeral and holding Molly and me on each hand – before we were rushed away to Grandma's house on the other side of town, to working-class Hunslet.

Tom also vaguely remembered our father tossing him up and down. None of us knew his date of death; presumably five or six years before our mother's. The three of us remembered our mother in the selective and highlighted way which memory imposes: as gentle, soft-spoken, firm in controlling bad behaviour – and *down*, inescapably in low spirits. A consumptive combination.

Another memory now surfaces, like a black tadpole; it was sharp and sad when I wrote of it almost ten years ago. Yet it has only now, as I finish this Prologue months after I began it,

1

wriggled out again. It had given a slightly disconcerting shock to a child.

Her face had become heavily lined, of course. But the lines were ingrained, dark grey; from years of cold-water washes. She could have boiled a kettle on the one gas ring but would not have not felt able to afford that. And must have hated the fact.

What if neither had died? What sort of life would we all have had? What relationships? The Morels of *Sons and Lovers* always surface when I wonder about that. A father not of the rough working class but very much a working-class NCO type. A more genteel mother. Tensions?

What had set firmly before our mother died was a typecasting of the three of us across the extended family: Tom quiet, serious, reliable, a model older brother; Molly rather frail and to be sheltered; me 'a bit of a lad', which meant 'something of a handful', but not ill-intentioned, not 'a problem'. Those were the common tags until all the generation before us had died.

We did not see again that bare little stone courtyard cottage in Potternewton, a part of Chapeltown; the poverty-stricken widow and her kids had gone; it would revert to a landlord of whom we knew nothing. By the evening of that day we reached our separate destinations, Molly and I to families of Hoggart relatives in Leeds, Tom to an aunt in Sheffield who had eleven children. A twelfth 'wouldn't make much difference', but it was still a kindness. Our mother's relatives, the Longs from Liverpool, mid-middle-class shopkeepers and the like, made no offers.

Astonishing that during all the years afterwards not one of us asked for her death certificate so as to have details of where she was buried. Even more astonishing is that, as I have just now rediscovered, I wrote only ten years ago that I would not try to find out where she had died. 'Probably St James',' I said rather offhandedly. I now find that almost inexplicable, even perhaps a matter for guilt; especially since the past has always been a pre-occupation, insistently present to me, marked by the sense of decades passing like the chapters of a puzzling book turning over of their own accord. Why didn't one of us do something about finding exactly where the mother who had so suddenly left us had been put into the ground?

Going round and round the question ever since having the death certificate, I can only conclude, though insecurely, that we were all suffering from what today would undoubtedly be called 'trauma'; that we were frozen within, lost. It had been, it had had to be, a very enclosed home, we had clustered round her from the moment she had been widowed, striving to manage on a pound a week from the City Guardians (Public Assistance). From the moment we turned away from the grave we had blotted it out, or just let it sink, for all those decades. But why, oh why, had we taken over sixty years to feel able to reach out and make that connection – and even then only when prompted by one of Molly's daughters? I can find no wholly satisfactory answer, only that rather fashionable excuse above, 'trauma', which is a fancy way of saying 'shock', and that is obvious.

The constant self-censorship of memory; and the inaccuracies. I thought I was the one who had found her dying on the clip-rug in front of the fireplace; Molly seems to remember that she did. One of us has taken over the memory from the other, absorbed and adopted it.

Now that I had the death certificate, I set off to find the grave. That proved much more difficult than the first step and a minor example of the ways of price-conscious, end-of-century England. It took several weeks for the Records Office up there to respond to the question: just where in that graveyard is our mother buried? They couldn't easily say, since the records were not yet computerised. They could put someone to searching for the entry by hand, but I would have to pay that person by the hour. One would have thought that an answer such as that would have stuck in the throat of the minor official who had to send it.

I told the town clerk that this response seemed not only dilatory but bureaucratically unfeeling. What if an old person living on only a state pension had sought the information? The town clerk agreed and told the Records Office so; they reacted smartly. Well, smartly for them – in two or three more weeks.

They said they had now discovered that no records were kept of that particular cemetery. Perhaps the vicar of St Michael's had them.

The vicar was quick and helpful; before eight o'clock on the morning he had my letter, he telephoned to say that the city had taken over the graveyard some decades ago, when his church had been rebuilt a mile away; he had no records.

So that was why, with a friend, on a cold, grey and dank day, I sought the graveyard in a Potternewton now tatty, run-down, ridden with drugs and prostitution, one of the Yorkshire Ripper's haunts. The front of the churchyard was almost hidden behind a façade of shops which mirrored the district, knew the tastes and limits of their customers: mostly cut-price.

Once inside, we found a desert, a desolation. There had been, near the front, a few fairly expensive graves; expensive for that area. The marble from those – we used to play on some we called 'potted meat', tan-coloured slabs – had long gone and only splinters remained. Hardy's phlegmatic acceptance – 'Why should death rob life of fourpence?' – as skilled urban theft. The rest for almost 100 yards back was all broken flat stones and what once were uprights with their inscriptions. A scatter of used syringes and used condoms; a few ragged trees wept over it all.

We looked as closely as we could but found no 'Hoggart'. Then my friend said what I had not had the wit or the wish to recognise. That area of dirty, damp, dogshit-spattered earth, a few yards wide and long, up against the far back wall, would be where they put the paupers. But no markers, not even a simple marker for each plot recording which half-dozen had gone into the one hole. The casual, blind cruelties some local authorities could commit!

I heard sometime later about what seemed to be called 'Penny Plots': spare land near the hospital was, by agreement with the local authority, used for pauper burials. I do not know if that story is true and, even if so, it would not seem to apply to our mother's burial, since her death certificate places her in St Michael's. Which was marginally less shocking.

By this time on that bitter day I was not near tears, but just stood there suffused with grief and dimly hoping for the way to a sort of expiation; at the thought of that family, the children dispersed and the mother buried, all within two days, and no record at all. Somewhere in that few square yards of mucky mud she lay, had lain for more than six decades, and I was only now paying some sort of due.

There then came to me, unexpected and unsought, the picture of a skeletal figure, deep down but facing upward, still connected, still belonging, after all those years.

I have felt the need to say all this for two reasons: because, as I said in the Foreword, that belated search for our mother, coming to the fore as I went into full old age, was one – perhaps the main – impulse which set off this book; and that, thinking over it all, I now realise how strong a force the empty end of that search was in making me try to think more clearly about the mosaic of interests, of likings and dislikings, experiences good and bad, relatives and revelations, which go, year after year, towards composing what we call a personality, a character. Given my – our – deprivation, the sense of the place of family life is particularly important.

So there it was; that sad walk in Potternewton was my true moment of beginning.

PART ONE

THE GRAND PERHAPS!*

That fruitless visit to the cemetery set off an unusual and unusually long wondering about unworldly things.

In the course of it I realised for the first time that people who habitually live within that condition of thought which can be loosely called the metaphysical, of whom I am not one, have always seemed superior, probably in intellect and certainly in the setting of their intellectual compasses. Related to that, perhaps essential to it, is often their pleasure and capacity in handling abstract and theoretical ideas.

I frequently remember Bishop Berkeley's assertion that he who has not meditated much upon God, the human mind and the *summum bonum* may possibly make a thriving earthworm, but will most indubitably make a sorry patriot and statesman. I have not habitually thought much about the *summum bonum*

*'Bishop Blougram's Apology', Robert Browning.

except in secular terms, have never had the wish to be a states-man, but refuse the label of a thriving earthworm.

I have always also rejected Brecht's crude 'grub first, then ethics'. Truly, vulgar Marxism. It is one of the few astonishing gifts of humanity that we can occasionally and against all the odds put ethics before bread. My formulation would be 'ethics first, then maybe metaphysics'. The sense of moral compunc-tion, whether honoured or not, insists on putting itself forward. To look back again to the Foreword here, the insistence on 'manifestos' based on ethics is rooted in earthly 'reflections'. Like ragged wallflowers, they push out into a world beset by the galloping, rampant weeds of self-love.

1

'The Heart has its Reasons' On Belief, Unbelief and Morals

'For I will consider my cat Jeoffry
For he is the servant of the Living God, duly
And daily serving him'
Christopher Smart

ORIGINS, ENTRANCES, DEPARTURES. When I was about seven or eight, I suddenly realised the nature of the human universe. It was entirely cyclical (as Vico proposed three hundred years ago, but I only knew even a little of that when I read Joyce's *Finnegan's Wake*). What I decided all on my own was that we never knew as we died that we had died; we simply started a new life at the exact point where we departed the other. Endless successiveness. Not a heartening or saving fancy, and no doubt common, played with by many another child.

I seem unable to acquire religious belief. I do not feel like mocking any form of religion; I do not, like one sucking a hollow tooth, nag at what many would call my deprivation. Did I believe in the Primitive Methodist God during all those childhood years? I think not. I loved my blind-from-birth Sunday-school teacher. I accepted in a sort of uncommitted way what she told me about Him, but that did not connect with any 'felt reality', 'felt sense-experience'. Why did I so regularly go to chapel, then? Because, first, I was told to go. I did not complain. Its small, enclosing world provided treats (especially the Whitsuntide outing), company, a sort of composure, even an order as against

9

the rough markets outside; though not one with much meaning, much grip.

Even now, though I respect friends who remain or have become religious, I do not envy them. I am gently moved by Christopher Smart's homage to his cat Jeoffry. I take serious note of Cardinal Newman's injunction on answerability: 'We can believe what we choose. We are answerable for what we choose to believe.' I cannot accept from him that, if we have no belief in immortality, not only love but every living force maintaining the life of the world would at once be dried up. My whole experience – of love, of self-sacrifice, of the sense of the comic – cries out to reject that conclusion. Wherever else it may come from, the sense of moral responsibility finds one source in the reality of love at least as much as that of cruelty.

Plato's image of the cave, at whose back wall we look, seeing shadows that we assume are 'real' places and events, speaks to me more than early nonconformist imagery. It suggests our world is an illusion, which is what many of us sometimes feel without knowing how and, even less, why. Plato's metaphor is empty unless it is proposing: 'Turn around and face the real world.' But what meaning, what truth, does that 'real', 'true' world have? Have we, if anyone, internally created it? If another, is that creator daemonic or divine?

Before such bewilderment it would be foolish categorically and without qualification to declare myself an atheist. That is to declare something we cannot know. Better to say I am agnostic, but not as an insurance policy in case there does somewhere, sometime, presumably after death, prove to be a Divine Originator.

Such a decision is not ignoble; it could be brave, rather, but not pugnacious. It is better taken in humility, rather than as an act of modified defiance or to hedge one's bets. We may not ourselves be able to declare for a God; but neither can we firmly declare against. This is not to adopt Pascal's wager, in accepting faith: if we are proved right, we are saved; if not, there is no loss. Some of us cannot in comfort place the bet. Nor do we necessarily accept

Emerson's rebuke, that it shows 'temerity . . . to believe in nothing'. Temerity before whom or what?

I do not feel courageous in assuming this position, though probably, to some of my believing friends, I seem rather pigheaded, stubborn, even sinning against the light. After all, many people cleverer than I find no difficulty in believing in the existence of God; if them, why not me? The question does not sufficiently recognise individual responsibility. The position is harder to maintain as you face the decline of the idea of inevitable Progress, as you see the spread of a rootless relativism, and perhaps simply as you grow old. Those same believing friends rebuke me if I say that it must be helpful to feel shriven by having made a sincere confession. It's then just as hard to go on, trying to be more virtuous, they reply. Yes; but if I became a Roman Catholic I would regard that confession and conditional restart as a gift.

As my wife and I travelled, a quarter of a century ago, through the man-rejecting mountains of Afghanistan, our illiterate Muslim driver wound down the car window so as to allow a wasp to escape unharmed, saying as it made away: 'Go with God' – that, too, simple and dignified as it was, sounded like an implicit rebuke to our own position. Yet still . . .

Compared with judgements on Love (more for than against) and on the Family (more against than for) there are in literature, discursive or otherwise, many more assertions of the need to believe than there are defences of doubt. Montaigne asserted that: 'Man is a being born to believe.' Emerson, schoolmasterly again, laid down that the affirmations of the soul insist on belief; a universe quite different from mine.

The procession over the centuries is long, especially from those who came to belief after great turmoil. Mark believed but asked God to help his unbelief; Tertullian believed because it was impossible. Blake's condemnation was frightening: 'The bat that flies at close of eve/Has left the brain that won't believe.' Tennyson believed where he could not prove. Jung was defiant before any questioner: 'I do not believe . . . I know.' Such thoughts of others occur more and more as one grows older.

Some are beautiful, some tantalisingly paradoxical, some opaque; none help much.

So: more thoughts on God, Belief and Death than on almost any other Great Questions: 'The heart has its reasons, of which reason knows nothing' (which could be accepted by an atheist or agnostic); a great many people recall like a charm one translation or another of that thought of Pascal's.

Some elements of Christian belief are very beautiful. I know a few Catholics who accept what one might call an aesthetically Pascalian position: they provisionally believe in the beautiful elements as possible symbols which possibly point to truths we cannot in life 'know'. Very sophisticated. My own imagination recalls at some point every day – driving, shopping, just before sleep – the beauty of the language and music of the hymns and prayers and oratorios which sounded throughout Methodist Hunslet every Sunday: 'O God, our Help in Ages Past'; 'Nearer my God to Thee'; 'Abide with me'; 'Jesu, Lover of my Soul'; 'Rock of Ages'; 'Now the Day is Ended': 'Praise my Soul, the King of Heaven'; 'I know that my Redeemer Liveth'; and even the Bunyanesque/Sally Army clarion call: 'Onward, Christian Soldiers . . .'.

Which brings us back to the origins of belief. Of many much repeated urgings-on-the-way, one said to be used by Catholic priests with young converts or doubters is: there must be a First Cause and that First Cause must be by definition greater than ourselves in intelligence and understanding. The games that First Cause plays are sometimes so odd that one can still withhold belief. I do not fancy profit-and-loss games with a Maker. At this point, Dostoevsky's Ivan Karamazov comes to many minds: Ivan will not accept that the sufferings of children are necessary to pay for truth; even truth is not worth such a price. Related is the conviction that, if I were to join the Roman Catholic church, I would be of the Péguy persuasion.*

---

*Charles Péguy, French Catholic and socialist, refused to accept the doctrine of damnation (as do many today).

That is not a rejection of God, but a doubt about His observed way with the world. Yet for Him to do otherwise with the world, above all to intervene to prevent disasters or cruelties, would be to remove our free will, we are told. That seems right; but it exacts a high price and one often paid by those who can least afford it. Kant turned the thought the other way: how could such people be the children of God? 'Out of the crooked timber of humanity no straight thing can ever be made'.

Yet there is a beauty in the thought (is it developed in Kierkegaard?) that our constant sense of unfinishedness, of falling short, of being alienated from something other and better, is the best evidence we have that we are indeed fallen, cut off from something we endlessly regret losing – from a God who in this way still reminds us of our pre-lapsarian being. But that would not satisfy Ivan Karamazov; or justify horrors not made by man; or explain, except as aberrant, those, to whom we will return, who apparently have no sense of doing wrong, and so no sense of guilt.

The more one looks, the stranger it all seems. So we ricochet: 'We are, I know not how, double in ourselves, so that what we believe we disbelieve, and cannot rid ourselves of what we condemn' (Montaigne). We feel bound by the commitments we make but do not know why we are so bound; in logic, we know why only in a prudential, *quid pro quo* sense, though it feels more than that; and we continue to make commitments. We are, above all, haunted by the disparity between what is and what, again without knowing why, we feel might and even ought, to be. Montaigne again, almost inevitably: 'Man is the only animal that laughs and weeps for he is the only animal that is struck by the difference between what things are and what might have been.'

Some may 'play the odds', carrying on purely humanly whilst assuming they will just be able to get their feet in the door at the last minute. Camden's lines haunted Graham Greene and haunt many another: 'Betwixt the stirrup and the ground/Mercy I asked, mercy I found'; the image of last-minute repentance and possible salvation. Tartly partnered by Augustine's: 'Make me chaste, Lord, but not yet.' The scene of Lord Marchmain's sudden return to belief at the point of death in *Brideshead Revisited* is not persuasive; Pinkie's death in *Brighton Rock* is more challenging.

In the face of such strong, often ambiguous and very widespread feelings, it is not convincing for others simply to assert that man is 'a believing animal'. He may from the beginning of his time have looked up fearfully at the sky or over the ocean or down chasms and into caves. He may then have imagined a superior being whose voice came out of the clouds or the sea or the earthly deeps. That could be no more than aboriginal superstition, not belief as we would recognise it.

Even today, that sense that there is no safe place has to be faced. There is always the precipice, the pit, the marsh, the cliff, the ocean, the chasm; no sense of an abiding stay. I do not always or even much of the time feel like this; I do always feel slightly as if I am walking on the water. I am apparently one of those who seem to have no sense of the numinous, the existential, the transcendental, the awesome, the holy, the immanent. Whatever the dictionaries say, those words are all to me, and I suspect to many like me, without attachable meanings in experience. I feel more than ever now, in the light of the findings of this century's astronomers, almost unbelievably small, but, oddly and, once again, inextricably moral; or, sometimes, moralising.

Romain Rolland believed he could identify the sense of the 'oceanic' in man, of 'eternity'. If one is not aware of ever having that sense one cannot argue. Some of us do have rare moments 'out of this world', which may be interludes of total happiness. Those moments are unheralded and seem to be triggered by a set of explicable earthly circumstances: a fine day, a loving relationship, exceptionally good health, a moment which crystallises all – through touch, taste or sound. I can recall three such moments, one in a spring wood in childhood, one on a day's leave from the Army with Mary just before we married in 1942, and one at my Aunt Lil's deathbed twenty years ago. All three, even the deathbed, gave in different ways a sense that the universe was at bottom good. I do not know why.

Less radiant and also less worldly are those moments, of which I again recall three, when I have felt suspended, out of my physical being, meaninglessly detached from the body, from the mundane sense of myself; when I seemed as unknowing of my own personality and usual consciousness as a baby may be in the first few minutes after birth. But still I was aware that, down there, was that someone whose carapace 'I' (whatever 'I' at such moments meant) normally inhabited. No doubt neurologists have a word for it, and perhaps even an explanation (one which avoids the common packaging word 'syndrome', I hope). It is an entirely puzzling and in part frightening experience, not one which suggests a transcendent being, 'eternity', a godly power. It may be 'oceanic' but the ocean is the elemental, baffling, frightening sea of our primordial sensations.

Related to all this and perhaps more revealing is the capacity to say, though very rarely indeed, for it is an astonishing claim: 'This book has changed my life.' I was startled when E. M. Forster made it (about Leopardi's *The Leopard*); how could any one book change that dry, ironic mind? I could make a much lesser claim for the powerful impression given by a great number of books; by Tawney, Hardy, T. S. Eliot, Auden, for instance. Those modern works are simply picked at this moment from the front of the mind. None have the degree of influence Forster seemed to be pointing towards.

The larger doubts remain. The French express them in the most sophisticated manner. It is not at first entirely clear to me what Camus means by our commitment to struggling 'with all our might against death' – he's hardly the writer to mean 'put your faith in human Progress'. The rest of the passage makes the first part clear: 'Since the order of the world is shaped by death, mightn't it be better for God if we refuse to believe in Him and struggle with all our might against death, without raising our eyes towards the heaven where He sits in silence?' Simone Weil is as gnomic as Emily Dickinson, if less disjointed: 'We have to believe in a God who is like the true God in everything except that he does not exist, for we have not reached the point where God exists . . .'.

'So have I heard/And do in part believe'; like Hamlet, I continue to doubt. Probably many more than readily admit it may at times wish to believe, to acknowledge what Whitman called 'The maker's rage to order'. But with people like me it may be a lesser urge (Whitman might have said 'a related urge'), more a rage or a tic to put the *world* into order, to tidy its awful disconnectednesses. We are not among those, who may be more numerous than we expect, whom, in *Modern Love*, Meredith observes as 'hot for certainties [presumably existential or spiritual] in this our life'. Apparently, we are neither eschatological nor metaphysical; as I have hinted, perhaps by nature.

I feel deeply for and respect Newman in 'distress', when he surveyed this world and saw no reflection of its Creator. No arguments in proof of God's existence then enlightened him or took away his grief.

People such as I appear to belong more to Conrad's world of 'incertitudes': 'My efforts seem unrelated to anything in Heaven and everything under Heaven is impalpable . . . every image floats vaguely in a sea of doubt.' Again, God sitting up there in silence, 'paring his fingernails'.

Then Pascal surfaces yet again, very wittily this time: 'Denying, believing and doubting are to men what running is to horses.' Pascal's wit, as much as the more solemn precepts of some other believers, can bring an agnostic nearer to accepting Christian belief.

Most of us for almost all the time seem to live without 'spiritual horizons'; not only without belief but without much apprehension of unworldly dimensions. Malraux and Nehru in conversation wasted no time on trivialities, phatic communion, but talked of first and last things. Most of us live from little item to little item, day by day encased in creatureliness, from short horizon to short horizon; avoiding making judgements of others if not of ourselves, from one sensible (of the senses) experience to the next – food, sex, family, shopping, beer, sport, good weather, friendship, gossip, television; if we are lucky, interesting work; with probably some sense of neighbourliness but short of feeling 'my brother's keeper' and with hardly any 'Divine Discontent'; making only short-term plans, perhaps thinking only the conventional, kindly or ugly thoughts of our group; if we are lucky, living comfortably enough with the few to whom we are attached or thrown together with. We do not die of 'the roar which lies on the other side of silence'. George Eliot finishes that austere passage in *Middlemarch* by suggesting that most of us are saved from that death of the heart because we are 'well wadded with stupidity'.

That can be too harsh, as harsh as the easy dismissal of the faith of those who have never doubted. To refer to 'a simple faith' can be condescending. Tennyson's lines owe their force, even for unbelievers, to more than their limpidity: 'Leave thou thy sister when she prays/Her early Heaven, her happy views . . .'; do not confuse her with 'shadowed hints'.

It can, incidentally, be surprising, though the surprise is always at least slightly ingenuous and does not last long, to notice again and again that many acknowledged Christians seem distinctly un-Christian in their day-to-day doings, lacking in charity, worldly. Would one distinguish the Christians among us in our usual goings-on, not only in that justifiedly favourite Medusa, the City? The religiose version of being purse-proud, and the two often coexist, is church-proud or chapel-proud; worst of all is the mixing of conventional church or chapel attendance, the sense of social class, and of 'one's' political party.

Montaigne had a crisp judgement: that Christians excel at making enemies; 'zeal never makes anyone go flying towards goodness'.

One hears in the mid-1990s a high-ranking Church of England clergyman assert, with a force which did not lack relish, that Hell is eternal damnation and means precisely and physically that. He quotes in confirmation relevant passages from the

Bible. Fire and torment, for ever. Faced with such an outlook, one admires Péguy all the more. We are rarely asked to face such absolutism, are more at home, though not in agreement, with the misguided vicar who refused to have 'Dad' or 'Grandad' on a churchyard tombstone. Even in the mid-1990s, the superior authorities upheld his foolish religio-gentility.

Some quotations beset agnostics just because we expect little. They may not be true or the whole truth, but they capture something of the truth as we apprehend it. Such as Thoreau's endlessly quoted: 'The mass of men lead lives of quiet desperation.' Even more, for me, Wordsworth's limpid profundity on suffering as 'permanent, obscure and dark' and sharing 'the nature of infinity'.

Then others come to the rescue or give some comfort; comfort is sometimes needed, emptiness is no consolation. Tchekov: 'Man is what he believes', which can be read either way, but puts the responsibility where it should be, as so often with Tchekov; the pattern of our beliefs composes our sense of self, even for agnostics. And the non-believer E. M. Forster, quietly commenting that we would do well to behave *as if* we were immortal and society eternal. I see no logical reason why we should so behave, but am drawn to the moral decency of the idea. That way, 'we will keep more airholes open for the human spirit at its best'; I think I can recognise that. Strangely uplifting, then; a sort of blank cheque drawn on a bank we are not sure exists, but occasionally feel it might, and perhaps ought?

After death, what? It is intensely difficult, though perhaps only a relic of my early Christian education, not to believe that there will be *something* there. In life, I have an unshakeable feeling that those now dead whom I took as models are still listening; and that, when I go, there may be a sort of ante-room where I will find some of them and others of similar persuasions and questionings. And say: 'So this is it, then. I wonder what comes next'. Not actual hellfire, though. And probably no God. Perhaps only the silence of the endless spaces. Or not even the sense of silence; an end of consciousness.

'We die as we live; alone'. Like, I believe, many people, I find it hard to accept both poles of that taut announcement. We do not necessarily live alone; in the physical sense, we obviously die alone. And about afterwards, even for an agnostic, there must be that continuing questioning.

The idea that we shall in the hereafter meet again those we love is powerful in all classes, but perhaps especially in working-class people. Tony Harrison's poetry about his 'Mam and Dad' catches that tenderly. 'Not lost, but gone before' is a favourite farewell inscription; and logically follows the equally often invoked sense of a preparation: 'All these things are sent to try us.' One imagines the wife or husband moving aside to make way for the newly arriving husband or wife. Odd to muse: if there have been two husbands or wives is there ever any strong feeling about who sits on which side?

––––––

It now seems surprising how little influence school and university had on my approach to belief and morals. Elementary school offered, at morning assembly, a watered-down form of Church of England practice. The headmaster of Cockburn High (Grammar) School left soon after I did, to become an Anglican monk. But he was politely quiet about his own beliefs, much more interested in trying to make his young working-class aspirants interested in the intellectual life rather than simply in 'getting on'.

Leeds University, for all its considerable virtues, did not as an institution invite us to consider first and last things. Nor did Hunslet, except for the chapel. Home, though strained, was, when quiet, better than any of these places. It did not encourage us to think of God. How could a home such as that? It offered us, as notions to live by, the aphorisms which then permeated respectable working-class homes: 'Do unto others as you would be done by', 'Live and let live', and all the rest by which private life was to be guided; nothing about the public life; to that we hardly belonged.

Nowadays, we, the agnostics, count among those we most admire George Eliot; standing in the Fellows' Garden at Trinity College, Cambridge, observing how inconceivable is the idea of God, how unbelievable that of Immortality, but how peremptory and absolute that of Duty.

It is not difficult even for an agnostic to agree with Hannah Arendt: 'The pillars of the best-known truths today lie shattered; we need neither criticism nor wise men to shake them any more.' She speaks of the pillars of truth being shattered, not of belief being lost. She may well have implied and assumed this: that truths founded in religion must be the basis of morality, can only be founded in extra-human beliefs. Bertrand Russell plainly avoided words to do with religious conviction and ended with a sort of undeniable, assertive, but abstract and pokerwork-sounding motto: 'Without civic morality communities perish; without personal morality their survival has no value.'

The two – belief and morals – cannot easily be separated. Most moralities professed or neglected by Europeans have been founded on Judaeo/Christian belief. Only a minority would now honour that connection, whether out of lassitude or, more rare, convinced non-conviction. It is by now clear that, except in part from the home, I do not know where the strength of my own sense of moral duty (not always lived up to, as I have already and inevitably admitted) comes from; perhaps from a little of the same stance before life as George Eliot so much more impressively bore; probably, less loftily, from Primitive Methodism as it was mediated by precept at Sunday school, and at home by an upright, village Church of England grandmother. I would not like to call myself 'driven'. But those influences do drive.

'Conscience doth make cowards of us all',* Shakespeare could have added; and, occasionally, it makes stubborn, bloody-minded resisters, rather than cowards – or heroes. Conviction is

*Oddly, Beerbohm echoes this in *King George the Fourth*: 'The non-conformist conscience makes cowards of us all.' Shakespeare's version is grander.

not always or necessarily belief; but neither is it necessarily two-dimensional. And though morals, laid out as statements, almost always seem banal or Western-determined, that impression can be misleading.

We do not know enough about how the revolutionary ideas of major thinkers percolate into the very corners of societies, as with 'God is dead', which has inspired hundreds of related statements. The process of percolation almost certainly involves both distortion and dilution. To change the image: Hannah Arendt's pillars have probably been steadily eroded until they can no longer support any firm beacon of belief.

To a degree, sometimes to a high degree, a range of moral positions may remain with a great many of us after belief has gone. Hannah Arendt may be thought to imply that 'truths' cannot then be retained. This is a common position and no doubt accurate about the minority who have thought much about these things and then lived within their convictions. When the sustaining pillars collapse, they know themselves in the wide-open wastes.

Hannah Arendt wrote from New York. As she knew, a visit to provincial America reveals how little effect all this demolition seems to have had there. Church- and chapel-going are still common, and what are, in most people, Christian ethics are still invoked as bases for conduct. Perhaps conventionally invoked more than practised? In such places, the pillars of the best-known truths may appear not to be 'shattered' – but may by now be plastic substitutes and hollow; percolation may have done its work.

Middle America can show this condition more extensively than any other 'developed' society, but it affects much of Europe, too. One then wants to ask: how far down in most people do these beliefs go? Are they really still 'beliefs', or even solid ethics? Or are they incantations without live connections; habitual conditionings only superficially followed in action, and rarely practised under pressure?

The ways of, predominantly, lower-middle-class churchgoers

are interesting here. One is led to ask: how many really believe, deep down, have accepted the sense of awful commitments rather than of a guarantee whose costs are not greatly exacting. The puzzle is increased when one watches, at a Sainsbury's in a middle-class town, the queue of neatly dressed women, many (in Farnham) likely to be church- or chapel-goers, buying tickets – usually in the plural – for the National Lottery. What relation can there be between the professed belief and the actual wild, magical gamble (to talk of 'a little flutter' is simply an excuse)? This is at bottom a reversal, technologically corralled week by week, to the exercise of elemental hopeless hope.

As for likely action under pressure, there comes to mind, notably, Richard Baxter's question: 'What would a serious Christian belief do, if God's law against self-murder did not restrain?' Which echoes Hamlet on 'His canon 'gainst self-slaughter'; and the magnificent, as much Christian as stoical, injunction from *King Lear*: 'Men must endure/Their going hence, even as their coming hither:/Ripeness is all.' Right up to and through middle age, those lines, that stance, seemed to me unforgettable, affordable, admirable and enforcing; less so now, as one friend after another dies of cancer.

So, an English Primitive Methodist, or other Christian, background of regular chapel and Sunday-school attendance, now long fallen away, still leaves me and many others with a sense of 'right' conduct, many of whose origins lie plainly within those schoolings. There is a sense of Something to be kept up, perhaps also Something to be accounted for – to Someone. A sense of falling off or away, and so at times of guilt. Very individual and Protestant, as befits one of Luther's footsoldiers. Or is it more deep-seated in my nature than that? It sits also with biting every coin proferred by any collective congregation, and with a deeply rooted suspicion of the self-righteousness which can go with that. The idea of women – church- or chapel-goers one and all, I would bet – handing out white feathers during the First World War to men in civvies (whose conditions they could not know) is one of the most blatantly horrible British instances of that self-righteousness in this century.

I have never understood how Wordsworth saw 'good in everything',* though sometimes I half think I do understand. As when I admire those who see 'the good side of everyone', that fundamental decency my grandmother and some others in my childhood and after – such as my wife's parents – consistently showed. Were they simply lacking sufficient imagination to see the dark side? Not necessarily. Inevitably, they all had known grief and shock. They could have gone the other way, to the dark side; as some do. In my in-laws, the undemonstrative strain in their Lancashire working-class blood was one powerful antidote to overt emotion.

Reading again outstanding nineteenth-century reformers, observing the firmness of moral judgement, the dedication, the conscientious detail, I know that my own ethical framework is a shadow of theirs. Yet it exists. 'Conscience' exists.

Moral convictions of one's own, if they are not to be sadly solipstic, must give rise to trust in others, in others' ability to work by that light too; if only intermittently, by most of us. At this moment I usually remember E. M. Forster's idea of 'rent', paid to sustain the idea of virtue in what might seem unlikely people and places. Masefield has a little-known, curious, odd, but equally apt and homely passage in *Odtar*:

> I have seen flowers come in stony places
> And kind things done by men with ugly faces,
> And the gold cup won by the worst horse at the races,
> So I trust too.

So one comes upon those qualities which I earlier described as banal when simply put down: feeling for others, generosity, charity, no unkindness, malice or snobbery. Very simple and no good as merely laid out like this; they have to be lived out.

*As in *As you Like It*, II.i.12.

One is bound to wonder how far the sense of shared convictions, of 'best-known truths', has by now become fragmented in some parts of society. Here is a small but typical instance. A couple of years ago we were at a county fair in Guildford, in prosperous south-east England. Nearby, two men, each with a boy of about ten, greeted each other. Lower-middle-class minor executives, from the look and sound of them. One, with a macho smile, almost casually set his boy to square up to the other for a fight. The second boy's father then encouraged his son to do the same. It was as if they said to themselves: 'They might as well learn that's the way the world wags. You have to fight your corner or go to the wall.'

It was as if all family influence, all talk, all writing, all efforts at education, all broadcasting about the nature of a civil society had passed them by. Perhaps they and their families had no such hinterland. Perhaps they themselves lived in a totally catch-as-catch-can, aggressive commercial world. Did they conduct their homes according to such principles, in so loveless a way? Or did those attitudes belong to a separate compartment? Did what we saw belong to a code of practice reserved for the world outside? If the schoolteachers tried to do anything to 'gentle' those boys, would they be doing it against the odds, against the fathers' crude machismo? Would some of their teachers by now expect no more, no better? This is the point at which some people – some readers – will interject that most people have to live in 'the real world'; an insensitive and reductive phrase brought into service today whenever any aspect of behaviour is called into question, judged; and which, I suspect, will echo through this book, as the opposition.

If we no longer learn our morals from Church and Chapel, doesn't that duty now fall first, and more strongly than ever, on the family? The answer must be yes. But how many people – from those in tough urban areas about which we hear so much but do so little, up through those lower-middle-class fathers at the Guildford Fair, and so to those among the prosperous middle class who make a lot of money from sharp practice – how many are now offering their children substantial ethical guidance, hand-holds, with which to manage their lives, their attitudes towards others and themselves? Perhaps many – perhaps even most – may not propagate in their children the laws of the jungle, but may lack the conviction firmly to counsel anything more positive. Nor does much in the overall unregulated thrust of society help. Family may not win over classroom, classroom may not win over the cultures of school playground or street corner. Not everywhere; but perhaps – probably, I hope – in more places than we now recognise.

Precepts disconnected from experience are likely to be heard only by those already inclined to listen. The introduction of 'Moral Teaching' in schools is likely to mean: From Stern Injunctions through to Sentimentality, Cracker Mottoes. Morals have to be experienced, felt on the pulses, practised or at least seen in action. The experience of good literature may be an aid here, too, though that is not certain; and few even among the well-educated, except for a small minority, recognise or read good literature (rather than the month's best-seller) today. Is the phrase itself – 'good literature' – still available?

Probably in every age, the models most groups of young people offer to all but the more independent-minded of their members are of styles not substance. The process of fragmenting with coalescing has evidently increased in the last few decades. For evidence, track the sixth-formers of many a 'good' grammar school to their half-hidden lunchtime haunts for fags, pot and Pot Noodles.

This is more and more importantly a multi-divided than it is a multi-cultural society; each part is served relentlessly by commerce, advertising, public relations; by age, by sex, by status; it has no coherent set of guidelines for all as to their behaviour towards others, except those of the current gang or group, the 'everyone's doing it now' pack. But, yes, in some there remain ethical echoes from the past. Perhaps, again, these still affect more people and are stronger than we are led to assume in our darker moments.

If not Church and Chapel, if not the home, then the only generally available source of early moral guidance must be the school, if the teachers will accept that role. Some will not, either from a nervous or stubborn unwillingness to deviate from solely teaching 'their subject', or because they are as puzzled as most others, or on ideological grounds, by which all 'teaching about morals' is seen as a means of sustaining 'the hegemony', propping up a society rotten at the heart. There are then no standards – in life and, it follows, in art; all is a confidence trick. At the extreme, some such teachers' lessons on ethics are to the effect that this is a society with no worthwhile ethics at all.

Some teachers do their utmost, not necessarily to inculcate Christianity, but to argue for the rightness of what had best be called 'humanist' ethics, and, in the best examples, to show those ethics in action day by day. Again, in the light of the prevailing cultures, their efforts may have only limited success, and even less when some of their pupils come from homes and districts which offer no moral guidance by word or, more important, deed. These are recurrent dark thoughts but, given so much evidence, lighter thoughts have to be hard-earned.

This matter, of where and how the moral sense emerges, preoccupied Auden; notably in the figure of his ragged urchin who knew no world where promises are kept or in which one could feel pity for another's grief, could weep because another wept. An evocation of the deserts of the heart, of the lack of an exact moral compass.

Looking across the people I have met in a lifetime, I sometimes wonder whether 'the moral sense' is in some innate, in others not, and hard to convey. If someone is kicked to death without apparent cause or remorse, the kicker is likely to be described as a 'psychotic', which, though it sounds 'professional', can be replaced by the more open words 'psychologically maimed' or 'deranged'; it is no more than a label, does not clarify the nature/nurture question. Can material comfort help the humane spirit to emerge? Was Forster right to say: 'Money pads the edges of things. God help those who have none'? Perhaps, to some extent. Yet there are plenty of well-brought-up and well-to-do ne'er-do-wells, and virtuous poor.

Meanwhile, in 'developed' societies as elsewhere, many forms of cruelty are endemic. How do detectives who regularly deal with the worst cases survive, or some prison warders? Discussing this, a detective said to me: 'You must bear in mind that most criminals are not very bright.' Curiously, that came as a slight relief, obviously to him, and then to me.

Is a developed moral sense a product of intelligence-with-imagination, the capacity to feel another's pain, to empathise, to assume a human 'belonging'? One feels like not trusting anyone who cannot occasionally laugh at the sheer lunatic awful oddity of the world. That ability too is an aspect of the imagination in action. Yet, as I recalled a moment ago, many people neither intellectual nor apparently very imaginative have a lively moral sense. Was Auden's ragged urchin wholly conditioned by family or neighbourhood or the prevailing culture? Or was he by nature incapable of fellow feeling? Auden seems here to place the blame on faulty 'nurture'; there is plenty of evidence elsewhere in his work that he did not underestimate the power of 'nature'. That debate goes on; a particularly rhetorical and combative modern version is to be found in Edward Thompson's 'An Open Letter to Leszek Kolakowski'.

I used to think that the common cry in childhood: 'It isn't fair' indicated an immature refusal to accept the reality of life. 'No, it isn't, and the sooner you realise that the better' seemed then a proper, if harsh, response. I now prefer to think of it as a natural and certainly outraged cry: that the world *should* be 'fair'; a moral assertion.

In some people the moral sense does seem innate, of nature, just taken for granted. They are able to say or assume, as though drawing from an elemental source: 'To live is itself a value judgement. To breathe is to judge.' One does wonder, though, whether Camus there meant 'To continue to live . . .'. Such people do not necessarily belong to any formal religion; most seem like that from birth. And some are upheld by a faith, such as the woman we know who was widowed in her thirties and left with two young children, and was struck by a terrible wasting disease in her forties and from then for some decades has been confined to a wheelchair with very few muscular functions working. But she reads and talks and listens with more cheerfulness and enthusiasm and friendliness – at least in public – than most of us muster. She does have that deep religious belief, but I am unwilling to think that is the only foundation for such stoicism in the face of personal tragedy.

Others seem to arrive at that conviction chiefly as a result of reflection on the *summum bonum*. Whitehead was more sure here than many of us can easily be: 'To be a full human agent . . . is to exist in a space defined by distinctions of worth.' Iris Murdoch joined him half a century later in adding that innumerable forms of evaluation haunt our simplest decisions. Dostoevsky's Aloysha has his revelation in adult life, as he awakes from a dream; it had given him 'a passion of pity' for the poor and downtrodden, a feeling he had until then hardly known.

At this point one also remembers Vaclav Havel, who retained in full force, even after years of horrible evidence that individual morality may be a myth, the belief that it does exist, who still saw politics as practical morality, service to the truth, essentially human.

Newman called those with an instinctive faith 'the once-born'. Sometimes, the 'once-born' seem more likely to be dutiful diplomats than explorers of the human condition; or like 'smooth smilers' whom no experience can shake. Yet others, at whom we will look more closely later, are purer spirits.

Behind all said so far is the implication that in some ways the main ethical principles cherished by humans – whether through various religions, which obviously have great differences, or by professed humanists, agnostics or atheists, or by those who think on these things without any beneficial buttressing from belonging to a creed or following a philosophical formula – that these often diverse principles have at their heart a considerable congruity in charity, as in Lear's: 'Oh, reason not the need!;/Allow not nature more than nature needs,/Man's life is cheap as beast's'; which is an archetypal first-marker, and is partnered by 'There but for the grace of God go I', another basic cutting-down-to-size.

At another extreme are the *unco guid*, the over-insistent moralists, who clutch their own sense of virtue around them like a drab but all-enveloping cloak. They turn every whim and small event into a moral issue. They are masters of the mixed mode, of critical language and the minatory tone of voice. They have to inhabit a world totally secure in its own rightness. Even the smallest fancy or prejudice must be set against the one right way; or chaos would come again. They have a thousand ways of rejecting with moral scorn anything of which they disapprove or simply do not like, from beer to a choice of wallpaper (someone else's choice). I was brought up in the company of one such and can still hear the grim voice like the growl of a dog which won't let go.

An archdeacon insists with vigour that, literally, for a man to look on a woman with lust, or vice versa, is as sinful as actually to commit adultery. That is itself an immoral position-by-prescription. The moral position is to recognise that either the man or woman may have been taken by surprise by the old Adam or Eve but has not even contemplated doing anything about it. That's a virtue – the choice of fidelity against temptation – which such elders of the Church do not understand. 'Nothing is more unpleasant than a virtuous person with a mean mind', Pascal noted; and Bagehot: 'We never do evil so fully and cheerfully as when we do it out of conscience.'

In reverse: to understand all is not to forgive all and, without repentance, may encourage worse. There is a sort of over-easy kindness, a self-indulgent readiness to forgive; and, conversely, a virtuous severity which knows better than other people what is good for them. At the extreme, such people are likely to refuse a cigarette to someone dying of cancer.

Tangentially, the odd, old feeling remains: that a person who

29

writes elegantly and perhaps persuasively about morals, or creates such dilemmas in dramatic action, will be for that a better person. Not so. We can see the virtuous road; and pass by on the other side. That is, once again, our freedom of choice. But perhaps something remains, to nag. It exists, and we fall short; that may be the half-hidden feeling, as we brush it away again. I wrote of this at greater length in an earlier book and expect to do so again; clearly, it occupies me.

One comes back to less complex things, in which our behaviour towards others and just as much to ourselves is being constantly tested, day by day. Basic tests? In whose examination system? Shall we agree on this, from John Rawls, at least for a start: 'The best way to cause people long-lasting pain is to humiliate them by making the things that seem most important to them look futile, obsolete and powerless.' The due, uninvoked word behind that assertion is 'charity', that moving out by the spirit to a soul in misery which can sometimes prompt even the most dried-up personality to an act of love. As when, in *Middlemarch,* the desiccated stick Casaubon, his marriage a sham, comes upon his young wife Dorothea sitting downstairs late at night and in despair. At such a moment even the most unresponsive may feel a flow of sympathy. Casaubon, now fully aware of the misery of it all, relaxes his bitter stiffness and most gently urges her to bed.

Then, as ever firmly impressive, Montaigne: 'All moral philosophy is as applicable to a common and private life as to the most splendid.' And again, this time being even more nobly responsible: 'If I can, I will prevent my death from saying anything not first said by my life.' That is some distance away from the stirrup and the ground. More in favour of the long haul. And how impressively he makes a movement from the down-to-earth to the metaphysical, and vice versa.

In such a world, such a troubling and often shaming world, 'endurance' in the face of unacceptable behaviour is not the first word that comes to mind but makes one useful foundation. Arnold, at his most rhetorical, wanted his body to be found by the wall as the fort fell. T. S. Eliot was more resigned, but as firm: 'For us, there is only the trying. The rest is not our business.' Kipling is rightly remembered for his advice after failures: 'Stoop and build them up, with worn-out tools.' Shakespeare's *Henry V* had his tight motto: 'Holdfast is the only dog, my duck.' To those one can add Cobbett's brisk, almost brusque, straight Englishman's: 'One may not do evil that good may come.' Yes; stand fast for that, so long as one can recognise evil when one sees it.

To go on going on, and to try to keep one's promises: 'To breed an animal with the right to make promises – is not this the paradoxical problem nature has set herself with regard to man?' Long after Nietzsche, the thought has engaged many poets. Auden was lyrically reflective on the cardinal distinction between the repetitive but wordless notes of the birds, and human, promise-laden speech. His friend Hannah Arendt joined him: 'The remedy for . . . the chaotic uncertainty of the future, is contained in the faculty to make and keep promises.' Robert Frost too had promises to keep; and miles to go before he might sleep. I still wonder why, and get no further as to the purpose of the journey.

'You can fetter my leg but Zeus himself can't get the better of my free will'. One remembers here the heart-rending mutual betrayals of the lovers at the end of *1984*; and cannot share Epictetus's conviction.

The most challenging, puzzling and at times inspiring quality of all is 'moral courage'. Not 'physical courage'. That need not be undervalued, has several complex forms and characteristics, but is at bottom simpler than 'moral courage'. Malraux thought it a banal consequence of the feeling of invulnerability. A starkly honest Ingush proverb adds: 'He who thinks of the consequences cannot be brave.' Certainly dramatic heroics seem exceptional; some of those who have experienced the need for courage in war might rather call their response a frozen stubbornness, which may make them just press on, or simply stand their ground.

'Moral courage' fails when, for fear of making others angry or disappointed, we do not tell them the full truth, especially if it casts doubt on their own acts or judgements. 'Moral courage', aided by mental muddle, fails when we utter one or more of the many forms of: 'If I don't do it [act to correct an ill] someone else will'; that can be used to justify ignoring almost anything from petty pilfering to inhumanity. 'Moral courage' fails when we refuse to 'blow the whistle' on corruption we see all around. 'Let someone else do it. I've too much to lose. Anyway, it's not my pigeon.' The examples are endless. Laziness, inertia, fear, self-interest, false pity, all conspire to create the failure to show moral courage. 'Moral courage' is essential in anyone in a 'position of authority'; its failure in just those places is endemic, in the disinclination to defend one's subordinates against one's own superiors, and much else.

A weak hold on the idea of shared values allows that failure to proliferate. Still, underneath we cannot help feeling we have failed, have let down someone else or some principle. Our twistings and turnings then are painful, to watch and to experience. We react angrily against someone who insists that a certain event does raise moral issues.

We who live in the comparatively free and prosperous world, and have 'a marketable skill' which will always be likely to ensure a job, should appreciate with great humility our freedom to exercise moral courage. It is easier to stand up to a bullying boss if you know you can take your cards and find a job elsewhere. In some countries that amount of courage could be costly or fatal, and only the heroic will be able to practise it, as I found when working for the United Nations. All staff members were 'International Civil Servants', not agents of their own nations. A grand concept. But those most under regular pressure from the embassies of their native countries, and who knew what might be waiting for them back home if they refused to do as they were told, sometimes thought my stubborn resistances came easily, were ethically smug.

One member of my staff, whom I rebuked for changing a resolution after I had passed it for publication, had clearly been put under pressure. He implicitly rebuked me in turn: 'It is perhaps easier for you, after all?'

Such beleaguered people, observing the exercise of what might be moral courage by someone from a more fortunate country, are inclined to call it 'moral posturing', 'easy self-righteousness'. They have a point. For the more fortunate, moral courage and self-regarding obstinacy easily merge; and the obstinacy may be greater than the moral courage. But it may help and, if it is recognised by the actor for what at bottom it may be, can reduce any tendency to self-righteousness.

By now, listening to the believers on the BBC's *Thought for the Day*, both the language and the thought – whether Christian, Muslim or Buddhist – seem almost like foreign languages and ways of thinking (though in some respects Buddhism is the most attractive). Yet some sense of external judgement remains.

How will I, when very ill indeed, face the end? By joining Henry James, after his first stroke, in the expectation of a great adventure, The Real Distinguished Thing now about to begin? By sharing Dr Johnson's dread? More mundanely, by calling out in hospital: 'Nurse, if it gets me better treatment, I'll pay to go private!'? I shall have to wait and see, as ever.

We have to be convinced that Dostoevsky was wrong: 'If God is no longer believed in, then everything is permitted.'

2

On Love of Others and Self-Love

'The least pain in our little finger gives us more concern and
uneasiness than the destruction of millions of our fellow-beings.'
Hazlitt, echoing Dr Johnson on toothache

IT IS OBVIOUS that I cannot speak of 'sin', have no logical,
semantic, or 'spiritual' grounds for using the word. No faith, but
a qualified sense of duty. Which leads me to ask, as often as any
believer, whether we can at least identify an overriding impulse,
a common tap root, in all of us.

The short answer is to be found in the sense of self itself,
whose activities start in self-preservation and move out into
a baroque density of related forms right up to the point at
which the sense of self is in some people transmuted into a self-
forgetful care for others; from awful cruelties to self-sacrifice.

It all leads then to the recognition of congenital failings, from
the simplest and weakest to what others may call 'the evil at the
heart of man'. The evidence of the domination of self is all
around, every day and in every way. As is, much less insistently,
the evidence that we can rise above ourselves: to the disinterested love of others, even of others not linked by blood. This
must be a sombre chapter, except towards the end, when the
saving qualifications are gathered together.

Shakespeare's use of the word 'all' in 'Sin of self-love posses-
seth all mine eye' is not accidental. The levels of self-concern are
in almost all of us boundless. The *Shorter Oxford Dictionary* has
seven long columns of small print on 'self-' compounds. Scott

echoed Shakespeare: one of his characters: 'concentrated all in self'. Self-love is related to self-regard, self-defence, self-protection, self-esteem (which can be upright or a type of pride), self-indulgence, self-justification, self-conceit, self-involvement, self-deceit, self-pride, self-preservation, self-respect (the first so far which is not easily tainted) and many others.

In the 'developed' world, the non-communitarian world, as compared with, let us say, parts of the traditional East, the most powerful impulse of all is individualistic self-justification. The communal East, though, often slips over, as if to the reverse side of a coin, into acts of dreadful individually or group-driven cruelty. In most times and places the constituents of self-love all seem to draw on that common root, a primary law of nature: save yourself. A further irony is that the Siamese twin of that impulse is our infinite capacity for self-forgiveness; it is as if most of us cannot without that partnering continue to live with ourselves.

The French outstrip us in coining punishing epigrams. Pascal is dry: 'Each man is everything to himself, for with his death everything is dead for him'; La Rochefoucauld is terse: 'Self-love is the greatest of all flatterers.' Valéry is more interesting, because puzzling: 'To be sincere means to be the same person when one is with oneself; that is to say, alone . . . but that is all it means.'

First read, that sentence seems positive and simple: to be sincere one must be the same person in company as when alone. It is implied that 'sincere' opinions uttered in a group may in fact be a form of insincerity, of self-promotion. Especially if you then go home and in the privacy of your room say to yourself: 'What a load of nonsense I sold them today.' Another person might reinforce his self-esteem by what could be taken for and might be mock sincerity; but then at home convince himself that he really meant what he said, was dealing straight after all.

The difficulty comes with Valéry's coda: 'that is all it means'. That is sharp, sardonic. Sincerity is then exposed as a dependent quality; one may be sincere about the meanest, the most cruel, the most stupid convictions. It matters little to plead that someone was 'after all, sincere'. Hence, I imagine, Valéry's tart final clause.

Montaigne expected no better from us than the ceaseless pressure towards self-satisfaction: 'The lawless flood of our greed outstrips everything we invent to try and slake it.' He admitted, being fair-minded, that some people are more self-aware than others, more ashamed of this overwhelming drive; and to some extent can control it.

An English example can enter now, with a declaration so flat and final that it tolls like a bell in its insistence on the supremacy of self-regard. So, Nelly Dean, considering the awful passage of life at Wuthering Heights: '"We must all be for ourselves in the long run."'

A less dramatic instance; a contemporary English form of self-justification. As when a practising Christian of the middle class admits, mildly but not very defensively, to taking advantage of some clear privilege (in educational opportunity or job-seeking, perhaps) and adds, as matter-of-factly as if she was observing that we must drive on the left-hand side: 'Ah well, in the end you've got to look after your own, haven't you?' (Nelly Dean's employer three half-days a week, a century and a half later.) The same person may thoroughly hate a cheat. We are back with the double mind, the split conscience, accepting minor personal fiddlings whilst at the same time denouncing them in public matters, and feeling no contradiction.

The instruments of self-love include flattery, humbug, deceit, fake sincerity, self-promotion, false modesty, aggression, lying, cheating for profit, gathering in selected, interested and exclusive cliques and peer groups, and so on and so on. The tools of the old trade.

In *The Neophiliacs*, Christopher Booker, recalling Hobbes somewhat, argues that self-love is a necessary element of the life force, of our need to propagate, to cherish and defend ourselves and our offspring, and that this – rather than anything more admirable – leads eventually to the development of the sense of community. He goes on to say that 'will' in free action, for example, practising sex for fun, perverts the aims of the life force. The free exercise of our desires is itself a form of self-indulgence, an aspect of self-love. Self-protection and wilful self-indulgence serve the same instinct. Yet the sense of 'community', his argument continues, even if it began as naked self-protection, has over millennia come a long way and to the good. It may now include even self-destruction for a common and disinterested cause.

By contrast, Matt Ridley, in *The Origins of Virtue*, sees humans as essentially, not by default, social beings, cooperative. Embedded self-regard leads nowhere. All progress depends on the sense of the social-political, not the personal-solipsistic. Of course, one wishes to believe Ridley; Booker also becomes more positive as his argument develops.

'There are but two schools; one turns the world into me; the other turns me into the world; and the result is the same.' Henry Adams is slightly unclear there. Does he mean that the entirely self-engrossed turn all experience into a poultice for the self? And conversely, that, by being entirely accepting and responsive to the world outside our particular culture, we may turn ourselves into its creature, and not know we have done so? And that both are forms of self-love? Perhaps. One might then have to add, grimly: 'But surely there is a third position?'

It is plain that the label 'self-love' can be no more than a catch-all which gathers together, points to but does nothing to explain, many if not most of our failings: from the smallest act of meanness to the worst excesses of fanaticism, from legitimised institutional cruelty to the underlying lonely despair of the salon frequenter (Prufrock); from a simple 'Thank God it's not me, anyway' to total, self-justified brutality (ethnic cleansing); from the pathetic self-justifications of the lowest little crook to those of the greatest of moral cheats. A complex plant with immensely tough, ramifying roots.

A relatively minor form of self-love can be fearful, afraid of what the neighbours might think, desperate to keep up appearances. Especially if, in an extended sense of the word, those 'neighbours' are today, through mass communications, aurally and visually far more numerous than we have been used to recognising and knowing how to interact with, being 'in touch with'. A distraught couple appear on the television news to ask for help in finding the murderer of their daughter. A heart-rending sight in itself, made heavier in its pathos because the wife had felt it necessary to dress up for the occasion, in twin-set and pearls. Understandable; but it most sadly suggested 'coffee mornings' with the neighbours.

Self-love is the mother of envy, jealousy, resentment, sourness and vengefulness. In those forms, its motto is the mean-spirited: 'There's no smoke without fire', especially drawn into service in cases of suspected adultery or petty theft. All those and other such qualities seek to express themselves, at one particularly low level, through talk about others in phrases, dismissive, reductive, which can be picked up and rolled along with pleasure from mouth to mouth. Their original author is soon forgotten but the remarks linger, become agreed facts, a substitute for personal judgement. There is safety in numbers; few have the strength to break ranks and say 'But this is a false judgement drawn from a faulty reading'. All such meannesses dry up the character of the gossiper, burn out generosity of spirit; they are a mental acid at work. Yet gossip continues to spread, like indelible black ink on a smooth, sloping, but porous surface, easy and quick to be recognised, since its habitual exponents must launch it soon into any relaxed conversation.

This – gossip – is the greatest single social effect of self-love, apart from hypochondria, which too has many varieties and comic/pathetic turns. Gossip is also one of the most depressing. Not anecdotage, which can express a love of the variety, the oddity, the perversity, the comedy and the sadness of life in and for themselves, and need not be unkind. It can be affectionate if the speaker has a good and generous eye for quiddities of incident, speech and gesture.

Yet anecdotage can be a type of vanity too. It can induce the Little Jack Horner mode – 'Oh, what a good boy am I in telling this tale.' It is then funny and also self-deprecating, falsely modest, insidiously ingratiating. This can apply to writing as much as speech.

Unabashed gossip, though, is inherently unkind, doing down; speaking ill of people behind their backs. A main communal tool of self-love, it reduces others by telling stories about their weaknesses, and thus minutely and temporarily reinforces the teller's own weak sense of self. 'Name-dropping', exaggeration, implied boasting and the throwing-in of occasional swear-words as a badge of 'blokeishness'; all those and many others are forms of talking to impress.

Some will often see through our posturings, however self-effacing they may appear to most and to ourselves: 'Our enemy's opinion of us comes closer to the truth than our own.' La Rochefoucauld again, and obvious again, but worth pinning down at this point.

The Americans are second only to the French as aphorists, and can be even more economical. Thoreau had the special metaphoric knack: 'It is as hard to see oneself as to look backward without turning round.' Not as promising for lingering over as some of the French masters, but more memorably pictorial. Emerson comes closer to the French in the hard, unmetaphoric mode: 'It is impossible for a man to be cheated by anyone but himself.'

We hardly ever know what main threads appear in gossip about ourselves: that we are always the last to reach for the restaurant bill, are vain about our hair, nourish a false sense of being passed over, think we are something of a Don Juan. We are never told, except by the frankest of friends or relatives, and then we usually hate them for that, at least for a time – until we have self-diluted the pain to a strength at which we can absorb it. But a sense of these opinions being in the common currency of gossip can sometimes be gained from the almost hidden, but complicit, knowing glance which someone whom you have not met before, but who knows some of your acquaintances, gives you; a belittling prism, a pre-set marking-down.

39

The shock when such opinions leak can be severe . . . even though we may be ourselves convinced that some, though rarely all, are mistaken. It is as if we had been set to make a crayon drawing of ourselves as a bundle of characteristics, and then acquaintances were asked to do the same. We are unlikely to recognise much overlapping. Worst of all is to overhear and perhaps catch a glimpse of ourselves being laughed at, even imitated.

Self-love does not in its origins indicate a disposition to vice; that has other sources, though the congenitally self-deluding may be led that way. Nor does it have much to do with the search for virtue; it is too blindly led for that, but the reaction against it by others may eventually prompt the search for more virtuous, less pulled-by-the-nose behaviour.

Chesterfield wisely warned his son that self-love 'draws a thick veil between us and our faults.' Self-love has an almost limitless range of expressions of tightly closed opinion, which nevertheless run in all directions. It is characteristically provincial, pinched-in, lacking in initiative, fond of ticking off rolling stones.

Self-love can look like self-defence, as in animals, but animals do not practise self-*justification*; they follow their instincts. Animals can draw on self-love in us. In 'Mr Gifil's Love Story', George Eliot nicely noted: 'Animals are such agreeable friends – they ask no questions, they pass no criticisms.' Some people love dogs because they are so evidently dependent and uncritical, even subservient, giving unjudging love, or what looks like love. Others prefer cats because they walk alone, own themselves, keep their distance, are not dependent, do not stroke our self-love, do not offer doggy-devotion. The differences are considerable and basic; yet some people love both.

Self-love has a long and brooding memory. A sudden excessive outburst of rage on what seems a minor matter may indicate that the abuser has been storing resentment about what seem to him slights but which you have not noticed. A long, open conversation is unlikely to yield much light; that kind of resentment is deeply rooted in the offended party's sense of self and puts the alleged offender at a loss. Memories do not and cannot concur and it would be fatal to say: 'All right. I hadn't realised that is how you felt. I do apologise. Please can we now forget it?' That sounds like patronage and does not excuse your failure to speak to him at the last public function, or worse, to introduce him to the important person he saw you talking to. The old-fashioned 'taking offence' and the even more picturesquely archaic, 'bridling', come to mind.

(At this point it occurs to me that some readers may be assuming that all these are habits of my own, disguised by displacement. No. Some are, others are not. I have mixed looking at myself with observing others. They have by now become mixed in my own mind, as they will be by most readers other than those who know me better than I know myself, of whom, as has already been pointed out as a general rule, there are bound to be some.)

At the bottom of attitudes such as these is conceit. Which can express itself, in public gatherings, by contraries; in a false shyness. Let them come to me; if they don't recognise me, so much the worse for them. Or perhaps you are tempted to drop in a word which indicates that you are at least a little bit known, not to be looked down on or ignored. Then there may appear a terrier-like rejection of all public notoriety, and a degree of self-dislike for having cared in the first place.

Self-love can be uncharitable, and the lack of charity leads to that silliest of hardly thinking attitudes: small-scale social misbehaviour, in the lowest to the highest. At the lower level is the public crudeness whereby, as you knock on an office door, a voice from within answers flatly: 'Come.' 'Come in' on a rising note would be different, not needing even a 'please'. The sister to that person is the receptionist who, as you arrive at her desk, does not look up but utters only: 'Yes', which is worse than 'Yes?', though that is rude also. The former manner is that of a boss, probably one who can hardly absorb the fact that he now has an office of his own; the second is the petty functionary's petty showing-off, an interruption to their implied, important busyness.

It is to be wondered that self-love in these circumstances, in this kind of society, can produce in others an elephant's memory for slights, rejections, rebuffs, hurts? Especially when practised by people whose public eminence should rule out such behaviour. As in the cabinet minister – this is one of the devices I have noticed in politicians soon after their accession to office – who has agreed to discuss an issue which closely concerns his group of visitors, but who, like someone who has secretly and deliberately failed to switch on a hidden audio receiver, soon reveals that he is not really listening, is merely waiting until he can dismiss you with a routine 'Thank you. So kind of you to come.' The first clue there is that his eyes do not really focus on you, are as if blind. If they do suddenly click into focus, this indicates that someone has broken through the protective film, taken him on. Roy Shaw and I managed this once, with a very grand secretary of state.

There remains the always surprising fact that, do as we will, some people will take an immediate and as if instinctive dislike to us, from the first moment of the first meeting or from the first page of one of our books, not in reaction to something we might subsequently say or write. This is more than the fact that some well-known people expect instant deference, attention like that of courtiers, and if they do not receive it will turn a cold shoulder; and more than the fact that some women (and presumably some men towards some women), often without knowing it themselves, seem to find some men physically, perhaps sexually, non-existent or off-putting. Those elements may be in play, but there can also be a deeper, probably natural and ineradicable dislike. No evidence; almost animal. It can appear in book reviews, where one sometimes sees, below the dislike of the book which is being judged, an only half-conscious dislike for the author – for his personality as seen in the book, since he may never have been met in person. When it happens 'in person' it can be startling, as when I realised over a committee table, and for no logical reason I could fathom, that Rebecca West's baleful glare was directed at me. Too powerful to be evoked by disagreement over the merits of a particular book, it seemed. Metaphorically, perhaps, the emanation of a deeply off-putting smell.

Gossip and anecdotage come together in one of the commonest forms of self-deceit. You are recounting an event which concerns you, but in which the rights and wrongs may be confused. You tell it in such a way, with such selectiveness, stresses and tones, that your hearer is being invited all the time to accept the whole picture without qualification, is implicitly asked entirely to share your sense of outrage. There are plainly omissions, slantings, a lack of any sense of the other side's case, so that the hearer is bound silently to feel that it couldn't have been just like that. But to interject so as to hint a reservation – nothing so strong as a demurral – is to risk giving great offence; few of us take the risk.

At the very extreme of that line is the person whose sense of being done wrong has reached so neurotic a pitch that he telephones even slight acquaintances to tell his story. Experiences such as this, in which our true reaction is also usually withheld, lead to a feeling that our lives are at times false, untrue to what we like to think is our own upright self. In both of these Ancient Mariner instances, it is useful to remember for our own sake, but even more for the sake of those at the other end of the line, a little-known English expression: 'We should all learn to swallow our own smoke.'

That is related to self-righteousness, which was briefly looked at in the early section on morality. It needs reiterating here, as one of the most advanced forms of self-love, among the hardest to correct and the most unpleasant. It gives its possessor no rest, since he must straighten every jacket in sight, especially those of his immediate family. All in the name of an external virtuous level from which the accused is presumed to have fallen. Very hard to eradicate, this, since it claims to speak on behalf of that external virtue, rather than from the depths of the accuser's self-love. Virtuous indignation is more often than not pride founded on uncertainty; and specialises in T. S. Eliot's 'things ill-done and done to others' harm/Which once you took for exercise of virtue'. Or still do. This happens in important matters and no less in littlenesses which should not be expected to bear the weight of such judgings. There is an apt English proverb: 'When they came to shoe the horses, the beetle stretched out his leg.' Proportion is important. At the extreme, this condition is narcissistic, like that of a dog constantly looking at its own reflection, and barking at it.

Self-righteousness has to be distinguished from a genuine feeling that an injustice has been done, must be pointed out and if possible corrected, no matter what the cost. This is, as I have already said, one of the prime and least justifiably evadable – though often evaded – responsibilities of the person in authority. The practice of it, even against the most glaring instances of injustice, will certainly be called self-righteousness.

Self-justification, like so many other aspects of self-love, runs the gamut, from types which seem to mock the very self-respect itself of their exponents, to the almost religious in high-mindedness. Parliament can exhibit both in a single session. This minister, suspected of cutting dangerous corners, *will* insist that everything he has done was inspired by a single-minded resolve: to serve his country, or, at a pinch, his party. This backbencher, proved to have taken money for planting a question in the House, will, back firmly to the wall, resort to the young child's favourite self-forgiveness: 'I have apologised, haven't I'? The trivially regressive, and a startlingly true instance.

Another example, seen on television (whose ability to bring us sudden revelations into character is underestimated), saw a former minister unwilling to admit that a cardinal principle of a responsible Civil Service – do not destroy historic public documents, even those which show your own political party in a bad light – had been violated. Party loyalty won over general principle. Sickening. Come back, honest Cobbett.

44

Self-forgiveness at its extreme: a colleague's son, long suspecting infidelity by his wife, noted the car's mileage before she set out for the nearby public library. She returned late, saying she had met an acquaintance and talked outside the library longer than she had realised. The indicator showed thirty miles and the engine was very warm. Her husband challenged her. She replied not with a denial but with the ultimate cock-eyed, defensive reversal: 'What's become of trust, then?' No making connections. No sense that trust, to mean anything, can only be at the very least a two-sided pact; here only the thrust to fend off judgement.

Such defence of the sense of the self leads to a deep unwillingness to change one's mind even after being proved wrong. One can learn to conquer this, but it *has* to be learned, and painfully; kind people will provide escape lanes, as on a very steep hill, to allow you a more or less unbattered exit.

The defence of the deepest sense of self also leads, especially in major matters, to the hunt for culprits. Someone must be found to blame, against all odds and reason. This becomes worse where the person transferring the blame has indeed suffered a grievous loss. Someone can almost always be selected: the police for negligence, the local authority for bureaucracy, the boss, the neighbours, 'Them'; anyone to whom a hidden sense of guilt – 'if only I had thought to do such-and-such, this might never have happened' – can be transferred. Coleridge noted severely that the first defence of weak minds is to recriminate.

Schadenfreude is endemic and deep-rooted, though generally denied. When we hear of dreadful events, we believe we feel shocked and sorry, certainly, and in some respects we are. We are also intensely interested, and that is related to a sort of dramatic thrill. Few would admit this. Some might just admit that we can on occasions be relaxed about the misfortunes of others. Even of friends. Sheridan remarked that if others abuse us we will soon hear about it from good-natured friends; the obverse, that, of Bulwer Lytton's commendation of 'A friend sincere enough to tell [us] disagreeable truths'. Emerson was

45

harder, but one cannot easily dismiss him: 'A person seldom falls sick, but the bystanders are animated with a faint hope that he will die.'

It would be interesting to have a book of the most common escapist-clichés of self-love; starting with 'One won't be missed' – as we steal a wild daffodil or shoot an elephant. So that, eventually, there are none left, but we are not to blame.

On all this, Solzhenitsyin had best have the last, penetrating, word: 'The line dividing good and evil cuts through the heart of every human being. And who is willing to destroy a piece of his own heart?'

––––––

'The majority of men are subjective towards themselves and objective towards all others, terribly objective sometimes, but the task is in fact to be objective towards oneself and subjective towards all others'.

Kierkegaard

I am not entirely sure about Kierkegaard's second 'subjective'; all the rest of his sentence is plainly true and exact. Sometimes it seems as though humans divide into two main kinds: the mediators and the alterers, the compromisers and the 'realists', the acceptors and the changers, those who take life as it comes and settle as comfortably as possible within it, and those who cannot settle. Both have their strengths and their limits. Good novelists tend to be acceptors, as novelists, if not as human beings.

So far, most instances described in this chapter have been about forms of private self-love and their public expressions. Today, the outstanding type of collective self-love and so of group insecurity is racism and its concomitants, in which we reinforce our sense of ourselves by declaring certain groups not admissible, as when near-literate and foul-mouthed youths march through the cities in defence of the purity of British culture. I recalled earlier that anti-Semitism and other forms of racism are by now less evident than they used to be, but they continue; ask the Asian consultants in some hospitals. I once met directly and saw meted out to others rude and high-handed treatment from a Pakistani consultant. His attendant nurse was defensive: 'The British consultants gang up against him. He gets thin-skinned.'

The main function of the group spirit is not so much to assert: 'I am lucky to belong here', as: '*You* don't belong here. Go away.' Which may be seen among five year olds and so all the way along to old people's homes. Reverse racism, the urge to discover against all reason and evidence racial prejudice in others, is only the mirror image of racism, but fairly common and always insistent.

Extreme passions can have the highest of motives. Ideological claims and self-regard are both boosted by the mere membership of some groups. No more doubts, no more argument, no more debate: simply the collective shout of false courage. It is easy to explain away some who appear in the front-line of such activities; they are 'sick – neurotic – driven by forces they cannot control'. Still, they may be professionals; teachers, for example. It is a sign of the general weakening of our morally discriminating indicators that this should be so. Any group, whether of the left or the right, and even if from an indisputably useful if underpaid profession such as teaching (indeed, such behaviour comes worse from them, low salaries notwithstanding), which marches down Whitehall uttering that mindless – well, childish – group chant, 'What do we want? We want this, that or the other', has left the field of reasoned debate, in favour of verbal group mugging. Muggers prefer company.

At the far end of this line are the many kinds of zealot, carrying with them harshness, viciousness, cruelty of all kinds, some of it as casually executed as the breaking of a butterfly's wing. But not all cruelty comes from extremism; some is born of incompetence, laziness, carelessness, the hunt for profit – in professionals as in day-labourers. Many, perhaps most, of us can find some urge to cruelty, even to sadism, deep down; laziness may then save us.

Extremisms of all kinds, whether in stupid or intelligent people, are attempts at escape from the burden of complex feeling, of the calm but constant making of choices and judgements. Santayana advised that intolerance is itself a form of egoism, and to condemn egoism intolerantly is to share it. So keep calm, but don't deviate. Remember that once a rigid idea, especially of 'duty', has got inside a narrow mind, it can never get out – as in some regular officers in the armed forces, some priests, some schoolteachers, some police officers; well, some people of all trades and professions.

Thank God for moderation, even if it costs a lot. In fanaticism, life has narrowed to a pinhole. It can only do that by removing from its vision all individual human and humane feeling. Self-justification has become total. To suggest that terrorists should be led through hospital wards, to see the suffering of their victims and be moved, is to miss the point. The first need of the terrorist is to furnish his imagination with a virtual screen of reinforced self-righteous plastic between himself and sight or thought of his victims. That screen is all the easier to fit if the terrorist is driven by an 'ideal'. At this point one says: 'Blast all ideologies, and many ideals.'

There are, it would seem, some who do not need this kind of screwing up to what the religious would call sin, the Iagos, those who can declare: 'Simply the thing I am shall make me live', and 'Now God stand up for bastards'; those who have no compunction. Most of us never meet masters of this mode. We do come across the minor talents, the easy liars and cheats; who entirely casually set aside all forms of debt, financial or worse, even those most harmful and painful to their creditors. I can recall only three such unhappy evidences, two by women.

Such people show the inadequacy of the assumption that no one ever admitted a wrongdoing except to argue that it was done with the highest of motives. They do not need or recognise that escape route. They blink or stare at you steadily, unfeelingly. They lack warmth and have only heartlessness. To hope to elicit simple, humane charity from them would be like trying to milk a duck. Their motto should be Devereux's: 'Stone dead hath no fellow'; or perhaps: 'No one alive hath a fellow.'

One may be tempted to think: 'People such as that are at any rate not humbugs.' A sad reflection on most of us, and two-penn'orth of dubious honesty (more accurately, of uncaring, self-regarding frankness) stuck on them.

———

It is much harder to write about lack of self-regard than about all those positive and dramatic forms which have so far occupied this chapter; less dramatically interesting, too, like turning to tap water after gin. Still, a good deed in a naughty world does cast a light. Looked at straight, without the need for melodrama, the light can be bright.

'The soul selects its own society.' That can be read in two directions, so does not help much; it is more likely than not to be interpreted dourly. In Shakespeare, as so often, we find greater and teasing subtlety: 'Self-love, my liege, is not so vile a sin as self-neglecting.' Conrad, also as so often, is sombre: 'The ardour for reform, improvement, for virtue, for knowledge and even for beauty is only a vain sticking up for appearances, as though one were anxious about the cut of one's clothes in a community of blind men.' That is the interested/disinterested type of self-love; and better than its unqualifiedly interested other.

Our own self-love may lead us, especially when faced with what looks like selfless virtue, to rush into insufficiently qualified judgements, once more the evasion of complexity, undervaluing those who break our prior notions of how they ought to be, those on the other side in particular disputes. We consign them to preconceived slots, make them into two-dimensional figures. We dislike an individual's whole public manner and then discover he has great reserves of active goodwill. We know this middle-aged woman is grievously superior in style, bossy, and then discover she has unobtrusively nursed a relative for years – far beyond any demands her public image, created and maintained by herself, might have suggested or prompted.

I have known two people, one in wartime, the other in civilian life, who seemed selfless. They were separated by time and distance but both happened to be called 'Humphreys'. Association being strong, I have since half-fallen into assuming that anyone called 'Humphreys' is naturally good.

Exceptionally, self-love can transmute itself, or push its appearance so far down in the practice of the personality that it is hardly noticed, and fuels the owner's capacity to do remarkable things, often for the public good. At this point someone is likely to say: 'Ah yes, so-and-so has done wonders for education, the social services, medical matters. But when you begin to know him closely you realise that at bottom it is all inspired by a form of conceit, far more sophisticated than you or I could handle.' So what? Freud gave us a much-adopted word for this but we have long known it exists. And a good thing too. The masked hypocrite may grow into the virtues the mask seeks to express.

Clearly, it is enormously hard to face in ourselves all the forms of self-love. Sometimes, to return to an earlier theme from a different angle, one wonders if to recognise them depends on intelligence, that some people do not sin against the light but are unable to recognise any light. Some of the exculpations for wrongdoing are so low-level that you wonder if such people could ever be persuaded to *see*. This is true not only of undereducated people. The excuses on television of a senior member of the board of a failed merchant bank were cleverer, smoother, more smartly evasive than those of the small-time trading-floor 'criminal' (his word) from his organisation, but no better at bottom. Yet we all know people who are not 'bright' but live by good rules; others of similar intelligence may find it hard to obey such rules when they meet unmanageable troubles.

The slope is uphill all the way and sometimes there seems no justice. Wordsworth's lines stick in the mind: '. . . Oh Sir,/The good die first,/And they whose hearts are dry as summer dust/Burn to the socket'. A lament for those who tried to surmount or had no problem in surmounting self-love in themselves, and paid for it.

There are a few rules of thumb. Trying to teach oneself patience, not to rush to unqualified judgements, not to under-rate complexities, not to be territorial, not to invoke irrelevant or 'on behalf of' claims to virtue. Self-examination is not necessarily solipsistic. To eradicate bad habits is like trying to get every last bit of dandelion root out of deep ground with a teaspoon: impossible, but you can reach a little, and sometimes quite a lot.

In his 'Remorse begets reform', Cowper echoes Montaigne's more poetic image: 'Repentance begs for burdens'. To feel shame is a step forward; and the capacity to blush is the sign of residual decency. As we saw earlier: Iago never blushed.

Many writers have persisted in believing that this kind of virtue, or elements of it, can be learned. Whatever he may have said in the depressed passage quoted earlier, Conrad was sure of this; it was one of his primary principles: 'fidelity'. You steered straight; you ensured the light on the river mouth blinked to time and without interruption; you were the last to leave or went down with the ship. You went out into the snow like Captain Oates. You did not break ranks in a crisis and scuttle for your own safety. As children, we were moved to admiration by such examples and injunctions. When, as adults, we heard, from an acquaintance whose eight-year-old daughter died there, that the first people to jump from an aeroplane which crashed at New Delhi were the stewardesses, we were shocked into a dreadfully sad wonder. They were called to show more self-abnegation than they proved capable of; training had not worked. Echoes again of Orwell's terrible song towards the end of *1984* – 'Under the spreading chestnut tree/I sold you and you sold me' – under duress, many of us might in the end betray each other. What would we – I – do?

A byroad here leads to wondering about the influence of suc-cess on character. Some argue that success improves most of those who achieve it; they can relax and think less about them-selves. Trollope believed nothing makes a man so cross as success. Perhaps he meant 'arrogant and impatient', as in some big-business men, high-level politicians, temporary 'celebrities' and inflated small-scale bosses?

So one comes back to the first step out of the coil of self-concern: recognising the need; and its difficulty. Goethe is a tonic: 'Know thyself! If I knew myself I'd run away.' Other writers in that therapeutic line include Pascal and Montaigne (of course), Stendhal, Flaubert, Sterne, Forster. A good step further is to recognise, but it is really all too obvious, that when we are at our most firm against bad habits in others, we are usually so absolute in our denunciation because those are un-acknowledged faults in ourselves.

Looking back on all the above, I am at last forced to the con-clusion that, as in thinking about morality, democracy and much else, the first and continuing need is for tolerance (inexorably linked with the moderation mentioned a few pages back), toler-ance towards others and to ourselves, the recognition of the slowness of progress, that we are all in the same boat and most trying to row straight. All this, and recognising also the impor-tance of the search for self-knowledge.

'How shall we expect charity towards others when we are uncharitable to ourselves.' Centuries later, Auden underlined Sir Thomas Browne: let us learn 'to leave ourselves alone'. Don't nag or 'go at' yourself; it never helps, and the loss of face can be borne. Arnold was acute in recognising Shakespeare's security within himself. Wordsworth's Happy Warrior was skilful in self-knowledge.

Camus spoke briskly of the imaginative inadequacy of the need to be right: 'the sign of a vulgar mind'. Better to try to live within as full as possible a consciousness of our own weaknesses. If he avoids that clear pitfall, then happy is the man who can still sit securely within himself. This is not always, or easily, dis-tinguishable from smugness, but it exists.

Milton made a more positive point: 'Oft-times nothing profits more/Than self-esteem, grounded on just and right/Well-managed'. Nietzsche turns that over: 'He who despises himself nevertheless esteems himself as a self-despiser'; and: 'Every man has his price – even if it's a call on his vanity of virtue.' Dr Johnson had already observed that a man who declares his faults does so to increase his plain virtues; he wishes to show how much he can spare.

Emerson was wry and puzzling: 'It is very hard to be simple enough to be good.' Like Billy Budd? But he was partially locked in by a speech impediment. The good individual may not be 'simple' but is likely to lack many of the tortuous complexities of those mired in self-love. His emotional blood runs more coolly, as if clarified. He lacks envy, spite, malice, unkindness and other elements which indicate insecurity in the self.

'Self-forgetfulness' is another phrase for all the above. Nietzsche caught it beautifully: 'One must learn to love oneself . . . with a wholesome and healthy love, so that one can bear to be with oneself and need not roam.'

Each of us, if we are lucky, will have our own list of those who were good to us beyond the call of duty or self-regard. For me, the line is long: my grandmother; stout Miss Jubb of the Leeds City Board of Guardians (which looked after orphans); the tired, but insistent to the education authorities on my behalf, headmaster of my elementary school; Mr Curry, the blunt and attentive English master at Cockburn High (grammar) School, who, among other kindnesses, organised a whip-round so that I could go to Stratford for a week of Shakespeare; Bonamy Dobrée at Leeds University, who gave many unexpected benefits, practical and less obvious, but imaginative, as well as an example of the Happy Warrior; the manager of the cheap Sunshine Grocery Stores in Hunslet (I delivered for him on Saturdays), who took me to 'high tea' at his lower-middle-class home, where north-east Leeds then petered out in cheap, owner-occupied housing estates. He was, I think, inspired by a not fully aware hope that I might glimpse to what I should aspire. It proved to be, in fact, a sort of 'low high tea', most carefully measured out. He would not have been well paid, but standards had to be maintained. From that tricky piece of social managing I also learned something.

And those two Humphreys: Arthur Humphreys of Leicester University, who seemed to have been born with not a single mean bone in his body; and Captain Humphreys, the Brigade Intelligence Officer in Italy. He took over an execution squad which ought by rule or custom to have been the duty of his lieutenant, me. It was, he said, rather too much too ask of a young newcomer. If he is still alive, I salute him.

Here we begin to come yet again upon those whom Newman called 'the once-born'. Sometimes the once-born seem merely like people with an unadventurous spirit. That is not good enough, is belittling. Some people seem not only to have been born with a strong moral sense but to have no difficulty in living it out; people to whom acting well, even self-sacrificingly, seems as normal as to breathe, who have an instinctive largeness and generosity of spirit, steadiness in the face of all diurnal temptations. They have no wish to 'bring down' (a savage, animal phrase) anyone who may after all be living in the truth, or trying to. Not the steadiness of the half-shut eye, this, or the softness of people who refuse to see ill under their noses. Rather, an ever-ready willingness to take risks on possible redemption, a sudden access and act of goodness. Forster's concept of 'rent', and Masefield's 'trust', again come in here, which we should honour willingly, even if we doubt another's honesty (that of a suspicious-looking taxi-driver, say), just in case they are indeed honest. If they are, to doubt them would be to commit a regrettable fault ourselves, and would damage their own sense of probity. The epitaph for such people is that of Marty over Giles Winterbourne's grave in Hardy's *The Woodlanders*: 'You was a good man and did good things.'

At the far end of this line is the spirit described in a poem by A. S. J. Tessimond in which the narrator knows that his enemy, thinking himself unsuspected, is about to kill him from behind. And he lets him get on with it. A refusal to make any retaliatory gesture. Cowardice? Inanition? Indifferentism? Pity for the miserable creature? The Greeks, if not Freud, perhaps have a word for that too.

Philip Larkin, surprisingly again in view of what sometimes seems a curmudgeonly spirit, comes in now with a most gentle passage: 'We should be careful/Of each other, we should be kind/While there is still time'.

I recently met, for the second time in a couple of weeks, a man who worked in the paint shop of a garage with four or five others. His head had been completely shaved since our first meeting. He explained that one of their number had been found to have cancer, had had lengthy chemotherapy and was now bald. He was due back to work next day. His 'mates' had all shaved their heads against his return, so that he didn't feel 'all that bad'. 'Mates' is often a conventional appellation, an expression of easy blokeishness among working-class men; here, it was transformed.

All begins in honesty towards the self; Auden, though he thought Robert Frost unlikeable because intensely conceited, also acknowledged Frost's honesty, by quoting his laconic admission: 'I have been acquainted with the night.' We feel much the same respect on reading Hopkins's economically vivid description of his deeply depressed state: 'Like a clod cleaving and holding only by strings of roots.'

At this point we also see that self-love can become blood-brother to self-hatred, to 'swallowing a toad every morning' as more than one French writer put it. The two can meet and recognise each other at few, but terrifying, intervals.

The most critical observers can be the most cheering: 'My bodily endowments are, in brief, in close harmony with my soul's. There is no agility, merely a full, firm vigour, but I can stick things out.' Montaigne had the right, as few of us have, to say that.

Schiller noted, as did Nietzsche later, one of the hardest attributes of all: 'Man only plays when in the full meaning of the word he is a man, and he is only completely a man when he plays.' Lawrence caught the condition neatly: 'A man in his wholeness, wholly attending'. For Kierkegaard, the best search of all was for 'authentic selfhood'.

Pope broadened and rounded off this whole question in the most assertive and pragmatic way: 'True self-love and social are the same'. One fervently hopes so, whatever the evidence against. To accept this involves much reining in of our own self-love, but takes us back to post-Hobbesian potentialities.

That is, I think, the best I can do.

PART TWO

LIVING IN THE PRESENT

From first and last things to the everyday social ground, the political. From memoir to manifesto; in part.

Yet most words for denouncing social ills are out-of-date, regarded as hardly applicable any more. A Labour Prime Minister's advisor says simply that he agrees with the making of a lot of profits, that to him that is 'not an ethical question'. He seems sure of not being challenged. I will, on the contrary, try to redefine some of the lost words.

We now have abundant evidence that authoritarianisms of the left and the right comprehensively damage or destroy human rights. The only alternative is the attempt at democracy, and, unless and until we can think of a better combination, of democracy living with capitalism, but always reining it in. Such a middle way is not a compromise; a continuing challenge, rather. Not a disposable, because old-fashioned, approach, but modern (or even post-modern), the acceptance of inevitable unfinishedness, a laying of planks across the endless and continuing bog made from the tendrils of human selfishness, of all kinds and at all levels.

So it is the main and inescapable business of an open democracy to control the natural impulses of capitalism, to turn them to its own purposes. The current myth, that unfettered capitalism will eventually raise the material standards of all, at no social cost but with greater social justice for all, is just that: a myth, a dangerous and damaging myth. A democracy may live with capitalism, but on its own terms, not those of capital. It does not have to be friends with capital; instead, a wary relationship.

3

The Uneasy Alliance:
On Capitalism and Democracy

'– So God help me, I can perceive nothing but a certain conspiracy of rich men procuring their own commodities under the name and title of the Commonwealth'

Thomas More

'. . . This is done chiefly by suppressing, or at least keeping a straight hand upon, the devouring trades of usury, ingrossing great pasturages and the like'

Francis Bacon

'The blind sentence passed by the economy, that mightier social power which condemns the greater part of mankind to senseless wretchedness and crushes countless human talents, is accepted as inevitable and recognised in practice in the conduct of men.'

Horkheimer

THE MORE THAN four centuries which run from Thomas More through Francis Bacon to Horkheimer have produced an eloquent parade of demonstrations of just those ethical questions, of denunciations of unfettered capitalism, its humbuggery and insensate egotistical thrust. One can't say that the contemporary political advisor quoted above has answered and rejected them; he seems rather to be unaware of the whole historical debate.

I recalled earlier that in the second half of this century, Vaclav Havel has spoken most lucidly about the deep relations between democracy and morality. By cradle-socialists such as I, the words of those authors right up to Orwell and Havel are repeated with relish; perhaps too much relish sometimes. In the prosperous West, capitalism has learned to wear velvet gloves, and is flanked by smooth-talking PR people who aim to convince us that this is the best of all possible worlds; they can shrug off the more intemperate old-style objurgations. We now need different tools; still passionate, but now more surgical than rhetorical.

These last two decades in particular have highlighted what Edward Heath called 'the unacceptable face of capitalism'. I imagine my identification of an unacceptable face would appear much earlier than Sir Edward's. But his was one of the last liberal judgements by a Conservative statesman before we were swept into an increasing wave of capitalist practice which not only pushed at the very limits of the acceptable but found new and ingenious ways of going beyond them, of redefining the acceptable. To accept this, as so many did and continue to do, through the silly phrase: 'That's the real world, after all', is bad language and bad thought. The 'real world' has been redefined as 'shifty, shoddy, immoral'. The real 'real world' is just as much the arena of affection, friendliness, mutual help, disinterested satisfactions. From top to bottom, the last two decades encouraged that strain in English life which runs, brutishly, from high-level boardroom peculation to football hooliganism. As my first battery commander in the war, a major and a low-level crook, liked to say: 'We didn't create the biggest Empire in the world by farting around politely.' Discovered with his hand in the battery's cash box, he was moved to the other side of Italy and, as is the fashion, promoted; to lieutenant-colonel in charge of a 'glasshouse' (soldier's prison). The British Way: when in doubt, avoid a scandal; kick the culprit upstairs, and best hopes for the men he now controls.

These last years have cast into the wings that other English strain, which values the honest, is charitable and tolerant. It will take years to reverse the process. We haven't even begun adequately to assess the damage, let alone decide how best to undo it.

ON CAPITALISM AND DEMOCRACY

It is almost but not quite otiose to say that galloping capitalism is, to look back to the last chapter, one of the ranker growths
of self-love. This is worth saying because those of us who want
the practice of capitalism to be made more rigorously subject to
the honest interests of individuals and the community should be
careful not to luxuriate too much in our denunciations. It starts
much earlier; it starts with greed, cupidity, in almost all of us,
and flourishes at all ages and in all parts of society. True,
it flourishes in some parts more than others and in different
ways; the different 'cultures' – which here means accepted
habits – of each class can encourage or discourage but not
entirely remove it.

The instinct is there. But nowhere is it practised by everybody.
I have written elsewhere with warmth about important elements
of working-class life before the war, elements which were family-
and community-centred. Some critics thought those passages
'romantic'. They were not; they were true to the 'respectable'
working-class to which we belonged. Others may have known
other kinds; they all existed. We, too, had our loutish neighbours. Those critics remind us that some, especially on the far
left, fear any emotion which is not denunciatory.

In all parts, there are people who have no urge towards
money-making, who would not wish to exploit others in any
way. Yet one must in fairness go on to describe how exploitation
is practised in the backstreets as well as in middle-class avenues.
It is a necessary justice to recognise that capitalism is not only
practised by 'fat cats' – though they are 'better' at it than others.
At a lower level, it is common on council estates. A favourite
catchphrase used by small-time working-class crooks about
those they can easily fool is, predictably, 'There's one born every
minute.' Glib glee about people usually less quick-witted and
'fly' than they are. There is a straight and unbroken line from
working-class 'fiddling', 'knocking off', 'liberating' other
people's goods, to the most unacceptable faces of capitalism. To
recognise this should not blunt the attack on major unacceptable
practices both institutional and personal; it does bring us back to

elemental human nature. Overemphasis on big bogeymen tempts us into cartoon thinking. A sense of relative degree is essential, especially to reduce priggishness. Always remembering that the differences in degree can become so large that they enter, high up, the 'wholly unacceptable' area. They will then have their most assured self-justifications.

If there is an acceptable face of capitalism, it is to be found in the spur which can there be given to individual initiative and inventiveness. This is something of which we are always reminded when the system is being defended. It is more rarely admitted that capitalism's killer instinct is, as we have already noted, to go not only to the very limit of those 'civilised' rules, but further, if that can be done without severe penalties. Historic and modern examples are easily found. Reading about the history of the great Chatham Docks, the Navy's pride, I was only mildly surprised by the centuries of corruption of all kinds and at all levels practised there.

To 'be competitive' is only exceptionally to build a better mousetrap or make two blades of grass grow where one grew before; it is more often to cut corners of quality successfully, to be aggressive to the limit (advertisements for salesmen routinely ask for 'aggressive marketing skills'). It is to bend the rules wherever you can, cook the books, give backhanders, be economical with the truth. A long way from the simple expression of initiative and inventiveness.

The 'entrepreneurial spirit' itself is, then, partly by nature, partly by nurture, found right across society; but rather unevenly. Somewhere above the middle of the lower middle class and on to the mid-middle class it begins, single-mindedly and publicly, to flourish. There, you meet people who believe money should be made to 'breed money', that it is interesting as well as profitable to 'turn your money over' (a strong, earthy image for what is so often a markedly unearthy occupation).

Nowadays, people at the lower part of this level repeatedly loot their apparently inexhaustible attics and hire a place at the nearest car-boot sale, or a pitch at the weekend open market. Or they set up small businesses, often with a bank loan, and open an 'arty-crafty' shop full of the latest fashions in 'collectibles', or offer free-standing baths in the Victorian manner, or second-hand fine furnishings, or discarded designer clothes.

They need not be led merely by greed, money-grabbing; many also find these initiatives enjoyable, fulfilling, even sensual, almost but not quite disinterested. The more greedy and watchful exist and are instantly recognisable, especially in their fondness for minatory announcements: 'All breakages must be paid for' (particularly common in 'collectibles' shops), 'No cheque sales under £10', '2½ per cent commission on credit card sales', 'No unaccompanied children, no dogs, no food or drink to be brought into the store', 'All purchases by cheque must be accompanied by a form of identification'. A petty nightmare world, no doubt with its justifications. It could have been inspired by bitter experiences with careless and dishonest customers.

Matters are rather different lower down the social scale, though not as different as they once were. Especially under the impact of the last twenty years, working-class attitudes to individual entrepreneurialism may be changing, adjusting to this much more catch-as-catch-can society. One hears in particular of miners who have received a redundancy payment; not a great deal to a middle-class businessman, but more than the miners have ever before had in their hands at one time. Some make good use of it; others fall into the claws of the variety of vultures who appear on such occasions, not all from outside the miners' own area. Such people always find their levels of victims. Nowadays, there is money to be drawn even from one-parent families living on social security; the 'underclass' are, relative to their income, cheated as much as the rest, or perhaps more. And their very existence refutes the favourite cliché that if free capitalist enterprise is given its head, then wealth will trickle downwards; the gap between rich and poor widens. I use that much criticised word 'underclass' deliberately. It is more accurate than any other and, though some wish to change it out of a misplaced wish not to hurt those it identifies, should not be replaced by something more emollient or cosmetic. That is misleading.

In many, perhaps most, members of the old-style working-class, sophisticated entrepreneurial habits were uncommon. This may not indicate lack of initiative, 'shiftlessness'. Not surprisingly, a common ironical, but not envious, expression about lack of choice was: 'Opportunity would be a fine thing!' The culture of the hired hands, the wage-labourers, stressed that 'common cause' rather than competition was, had to be, most often the rule. You could not hire skilled labour, so you exercised a sort of labour barter if you could. If not, you could still have your pride. In our districts, before the war, a very old widow living alone on her exiguous pension found survival difficult, and was too old to continue as a charwoman. She baked a few good currant teacakes each week and sold them for a copper or two from her kitchen. Boiled ham cost 3*d*. (just over 1p) for 2 ounces then; she managed. We couldn't even afford them, I have just remembered. She used to give us occasional leftovers.

No such rule is universal. Working-class districts of the old kind had and today's large estates of council houses have their own internal range of small entrepreneurs. Taken together, they are in a minority; but they are varied. The weekly house-to-house insurance collector has almost gone; the woman who runs a 'club' by which you take out a 'check' to be paid off weekly so as to have new clothes for high days, holidays and special occasions, still does her rounds. Or has been transformed into those who take orders for goods from the increasingly glossy and numerous mail-order catalogues.

These can be complex operations for the dealer and the customer, and some people – especially those bringing up families on their own – soon get into difficulties. Then the loan-sharks move in, with their illegally high rates of interest. The growing number of 'credit unions' in some districts are working hard at making these activities less rewarding, but meet increasing difficulties.

The men who still offer, usually in pubs and clubs, things

which have 'fallen off the backs of lorries' (stolen at work, or the proceeds of burglaries passed on by fences) can seem like helpful, organic small sustainers of the community. In our part of Leeds – a typical home of the aspidistra, hand-cart, borrowed cup of sugar, and canary culture – these uncovenanted odds and ends gave us a bit of a lift.

My Aunt Lil was a repository of the more decent working-class attitudes, an exact sounding board. She also exemplified a number of happily accepted, comfortably lived-with contradictions in those attitudes (in his recent excellent book, *Classes and Cultures: England 1918–1951*, Ross McKibbin describes a variety of these). My aunt would not condone cheating, was indeed upset by it. She would accept from a friend's husband or a neighbour, especially in the late 1940s, a large tin of fine ham or a chicken which had found its way from the dining-car of one of the Leeds–London expresses. She appeared to feel no qualm in that kind of dealing, but would have been 'mortified' if called unscrupulous, a thief. I put that verb into inverted commas because, it suddenly occurs to me, it typifies the way working-class language could suddenly shift into polysyllabic words of weight. From where did they come? The Old Testament (Samuel), Church or Chapel, the local Big House of Long Ago.

Was this range of attitudes a hangover from the scarcities of wartime, when, for the family's sake, bending the rules often seemed justified to many? Perhaps. More likely it was within a much longer tradition, by which it was felt justified to cheat (but not too grossly, and anyway that might lead to prison) the boss who was believed to have grown fat on the labour of your kind; and especially unseen corporate bosses such as those of British Rail.

Today we have, on the one hand, the communal and familial, which can still exist; on the other, less holding together. To that has to be added a fact it has become 'undemocratic' to mention: many people, and not simply the 'underclass', still living in those large working-class housing estates, are easily duped, not well equipped to deal with smooth falsehoods. Their disposition is to believe what people say, especially if they are from their own area. The most successful operators in working-class areas are themselves from the working class; they know the tones and accents of deception most likely to succeed; and the inhibitions. The streets are thus ridden with small cheatings. Even now, it remains unpleasant to see one's relatives so frequently conned. Very few of them are likely to say: 'Pull the other one'; and virtually none would add: 'Get off with you. *Which?* says it's a rotten machine.'

Nowadays, those who are buying their formerly council-owned houses are particular targets. They tend to worry about the upkeep. They can be easy prey for the lying roofer who tells them replacement is urgent, for the man who says their front drive is dangerously 'past it', or the one who insists that they are foolish not to have their inner roof area fitted with insulating felt, and then grotesquely over-measures the area. In carpet-selling, this particular trick is so common that you wonder whether the salesmen, no doubt on commission according to sales and therefore harried, are equipped with a self-adjusting tape measure which increases each estimate by about 15 per cent, at the very least.

Another pronounces that the fairly new washing machine needs expensive repairs. If the owner points out that it is still under guarantee, he is told the small print rules out the sort of breakdown the machine has suffered. The double-glazing salesman will be hardly prize-able off the settee until he has clinched a sale. The roofers and other heavy workers will ask for some of the cost in advance, probably a large proportion, 'for materials', and then either do a dreadful, corner-cutting job or disappear into the night; along with the insulation-felt man and the crooked washing-machine engineer.

The men who appear before Farnham Magistrates' Court for nasty little deceptions are often described as 'roofer and tiler'; those seem to be in the front row of today's working-class cowboys; 'By Self Appointment – Crooked Purveyors to the Working Class'.

When the fiddlers are found out, the commonest self-exculpations include of course: 'They all do it – but the big boys know how to get away with it'; 'Everyone's at it. It's natural, you'll never stamp it out.' The urge for self-justification is there in all but the entirely incorruptible. This is the pettiest level of free capitalist 'enterprise'.

In totalitarian states, though, fascist or communist, corruption is congenitally at least as rife. Before the collapse of the Soviet empire, visitors from the eastern bloc (always officials of one sort or another) who visited the UNESCO headquarters in Paris often brought hidden in their spare underwear quite valuable objects, such as icons from remote churches. They wanted dollars or, at a pinch, French francs or sterling; to persuade the best heart surgeon in their capital city to perform open-heart surgery on their granddaughter or to allow them to bring her to Paris or London. That was an actual case. So was that of the middle-rank Polish diplomat who was saving for an expensive American outboard motor on the urgings of his two mistresses. By another fiddle, he finally had his prize carried over in the diplomat bag. Some 'bag'. Later he was found out and demoted, posted to their equivalent of Ulan Bator.

To repeat what is all-too-obvious but not sufficiently made explicit: it is one of the plainer duties of society, and especially of those which profess a commitment to democracy, collectively to constrain, steadily and all the time, these instincts. Many, perhaps most of us, have a potential crook, small or large, hidden within, if not quite yearning to get out. After all, it could be 'fun'.

> If you are rich, you perhaps think that inequality is a good thing –
> that it fosters a spirit of emulation, and prevents things from stag-
> nating at a dead level. But if you are poor, you must know that
> when inequality is so outrageous, it fosters nothing but despair . . .
> among the very poor; arrogance and wastefulness among the very
> rich; meanness, envy and snobbery among the middle classes.

Shaw was a little slapdash there, but essentially right. I would only add that the qualities he notices in the middle class are often buttressed by insecurity and suspicion. 'Is he out to "do" me?', leading to: 'But, still, one doesn't like to make a fuss.'

Plenty of people know how to play on those attitudes. Or why should a charter airline, bringing back lower-middle- and middle-class holidaymakers from the sun, be able to buy on board passengers' remaining foreign currency at a rate 25 per cent worse than the banks at home will offer? No one argues; few people notice. Anyway, it would be a pity to spoil a good holiday by wrangling at the end. If anyone complains, a bland, computerised bromide of a letter is despatched. From such mean and nasty little tricks the line runs unbroken all the way up to the biggest of cheats.

Students who have worked during the vacation in factories supplying foods to all kinds of outlets come back shocked at the fiddling of the rules by the management. 'I'll never touch one of their fancy prepared meals [or sausages, soft drinks, hot dogs] again' is a common reaction. The presiding motto is: 'What the eye doesn't see.' A few years ago, a particularly greedy and short-sighted firm was peremptorily deprived of its large contract to supply hamburgers to Sainsbury's. The supermarket's regular inspectors found ingredients being used which were below the level specified in the contract.

Not all fiddlers, especially the increasing collectives of Pumblechook undertakers, are found out. They often take advantage of the vulnerability of their clients, at those disoriented times and at all social levels, to persuade them to buy coffins and elaborate accessories, far more expensive than they can afford. One large firm of undertakers, whose headquarters are in the United States, tried to justify these practices: 'With the best will in the world we are answerable to our shareholders, not to the public.' A strange form of 'best will', but the easy cliché came in handy. Another regular revelation on television, a grisly one, is the sight of their apologists greasily trying to justify their bosses' practices. There are pressures on all sides. One of the more unpleasant sights in this kind of society is that of the shareholders howling like hungry hyenas at a company's Annual General Meeting if their profits haven't been maintained.

Some contractors to local government use wrong proportions of sand and cement and so produce weak concrete; the local-authority inspector may go away with a backhander. That is traditional behaviour, which I met just before the beginning of the last war, building sandbag blast walls at a Leeds hospital; such habits continue. Some small- to medium-sized haulage firms and bus companies consistently break the rules as to main-tenance and hours served by their drivers; a few pounds in the hand each week to the drivers will keep them quiet. Fines imposed if their boss is found out tend to be modest.

Servicing the middle-class in that succession are the building societies – ours was Abbey National – which, among other prac-tices greatly loaded in their favour, used to charge heavily for 'our own survey', a once-over-lightly job designed only to ensure they could get their money back if you defaulted and they had to sell the house. If you had paid for a much more thorough and expensive survey, they would not accept it. 'That's business,' Roy Fuller, chief solicitor to the Woolwich building society, said to me equably. 'They're not breaking the law.' One of the rare gains from the wide-open competitive climate of the last decade or so has been the driving-out of some of those routines. These and many similarly paltry practices riddle society like advanced woodworm. Yes, I will, and we should, go on kicking against the pricks in all this.

As, for instance, a remaining bad practice among banks and building societies. That is, floating a new savings account at an attractively high rate of interest and then, once it has recruited many savers, quietly lowering the rate. Ignorance or indolence do the rest. Challenged, their smooth justification is: 'It is not financially viable to remain at "best rate" [widely advertised] at all times' – only until we have netted a few suckers by a loss leader.

At a somewhat higher, professional level, evidence of a change in social sensibility is easily illustrated. Recently, a new and valuable but expensive drug for the relief of Alzheimer's dis-ease was released to pharmacists. A survey revealed that across the south of England, the prices charged by chemists ran from about £150 to £200. Challenged, a spokesman for the pharmacists responded in this manner: 'They are professionals and have a right to charge what they choose.' Legally, they no doubt have such a right. But one used to assume that 'professionalism' meant practising a severe discipline with its own internal ethics, an integrity before both its demands and its community obligations of care; not to be swayed by external pressures of competition or sheer self-interest. Here, professionalism has been redefined to mean the accepted practices of a close, money-making cabal, free to profit as they will in a wide-open society. No ethical question there.

Moving even higher up the muck-mountain, one is excessively tempted to unleash a rhetorical lambasting on the 'fat cats' of the 1990s, on their exceptional greed and self-regarding insensitivity to criticism. My direct experience of them and, through service on various public committees, of other high-wire capitalists is limited, but probably wider than that of most academics.

Decades ago, W. H. Vanderbilt uttered what is today's tirelessly repeated anti-social rubric, the ever-increasing-salary-and-shareholding chief executive's brief, odious daily prayer: 'The public be damned. I am working for my stockholders.' The worst example of this attitude I recall is the decision of a giant American car-making corporation not to modify their cars so as to make them safer. Their accountants assessed the amount likely to be needed to pay compensation to those injured by the cars in their existing format, and set that against the loss of profit if the modifications were made. Profit won; the modifications were not made.

That kind of attitude appears particularly shocking in Britain when held by the chairmen of recently privatised public utilities, but obviously seems to them entirely proper. Most of them hastened the privatisation of their own enterprises: vastly increased salaries ('the rate for the job'), share options and other substantial perks beckoned, plus richly protective clauses in case they make a mess of things and have to go. The partial privatisation of the prison service and now of some local-authority schools is against all sense of the proper public domain, and in practice the privatised railways are now proving the same point.

The partner to Vanderbilt's declaration (again, particularly nasty in the mouths of bosses of public utilities) is: 'We charge, of course, what the market will bear.' That leads upwards as to prices. Leading down, is the practice of diluting/reducing quality little by little until the place is reached where the customers complain. At that moment, prices have indeed reached the still, unpassable point of what the market will bear.

Lower still, a favourite 1980s/1990s phrase is 'What's the bottom line?' There is always a language for the crime. At this point Solzhenitsyn comes in again, like a cold clean shower: 'Capitalism was doomed ethically before it was doomed economically'; at least the first half of the sentence remains accurate.

Worst of all is the apparent moral inconscience of such people, their deafness to the widespread disgust aroused not among their acquaintance but in the sort of people they now rarely meet, at the way they have manoeuvred to gain for themselves those disgracefully high advantages. Governments have carried on parroting that such practices encourage initiative; or they intone the mean little: 'Your objection is only "the politics of envy".' No: many people continue to recognise rampant greed when they see it. This truly is the blindly self-condoning, unacceptable face of capitalism.

'There's no art to read the mind's construction in the face': that is, all in all, right but not sufficient. One comes to mistrust the easy use of such phrases as 'hard-faced men'; some captains of industry have soft, almost babyish faces.

Self-justification, even of bad deeds, can make a face seem almost innocent, or just satisfied in and within itself. I know one such face; its owner is deeply read, especially in nineteenth-century fiction, especially about all those captains of industry and politics in Trollope and Disraeli. What is the attraction?

Entry to a more assured world for the tycoon? But those predecessors had their disgraceful falls. Perhaps a kind of substitute
shriving?

Trollope knew the ruthless, money-regarding faces well but
could, though very rarely, lack specific detail. In *The Way We
Live Now*, he says Melmotte had a 'wonderful look of power
over his face and chin', which leaves most of the work to us. The
weak word is 'wonderful', which tells us nothing but suggests the
face was impressive in suggesting power. For the rest, Trollope
merely notes 'the large heavy eyebrows'. A pity, because he was
elsewhere excellent at drawing such faces in detail.

In the faces of some of the six or seven tycoons I have met,
certain common, tell-tale characteristics did seem evident. Long
competitive practice had sometimes left its mark in the watchful
eyes, the tight line of the mouths, a humourlessness, or an over-
brief, unwilling response to something genuinely amusing, an
impatient incisiveness, or its imitator, a tetchy impatience. Yet
one of them had the good-natured, helpful expression of a local
parish vicar, and it seemed 'real'. Very puzzling. Of such puzzles,
more later.

More culturally interesting nowadays in the top commercial
people I have met is their need to be surrounded by a relatively
new breed of men and women: a range of 'special assistants' for
public relations or corporate affairs or some other fancy disguising label, often 'power-dressed', well-groomed, thirty-odd-
year-old women who will counter any criticism with their own
choral line: 'We must pay the rate for the job.' An elusive concept,
but one which appears unassailable to them. What is the rate for
the job of a devoted priest in a broken-down district; or a similarly devoted teacher; or one who gives night and day care to
the old and ill who are 'not even relatives'? The questions are
irrelevant. This 'rate for the job' is an entirely enclosed, self-
referring and self-evident, capitalist-escapist false-truism.

Even less attractive are the senior PR men and women;
especially when they laud their promotion of the arts. Here
humbug reaches its apogee. The 'chairman's wife syndrome'

may occasionally still be in play but is by now an overused joke. When discussing what might be the public acknowledgments of their great generosity, the PR men and women are as tough as carpet salesmen from a large but not over-scrupulous firm. Remember also their record – the defence of cigarette advertisements, of alcoholic lemonade, of greatly increased water rates; and their promotion of dubious new 'special offers' on telephone rates and a hundred other such dodges.

Sponsorship-seeking officers of artistic enterprises hoping for this largesse usually yield to kid-gloved bullying and concede gross over-acknowledgements. To paraphrase Sir Henry Wotton: 'A PR executive is a dishonest man paid to lie at home for his company.' With few exceptions, sponsorship in England is at bottom a cynical practice, though some of its agents half-believe their own humbug.

Class and profit can comfortably coexist if PR arranges it so. At one grand reception to announce the winner of a major book prize, the chairman of the sponsoring conglomerate had two pre-ceremony parties: one for the nobs (peers, tycoons and the like) in his private quarters; the other for the *hoi polloi*. The judges and the short-listed authors were with the crowd. Not qualified for nob status. That chairman knew his business culture precisely.

It must be hard for PR officers to manoeuvre honestly between such shoals. Some are honest, usually working in less predatory and profitable areas (for charities, say). For the rest, the enveloping miasma of double-talk and deceit has to be accepted. Not all find this difficult. A woman promoting hard-sell advertisements directed at children before Christmas blandly asserted on the radio that 'Kids aren't fools. They're not taken in.' Wasting her time, she was; or exhibiting pious mendacity.

It is a sad job, all in all. Which perhaps explains why, as they leave the Big Boss's sanctum and are out of his PA's hearing, they tend to mock him: 'He seems rather shy with strangers, but underneath he's a bastard. And he can hardly wait for his "K".' Typically, the bastard dotes on his daughter. Her photo is on his desk along with that of her mother. In England, the girl is sent to Benenden and given a horse or two; in America, it's Vassar and a Ferrari. The habit is rather touching; like the 'thumping crook' in Betjeman's tea shop, they feel love and seek love.

The 1980s and onwards saw all these attitudes not merely grow but be firmly approved. Each government promotes some and represses other characteristics of its society. It would be difficult to assess the damage done to some of the more humane elements in British culture during the Thatcher years.

It was reported that Michael Heseltine felt no embarrassment in telling assembled owners of small businesses that he kept himself afloat in his early days by delaying paying his creditors for as long as ever was possible. What did the creditors do, especially if they had no one they could subject to similar treatment? Some sank, presumably. The same man appeared to see no conflict of conscience in the Churchill family's accepting millions of National Lottery money for selling Winston Churchill's papers to the nation. 'If you find a Rubens in your attic, of course it's yours, and you sell it', or words to that effect. A small-visioned approach to a large, multi-dimensional ethical public issue. One of the tabloids completed the picture of a rapacious but only near-literate society by transmuting that sentence into: 'If you find a ruby in your attic . . .'.

An even more striking instance of the capitalist spirit at its most naked came from a wealthy elderly Frenchwoman whose family owned prosperous fine-art establishments in Paris, London and New York. Some years ago, we were attending a grand lunch after the wedding of a French colleague. Nixon and Watergate began to be talked about. The elderly lady irritatedly contributed, apropos the breaking-in and bugging: 'What's the problem? Of course they broke in and bugged. Anyone protecting their business would have done that.' *Pas de problème.*

To a buyer, '*caveat emptor*' may translate as: 'I'd better be careful.' To an unabashed seller it means: 'Fiddle where you can. It's his lookout if he's done brown. Every man for himself. There's one born every minute. Fuck you, Jack. Pull up the ladder', and all the rest of the shameless litany. The difference is crucial and provides another motto for our times. These are the days when to question the National Lottery is to be a whey-faced prude, and to challenge uninhibited arms sales is to be an earnest idiot. A Foreign Secretary who, no doubt in good faith, had promised to restrict or abolish arms sales to authoritarian regimes is simply mocked when he finds the pledge much harder to honour than he had seemed to assume. I recall an American high official brusquely and brutally putting down a close Paris colleague who had questioned the justice of the Vietnam War. Years later, he publicly regretted his considerable role in prosecuting that conflict. 'It's never too late', of course; presumably he felt better for getting all that off his chest. To do so in the course of affairs would presumably have been just too much.

It is a truism that some on the far left are deeply unwilling to recognise a fact noted earlier: at all levels, 'socialist' authoritarian states are as riddled with corruption as democracies. They rarely have checks and balances, either within the government or outside, in the public arena; no free press, no free broadcasting, no free universities, no difficult intellectuals, no unhindered 'gatekeepers', no network of self-regulating and vacuum-filling voluntary bodies; none of that network of checks and balances essential to any would-be democratic society and which can have great tensile strength.

We are back with these uneasy forms of society, the commercial democracies, as the least worst choice of government. But, to repeat, and repetition needs no apology, they have to be reined in and wrongdoing must be punished severely. That kind of freedom has, must exact, a high price if it is misused. It will be misused. As the screws of capitalism tighten, so commercial morals loosen; that is a fact of the free-market life. None of this need damage initiative or the true sort of independence. Nor need it involve flying great ideological flags on behalf of the Citizen's Democracy. It involves boring, slow, patient work so as to allow maximum freedom to each and maximum discouragement to the greedy and immoral; it requires a sense of due degree, control, moderation – on behalf of all. Then it may work. But usually only in part. Democracy is by nature easy prey for the exploiters of its essential wide-open spaces, as people like Rupert Murdoch soon discover. For our part, we have not yet learned properly to keep such people off the grass.

At its best, it may advance human rights, the cause of the environment, the greater rights of women, anti-racism, in spite of class or status or other forms of envy, and at all levels of society.

The last words should go, as at the start, to some of this century's most humane and democratic voices, clear, direct, but yet organ-voices against the unacceptable drum-banging of capitalism: respectively, Tawney, Titmuss and Orwell:

> [There can be] a taste of ashes on the lips of a civilisation which has brought to the conquest of its natural environment resources unknown in earlier ages, but which has not yet learned to master itself.

> It is the responsibility of the State, acting sometimes through the processes we have called 'social policy', to reduce or eliminate or control the forces of market coercions which place men in situations in which they have less freedom or little freedom to make moral choices and to behave altruistically if they so will.

> Capitalism leads to dole queues, the scramble for markets, and war. Collectivism leads to concentration camps, leader worship, and war. There is no way out of this unless a planned economy can be somehow combined with the freedom of the intellect, which can only happen if the right and wrong are restored to politics.

Good words there, and greatly out of fashion. As always, we are judged by our language. Today, enterprise is favoured over compassion, self-assertion over charity, aggression over pity. In the age of galloping relativism, to work for better days may seem even harder than we have usually expected. That is inescapable, and no cause for hand-wringing.

'The most may err as grossly as the few.' Dryden was right in that cautionary note on democracy. Yet there was no way by which I could have been other than a socialist. Not so much a 'Labour' man, if that suggests smoke-filled rooms for, sometimes, routinely justified corrupt, small, local practices, endless speeches all interspersed with 'Comrades!', a self-righteous you-done-me-wrong manner which is the obverse image of a bullying boss's style, and no more attractive.

A socialist has to try to live up to a richer idea of 'comradeship', to work against gross riches if others are poor, to look on the parade of divisive class practices with both a critical and a comical eye, to try to acknowledge some worth in almost all – even in the more rigid sort of Tory. Just as most country squires find it almost impossible to shake off their cradle-Conservatism, so I cannot and do not wish to shake off what I have called my cradle-socialism. For some of us, these dispositions are almost in the blood, not good and bad opposites adopted as we grew up. I learned from Edward Boyle and one or two other Conservatives something of the feeling for tradition, public obligations, duty toward the land and its inhabitants of all kinds, which could move the best of such people. It is a pity that these attitudes are relatively rare in today's Conservative politicians. We could do with more understanding and compassion for the poor and unendowed.

It follows that socialism rather than Conservatism is the natural foundation for a democracy (which is well defined by Kolakowski as 'the obstinate will to do better'), even of an open capitalist democracy; socialism which has taken the trouble to learn a few things from the more civilised aspects of Conservatism. Other political forms are of course easier to live within if you are born or arrive high on the hog, sufficiently encased not to see often and be shamed by the privilege and distress around you.

Societies claiming or aiming to be democratic habitually dig up their roots, and either declare them in good health, and stuff them back, or, more rarely, are tempted to suggest a literally radical, root and branch change of political plant. Since adverse criticism is always more exciting than the admission of a degree of success – especially in democracies – the critics outnumber the congratulators. Not a bad thing; but much truly sharp criticism is deflected.

We have already noted that a network of critical voices is essential. But they may easily drift into speaking only to those of their own persuasion and, insofar as they simply rub together, cancel out each other; or, at the lowest level, they are not genuinely critical but flattering voices, prejudiced or even irrational. A regular *Guardian* reader usually has criticisms of that broadsheet but, coming across the *Daily Mail* at the barber's, is likely to be startled by its rigid internal protective-emollient-with-anger coherence, a wholly different world from that we choose to enter when we seek to became adult, at least in judgement. To make that entry it is necessary to realise that literacy is not enough; a democracy requires critical literacy (so does a dictatorship, but there it is harder to practise, not on the agenda). Not to train citizens in critical literacy is, for a commercial open democracy, like throwing most of the population, at sixteen, into a shark-infested sea, with no more equipment than a pair of cheap, gaudy, plastic water-wings.

So it is important from time to time to run through the case against democracy. Its limitations are glaring. 'Democracy means simply the bludgeoning of the people by the people for the people.' Wilde's epigrams, meant to shock, almost always have an atom of truth, as where he points, above, to the tendency of democracies to become uncritical, self-justifying head-counters. This underlines once again that democracies need many and varied institutions through which citizens are meant to be able to express and bring to bear their considered thoughts, individually and collectively. Otherwise, less disinterested people will treat them as a mass and offer reductive mass guidelines, as happens most of the time, here and now.

Edmund Burke had a similar but even more direct way than Wilde's of putting the case: for him, a perfect democracy is 'the

most shameless thing in the world'. That is at least as shocking –
out to shock – as Wilde's assertion. 'Perfect' is presumably to be
read as 'uncontrolled, uninhibited, left to be totally loose,
unqualified, taken for granted, going to the limit of its inclinations'; and so settling at a low level because always conforming
to majority taste. Chesterton, as prone to startling his readers as
most aphorists, gives a deeper dimension and one largely dis-
regarded today: 'Tradition . . . means the democracy of the
dead. Tradition refuses to submit to the small and arrogant oli-
garchy of those who merely happen to be walking about.' That
sounds like a down-to-earth T. S. Eliot insisting, as do many of
Eliot's pronouncements on tradition and politics, on the sense of
the past and our increasingly neglected duty to be in touch with it.

Today, the democracy of the dead is an unknown concept. In
different ways, the service of the contemporary 'hegemony' is
preoccupying. Autocracies have to know how to create
hegemony, consensus. The search is particularly applicable
also to democracies. Aiming to rule not by *diktat* or force, they
must go straight for consensus and seek it in more varied and
ingratiating ways than autocracies.

One of the most disturbing of all such judgements came from
Coleridge; many people today will reject it instantly. It too
pointed to some of the more difficult functions of a democracy.
Democracy, he argues, is a quality, an attitude, the 'healthy life-
blood' which courses through the arteries of a society. It is not
the ruling government itself; if it were, we would have
demagoguery, populism, head-counting decision-making, not
democracy.

In characteristically disenchanted mood, Conrad did not
moderate his words. He regretted that 'the popular mind' lacks
scepticism and so falls for all kinds of flattery. Again, not an
agreeable or acceptable remark today; but right. When our emotions are played upon as those of a mass – at least one major
modern example is still before us in the late 1990s: the reaction
elicited by the death of the Princess of Wales – we fall then as a
mass into extreme sentimental bathos. Not enough scepticism.

Emerson uttered a despairing and, we must hope, mistaken
elegy; mistaken so far as concerns the more nearly workable
democracies: 'Every reform is only a mask under cover of which a
more terrible reform, which dares not yet name itself, advances.'
As in the label 'National Socialism' for 'Fascist Totalitarianism'.

The case for the inherent weaknesses of a democracy can be
easily made, which does not mean it is compelling or decisive –
rather, such judgements remind us that democracy is one of the
forms of government most easily taken for granted as 'a good
thing', so that criticism or warnings about its soft underbelly can
be dismissed as proto-fascist or given some other, more or less
sticky, tag.

Democracy has always to be a gamble. Its core is sound, but
day by day it lives on a mixture of half-truths and half-wishful
thinking. Its elected representatives are rarely willing to face its
inherent weaknesses; blind flattery is easier and gives a quieter
life. That some British MPs are fools, others self-serving, others
loud-mouthed toadies, others cynical even about their own role,
is true. That is the price of democratic elections, particularly in
a society where one in seven adults is functionally near-illiterate.
Most MPs are nevertheless reasonably well-chosen. Jefferson
was properly firm here: if we think the body of the people are not
fit to govern themselves (which has to mean above all choosing
well those who will cope with regular decision-making on their
behalf) we will have to educate them. Disraeli echoed that in
1871: 'We must educate our masters'. That task we in England
have still not accomplished well. A loutish strain runs through
the English at all levels, like a smell from the drains. One gets
used to it, except when it glaringly erupts.

There are less evident weaknesses among those who claim to
be democrats. We looked briefly at one example of these some
pages back, but it needs more attention here. There are many
who are in principle socialists, though living well. In practice and
in certain matters they will do something to help the country
arrive at a more effectively democratic condition; little that hurts.
Some are willing to accept higher taxes so as to provide better for

the less fortunate. Yet, in general, it is assumed that their own present standard of living must not fall, must be the new base level for all. They will wait for others to catch up but will rarely forego some of their own present advantages so as to speed up the process. This is not an instance of 'Pull up the ladder, Jack. I'm all right', but a less brutal, more apparently encouraging position: 'Here's the ladder. Do climb. I won't come down a couple of steps to help. And please keep things steady.'

We will take steps to protect ourselves and our own. Some of those moves are understandable. We may live, perhaps, in a district where the comprehensive school is battling against almost overwhelming social problems – pupils from many different ethnic groups, one-parent families, unemployment. The teachers do their best, but hardly any pupils reach a respectable GCSE level. We approve of the comprehensive principle. We would not choose private education for our own children, who, we are sure, are clever (we may be right) but held back. We move to a district where the state comprehensive has a more respectable academic record. Feeling guilty, putting in service as Governor of a local school, but . . . .

The great inadequately examined educational problem lurks just behind. Comprehensives were founded in the belief that they could help us live together more equably (that word is exact here), could reduce the divisions of class or cash. They would disadvantage no one; no one would feel inferior or superior, socially better or more intellectually gifted. But that is the sort of vacuum or social space which societies, even the small societies of schools, will not tolerate; there must be a closure. All may be equal but some are more smiled upon than others – very often in imposing the strict rules of the peer group rather than, say, respect for academic or intellectual matters. It is in the interest of the dominant group to make the intellectually or imaginatively gifted feel out of line.

As much as other public figures, trade union leaders know the slacker rhetoric of democracy. In action, some can be as aggressive, rude, restrictive, immoral as the most thrusting industrial magnate, and pompous: 'If it's good enough for the bosses, it's good enough for my lads . . .'. Sharp practice for the greater benefit of 'my lads', even though it may damage others' 'lads', or is against the larger public interest, socially, educationally, culturally – all that is as easily and as completely excused as that recurrent boss's mantra: 'I owe it to my shareholders.' When a senior trade union officer admits that the higher productivity for which he is claiming a wage rise is due more than anything else to technological developments, and that thus work has become easier (but profits certainly higher), we will know that negotiations have started at a clearer upland.

At such moments, I recall Fred Sedgwick, the Worker's Educational Association district officer for North Yorkshire for two or three decades after the war. He came there from a trade union office. He worked tremendously hard for little pay, travelled exhaustingly by public transport and, except by the habitually sour, was admired and even loved. He finally decided that he could be much more effective if he travelled by car and asked his executive for the smallest Ford (at the time the Popular). Enough members of the executive thought he was getting above himself – 'He'll probably use it to go to Bridlington for the weekend at our expense, and all that . . .' – to delay the acquisition for months. Of course, it transformed even his existing wide range of work on their behalf.

As to most of the big unions, I look forward to the day when the environment figures seriously and more often on their agendas. It was, I think, in Melbourne that we saw workers, led by their union, refusing to cut down a fine stand of trees in the cause of 'development'. Would that happen in England? If the 'fat cats' epitomise one kind of contemporary England, there is a continuous line from them to bulldozer operators making no objection to whatever they are ordered – often with a sweetener – to do in the name, again, of 'development'. Another unhappily hijacked word.

One of the weaknesses of English and other democracies – it is native to the form – is laziness. Dr Johnson was right in that celebrated blunt assertion: whatever our pretensions to political interests, a toothache troubles us more than the state of the nation. So it should; it is pretentious to claim otherwise. But, having admitted the predominance of toothache in this calculus, most of us ought to give more regular attention to the essential best practices of democratic politics.

Here appears another common and probably excessive hope, popular among some who do think about politics and with the best intentions. It is widely believed that today's citizens feel, and possibly are, dangerously divorced from the centres of influence; that governments pay less and less attention to the House of Commons in their decisions; that the Commons harangue but seem unable to put much pressure on the levers of power; that we have moved into presidential-style government; that global business and industry become more and more the unacknowledged instruments of force; that among 'ordinary' voters, disaffection, or sheer disenchantment, increases.

The more hopeful among politically minded people, especially those on the left, often put their trust in the increasing appearance of grass-roots oppositions. They quote various clearly dissident, indeed 'dropped-out', groups as examples of the rejection of the present disconnected situation, but fail to enquire into how such groups can connect with the centres and exercise of power instead of going round and round within their own fields of interest and protest. Even if a government were more aware of them, it would nod and pass on, registering them as harmless permitted deviations, against whom, if they become nuisances, the Home Secretary could act.

Other writers avoid the more dramatic fringe groups but cite the extensive and long-established range of local initiatives of all kinds, especially those committed to nourishing community activities. To them one adds voluntary bodies preoccupied with those major national or international interests already mentioned; obviously these can all be valuable, very valuable indeed as a main expression of that sense of common belonging which Orwell celebrated, though with ironic qualifications. But, again, what are their present connections with national or international decision-making? The collapse of the Soviet empire was hailed by some members of END (European Nuclear Disarmament) as a victory for their efforts. This would have been a wonderful outcome, but the claim is probably ill-founded. Gorbachev's dismissal of the claim is more credible; the forces he recognised had precisely to do with hard, practical economic pressures on a global scale, little to do with 'people power'. Nevertheless, we need be neither dismissive or depressive, as I shall try to show later. We must treasure all our forms of well-aimed voluntary activity, as crucial to a democracy. We have still to learn how to make them connect better with influence, power, authority. That will be difficult; we may have to seek, initially, different and less immediately gratifying forms and levels of connection.

———

The case *for* democracy? A sour but true commonplace accepts that societies constantly rewrite their history so that their own present form is seen as inevitable and right. The dead can do nothing about that. In this light, the Chesterton passage quoted earlier acquires new force.

Democracy, by nature trying to be honest and open, must always fall short in its achievements compared with its professions, and will always be beset by the contrast; it cannot live up to its own dreams. Authoritarian governments believe in the – forced – perfectibility of man; their own version of perfectibility. They assume and demand too much of everyone. They believe they can arrange over time for the average sensual human to be made average only in unsensuality, obedient behaviour; that most people can be screwed into a simulacrum of virtue or at least of good routines, as Stakhanovite citizen/workers or onwards-and-upwards Gauleiters. The rest, a small minority, are regarded as mentally ill. Ah well – only look at present-day Russia, after sixty years of such indoctrinations. Sad, because of the failure of a sort of dream; but also heartening for us as we go on trying to succeed differently.

Democracy is, in one sense, the best of a bad job. A poor conclusion? You will think so if you want instant and perfect conclusions and are perhaps prepared to go through blood and fire to reach them. Democracy will not attract those who would live by absolutes. It is always left somewhere in the middle, unfinished, never to be finished, mud-bespattered, always falling down and getting up once more. We repeat such clichés again and again; we have to, because they are right: the least worst form of government. It recognises and stands for, without regret or self-exculpation, the fallibility of us all. It can be sloppy by demanding or asking too little, but is the only individually reflective form of society and can sometimes with success ask for more than we realised we could give: in neighbourliness, community sense, careful rather than chauvinistic respect for the national interest, respect also for human rights rather than narrow-minded bigotry, intelligent and imaginative rather than prejudiced legislation, all in trying to pull up our communal selves by the bootstraps.

Most impressive of all: it can allow laws to be passed which are somewhat better, more civilised, than a referendum would prompt; a referendum is a two-edged weapon to be handled with great intelligence and selectivity. A referendum on capital punishment or for racist practices would, even today, approve both. This democracy has passed legislation opposing both; we do not sufficiently recognise or celebrate such astonishing achievements.

Democracy can be a level-headed way of running a country and so provide the best available checks and balances against those chief destroyers of civil societies already observed: extremism and its sister, intolerance, on the one hand; and an often lazy, self-regarding bureaucracy and citizenry on the other. But, as Conrad again sensed, the floor is very thin; we are almost always almost walking on the water. The gloomy Dean Inge was in one sense obviously right in declaring democracy 'only an experiment in government, and it has the obvious disadvantage of merely counting votes instead of weighing them'. But he

should have taken a further step; or half-step, as he would probably have said. The thinness of the floor even today was
distressingly illustrated in the commotion created by Glenn
Hoddle's remarks on reincarnation. By most of the press and
some of the government he was misinterpreted, freedom of
speech was pushed aside and his resignation as coach of the
England football team irrelevantly but successfully demanded.*
'It is a sin to make the State a school of morals.' Hölderlin was
in some senses right, too; in other ways, too unqualified. On certain moral issues a democratic state must take a stand, especially
to protect the more defenceless of its citizens; that is an element
of Mill's principles to which such a state must keep itself as
open as possible: it must intervene to prevent some from inter-
fering with the rights of others. For certain people, who
inevitably call themselves 'true' democrats, such moments will
hardly ever arrive; for them, the boundaries of intervention are
too difficult and dangerous to define except most rarely; almost
every limitation on freedom is suspect. They call for virtually no
governmental action except, most regrettably, in quite unavoid-
able cases such as on which side of the road we must drive.
That is their freedom, too. I prefer Habermas: 'Men are qualified for civil liberty in exact proportion to their disposition to put
moral chains on their own appetites.'

Democracy is never an abstraction. It has to be rooted in a
sense of our own particular culture, of its virtues, strengths,
limitations. That is the best soil for a true patriotism. It arises
from the people we have known, loved, respected as we grew
up, whether that was among the urban or rural working class,
or the conscientious and public-spirited among the middle class,
or the upper class.

Each of these levels has its false mirror image, and this
produces, as it does in most European countries, that narrow

*Mark Mazower's *Europe's Twentieth Century: Dark Continent*
tellingly illustrates the newness and fragility of even Europe's hold on
democracy.

and ignorant chauvinism which in England chants: 'We have the best universities/health service/armed forces/landscape/record of deaths on the road/educational system/social security/police force/sense of humour in the world', and, on the way to a football match on the continental mainland: 'We won the war! We won the war!'

Above that range, we meet one of the smuggest of all English ways of closing the discussion of tricky issues: 'I think we have the balance about right now. Yes?' Better always to be aware of our limitations as individuals and as a society; in all of them, in all of us, are the marks of both our imperfectibility and our inclination at the best to reach higher.

A democracy is commodious and hospitable but tends to insularity. It lacks awe, but is always preferable to a theocracy (that can be another name for various autocracies), which is by nature exclusive and so tends to selective cruelties. A democracy offers no quick fixes. It belongs to 'the real world', in an acceptable definition of that phrase. It offers no golden future horizons but may have some very bright pleasant moments; and some terrible. That is our fate, and democracy the best way for societies to face it.

My sense of Englishness was first founded on common strengths in part of the pre-war Leeds working-class. That was a largely urban experience. It also brought the extraordinary bonus I intend to mention, as needed, more than once: that even in tightly packed Hunslet we inhaled, as easily as the polluted air we breathed, a sense of the land. We knew the great Dales just outside to the west and north and knew they were ours as much as anyone else's, part of our patrimony. Airholes, yes, not aesthetic backdrops.

'Dullness is decent in the Church and State.' Dryden was right again. Democracy is founded in what can look like a decent dullness. Democracy is also deeply radical. It sticks to the radicalism of the middle way, the refusal to accept any form of unqualified absolute solutions. It needs great courage to fight, on behalf of its citizens, the big battalions of capital, of the City, and of all kinds of extremism, and the courage to try to steer straight against the more mellifluous voices from government, sometimes from the Church, and always from the voices which reflect only popular prejudice. At that point, a society may be on the way to becoming a civilisation.*

I began with quotations, chiefly about the limitations of democracy, and went on to vindications. We may end with other reminders of its present limits and possible aims. The debate goes on and always will and should.

It is not surprising that the arguments are often expressed in paradoxes. Pascal agreed that: 'The majority is the best way, because it is visible, and has strength to make itself obeyed. Yet it is the opinion of the least able.' For Chesterton, democracy means 'government by the uneducated, while aristocracy means government by the badly educated'. As so often with crafted paradoxes, the oppositions are skewed.

Nebuhr's paradox is, though, straighter and more hopeful: 'Man's capacity for evil makes democracy necessary and man's capacity for good makes democracy possible.' To which Emerson surprisingly and happily adds: 'The evils of popular government appear greater than they are; there is compensation for them in the spirit and energy it awakens.'

Kolakowski underlines the cost: 'Democratic socialism requires, in addition to a number of basic values, hard knowledge and rational calculation . . . it is an obstinate will to erode by inches the conditions which produce avoidable suffering, oppression, hunger, wars, racial and national hatred, insatiable greed and vindictive energy.' The key word there is 'avoidable'. Then, a good partner to Kolakowski: 'The first [basic claim about human existence] is that humans are typically unfree, dominated by conditions which they neither understand nor control . . . The second is that human life need not be this way.

*Some recent work on the stakeholder society looks more promising in this way than the usual back-to-the-drawing-board proposals.

The third is that an increase in knowledge is the way the oppressed can liberate themselves and thereby better their lot.' As an old-hand adult educator, I can only applaud that.

Last, some typically English judgements. Forster of course, with elegant verbal gin-and-bitters: 'Two cheers for democracy: one because it allows variety and two it admits criticism. Two cheers are quite enough; there is no occasion to give three.' Then Lindsay of Balliol on 'the thoughtful, practical idealism of the moderate Left [to whom democracy must be seen as native ground]'.

Finally, and as so often, Auden, warmly celebrating, in 'Horae Canonicae': 'Our dear old dog of a democracy' – which is fine, so long as the old dog isn't losing its *joie de vivre*, threatening to die from inanition on the living-room carpet, and beginning to smell a bit.

Even so, democracy, like the dog, remains homely if niffy, not grand. Good: for the great body of 'ordinary people' always have to pay for others' non-democratic delusions of grandeur.

4

On Classes and Masses:
The Cleft Society

SPIRALLING EVER CLOSER to the ground, from belief and unbelief through love and self-love, capitalism and democracy, we come to the actual world of pavements and people, shoving and pushing, shops and lamplights, of washing up and dressing down, of contemporary cultural phenomena which we pore over intently these days but seem hardly to understand much better. More immediately, we move now from the political life of society to the public life of the inner neighbourhoods and outer suburbs, and the private life of our convictions and prejudices. Less memoir, rather more meditation, much more manifesto.

I have been writing about English society, impressionistically rather than 'scientifically', for almost fifty years. Writing about English 'culture' in roughly both the anthropological and the Arnoldian senses; the two are inextricably joined. And especially writing about 'class', on which for almost all those fifty years I seem to have been swimming against the tide. Didn't I know, I have been told repeatedly, that the sense of class distinction has gone?

No; I did not and do not know that. I know the opposite: that one of the most common myths in England today is precisely that the sense of class has almost entirely disappeared, or is well on the way to doing so. This false belief is so firmly held that anger meets any denial. This is the routine 'Nonsense! I regard my cleaning lady as a friend' response. It is made all the more sharply by people who, usually half-consciously, realise that though some of the old forms of class expression have been muted, they have themselves benefited by what I call later the transfer of class to status feeling and distinction.

One could easily go on and on in indicating the resistance of the sense of class today. The class- and cash-divided National Health Service can preserve habits out-of-date fifty years ago. A friend, waiting with his trousers down for a consultant's inspection under the NHS, heard a specialist in a nearby cubicle berate his juniors: 'What do you mean by requiring a *private* patient to lower his trousers before I *invite* him to do so?'

The old myth, which I have noted in an earlier book, remains: that paying for treatment reduces the waiting list for treatment under the National Health Service. If it does that, it does so by queue-jumping through cash, ignoring need. There is a second common practice of which I have only recently taken the measure. A senior surgeon usually has a team under him. An NHS patient will be lucky to be treated by the senior consultant; a private (the word is misused) patient will assume that he will be treated by the senior, or would complain; that is also what he is paying 'good money' for, and it suits the senior person. By great good fortune, our younger son was immediately and successfully treated for a cancer by a surgeon who seemed not to stick to such habits; they do exist. The dental service is now an even worse case, especially in the way it bears on the poor, many of whom simply neglect their teeth.

This system therefore distorts overall treatment. Secretaries of state do not like to grasp the problem. Shadow secretaries of state may admit that there is 'spare capacity' in the private sector without seeing that that alone is a criticism of private health care; we won't treat you, whatever the urgency, unless you pay us handsomely. No wonder Bevan was disgusted, but had to yield.

There is, however, an increase in pseudo-classlessness, false togetherness of all kinds. Or, surprisingly, there is the opposite, a deliberate reintroduction of class divisions in places where we thought they had long gone or been modified. It is some decades since British Rail abandoned its Third Class, leaving only Second and First; and then, in the itch to lessen explicit class-insult, Standard and First. Standard and Sub-standard would be more accurate on several lines nowadays. (And why 'customers' is felt to be preferable to 'passengers' is incomprehensible except to the marketing director's ear.)

Railway operators do not usually fill their seats in the middle of the day, between the rush hours. So they have inherited from BR lower fares at those times, which attract especially pensioners. Both sides gain. But some bright PR person on GNER (the Great North Eastern Railway) has succeeded in convincing management that it would be attractive once again to have Second and Third classes. So now, on that line, you can travel Full Standard in a 'dedicated' carriage if you have paid a full Standard Class fare, with free cups of tea and more room, because those who have paid discounted fares in these slacker hours are in steerage, now more crowded than ever.

Is this an instance of the decline of the divisive, the class-distinguishing sense, fifty years after we began being told that class was dead? The railways still gain money from selling seats they would not otherwise fill; those who travel at a discount now pay for it by more crowded conditions, no doubt thought suitable to their status and not likely to cause a fuss. Only the small, class-fixated PR mind could have invented that.

GNER is not alone in inventing class divisions to boost charges. Virgin Rail is byzantine in its selective colour-coding of carriages; the staff often stumble as they read them over the intercom. GNER is probably more cheeky in defending such practices. A day return ticket to a town north of Leeds costs x pounds; for a journey 60 miles shorter up the same line, the same fare is charged. If charges were proportionate to distance, the shorter fare would be £4 cheaper. Questioned, the 'Customer Relations Manager' is not in the least evasive; shameless and jargony, rather: 'I would advise you that we are now a private business as per government directive and similar to any other business policy, we can and do charge what the market will bear.' Thirty-two words to say: 'Get Stuffed.' The only main cliché he omits to invoke is: 'We owe it to our shareholders.'

In certain respects, the undoubted blurring of some class differences may at first appear regrettable. Lionel Trilling greatly appreciated the hum and buzz of implication in English life, its dense texture (which is largely composed of class reverberations): 'The diminution of the reality of class, however socially desirable in many respects, seems to have the practical effect of diminishing our ability to see people in their difference and specialness.' Perhaps he had America in mind there. Certainly in 1950, when he wrote that, it would have been a premature judgement about these islands; and on the whole it still is, even though Trilling's compatriot Edward Shils not quite so many years ago noted 'the entry of the working class' into British society, as general prosperity increased.

Much as I admire Trilling's judgement, I think him only half accurate there. There has certainly been a lessening of some aspects of class-determined behaviour; of, in short, various manifestations of snobbery. Yet the sense of class difference is so deep-seated that such changes are still superficial; that sense finds other ways of expressing itself: in holiday habits, eating habits, sports activities, housing areas, marriages. Even as 'class' is to some extent weakened, so it redefines itself under a new name and with new intimations of difference. The sense of class is so deeply ingrained that we still do not notice it as we continue to exercise it, in old or new forms. Class sense becomes status sense; the emotional energy spent in sustaining one form now supports the other. That is the gist of my argument about class changes today.

Those changes affect different levels in different ways. I know almost nothing about the upper classes, except that they still exist, though, it seems, not quite as solidly as they used to. The middle classes are in some confusion, partly because their aspirations are now more difficult to define, but more because, like a currency flooded with somewhat suspect notes, they find themselves being, except at the upper-middle-class level, threatened with absorption by 'executives'; that title covers an enormous range of people, from important managing directors to salesmen on £16,000 a year plus commission, a Mondeo and a mobile. The very word 'executive' will, must, have its time but that has not yet arrived. Only a few weeks ago I saw advertised in a Farnham town café: 'Executive Ploughman's Lunches'. Made superior with a glass of chilled Chardonnay? Like Irish Coffee, the Ploughman's Lunch is a PR invention; we might yet see Executive or Business Class Irish Coffee, with double shots of spirit.

Many in the upper reaches of the professional middle classes still feel themselves secure. Travelling First Class from London to Farnham (paid for, luckily, since Standard Class was crowded that day), I was in a carriage occupied by only two other men, both obviously City types. They boomed confidently at each other. The younger of them was very pleased with life: 'Yes, Giles is taking Common Entrance this year, Peter next year. Peter's already a cracker at cricket. Giles got 90 and 75 in his Trial Maths . . . So I suppose it'll be Charterhouse. Better the devil you know, eh?' Not much shaking of the social foundations there.

Malicious observers are likely to say of the lower middle classes: 'They always buy their fluffy slippers at Marks and Spencer.' For what it's worth, that may be generally true. Their most important characteristic is their loyalty to established habits, their muted yet dogged resistance to most offerings which might change their ways of life. In this role, in attitudes not objects, they, rather than the aristocracy, are the pillars of English society.

Here is a contemporary change which especially attracts the lower-middle to middle classes at a certain time of life, and also shows a new and increasing divisiveness in elements of British society. Highly specialised, segmented provision is offered; in insurance, for example. You can now, and over the telephone, receive an advantageous quotation for many kinds of insurance;

if you fit the regulations. If your house is not more than x years old, if you are not more than x years old, if your car is not more than x years old; and so on. Be stereotyped for your own small and the insurers' greater profit. The trick is to refuse to insure anyone who might be more likely than most to make a claim. Most insurance companies have traditionally taken the rough with the smooth, had a wide range of possible customers and let the less vulnerable subsidise the more. Now the vulnerable must go elsewhere and pay higher premiums because there are no balancing offsets. Legitimate; but not what could be called a communal democratic practice.

Segmentation-with-concentration of a related kind is going on rapidly elsewhere. As in publishing. Increasingly, the large, accountant-led corporations insist on the selection by their editors, so far as can be judged, of likely best-sellers. They pay handsomely for them and, if they guess right, themselves make large profits. Their guiding light has to be 'effectiveness in the market' not 'quality of writing' – nothing to do with contributions to literature and understanding. So serious authors find it increasingly hard to place their books, their advances fall, the prices of their books increase, their publishers' profits are slimmer.

We are back again with a predictably small, segmented, minority audience. Mass-audience-seeking narrows the airholes for quality; verbal and intellectual inventiveness are reduced. Social compartmentalism increases; we are back again with the enclosed 10 to 15 per cent, and the great congealed readership mass.

Most interesting of all are movements within the working classes (to use that phrase in the plural is an acknowledgement of change, for it is not accurate to say they are not changing; or, conversely, that they have virtually disappeared). Many of their old ways remain much as they were – only listen to their speech, especially in pubs and clubs. In their habits as consumers – of everything from food to clothing, but *not* of opinions – they are changing fairly quickly. Someone has cruelly but accurately noticed: the only 'book' to be found in many prosperous working-class homes is the Argos catalogue – the archetypal consumer-society object.

There has been no significant lessening of Trilling's 'difference and specialness', of attractive variety, of interesting and often comical practices, vocabularies, voices, gestures, omissions and elisions. There have been superficial changes, much loved by trend- and fashion-hunters. But we still have, and will continue to have for as far as we can foresee, what Bulwer Lytton felicitously called: 'the shot-silk colours of society'.

Many of our more tenacious attitudes are not at all 'shot-silk' or felicitous, and some of the most unattractive run across all classes. Such as racism, from the mild to the virulent. Even late in life, the former Prime Minister, Harold Macmillan, entering a Commonwealth reception, had forgotten what the occasion was, and pronounced cheerily: 'A lot of nig-nogs here today, eh!' Lord Goodman, in many respects a liberal-minded man, remarked without hesitation at an international conference we were both attending on the 'surprising' assertiveness of many of 'our curly-headed friends' present. Both those instances are from about twenty years ago. Have racism and anti-Semitism weakened? A little. After fifty years, Caribbeans and Asians are more accepted. Anti-Semitism, being more deep-seated, more like a historic and even natural limitation, has lessened little. Have both learned to hide themselves somewhat better?

Most in all classes are, or were until very recently, deeply old-fashioned in their sentimental attachment to royalty. Forms change, attitudes remain. When they are not exposing royal weaknesses, the tabloids stroke the sentimental nerve. One night, a few years ago, the polo ponies stabled at Windsor were threatened by fire. The tabloids reported, or invented, the news that the Queen 'threw an old coat over her shoulders and went out to see if she could help'. That 'old coat' is a clever touch. Just like the one we have hanging behind the scullery door.

The popular reaction to the death of the Princess of Wales, as an index to royalist feeling, has been interpreted in dozens of different and often superficial ways – in support of or against the future of the monarchy – but all unable to leave it alone or to wait until the disguising dust settles. Many years will be needed before we can properly interpret it. One thing may already be said: after the initial resentment at what was thought to be the Royal Family's inadequate reaction to the tragedy, public opinion bounced back into the sentimental mode towards them. Several anti-royalist and pro-feminist commentators fired too soon and mis-predicted.

When we recognise that the Queen is dumpy, walks stoutly as if over rough moorland, is touchingly ill-dressed and coiffured, and has limited intellectual interests, we will have taken a small step forward; and perhaps we may then like our royal icons the better in that form.

More racism than we like to admit, more anti-Semitism, much support for the death penalty, sentimentality about royalty – all these unite the classes as much as the much-vaunted tolerance and pride in our long democratic traditions. Aided by their resistant attachment to out-of-date figures, objects and rituals, the English, whilst continually proclaiming their democratic credentials, will put up silently with glaringly undemocratic institutions and practices. As we have seen in the notoriously class-divided health service and educational systems, and the divisively weakened dental service, no longer a national service.

Thirty years ago, in a letter to me, Auden expressed his pronounced sense of traditional interconnections. Most of his observations would stand today, though perhaps not be readily expressed in public:

> As regards the bourgeois, I am, as you know, middle-middle class, and count myself lucky to have been born in it. Whatever their faults, the middle have realised and introduced into civilisation two great virtues, integrity about money and a devotion to work. The aristocracy did not pay their debts, and the peasants, naturally enough, reacted by cheating them when they could. The aristocracy thought work beneath their dignity, and to the poor, by and large,

work was pure work, i.e. had no element of play in it because there was scarcely any element of choice . . . I grew up in a family where there was always enough money to pay for necessaries, the butcher, the grocer etc – but any luxuries had to be saved for. Consequently, I have a horror of debt – I like to pay bills by return post and I have never in my life bought anything on Instalment.

Again – this may be rather neurotic – I feel guilty about indulging in any pleasure unless I can feel that I have done enough work to deserve it.

In many respects intellectually 'classless' and by then a New Yorker for many years, Auden nevertheless shows in that letter (as often in person) how much he remained 'of his class'. In a drive from Birmingham to the Malverns, he grew tetchily opinionated in an old-fashioned and uninformed way in response to any criticism of the public-school system, and suspected, in the manner of a retired local Conservative party chairman, the obstreperousness of the trade unions. He was not alone. He has been joined, almost conversely and perversely, by some long-serving communists who went to Oxbridge and will now defend the indefensible: the admissions procedures in many colleges. A liberal-minded high executive of the BBC will defend private medicine on the strangely mistaken ground we have already met: that by paying for his operation he has 'made space for one more to be treated on the NHS', and was not queue-jumping.

We have endless, subtle, unspoken points of recognition. A man of the lower-middle class, obviously used to some degree of management, the sort who soon after joining the wartime army would have been noted as a likely corporal, occupied a hospital bed near me for a few days. He was courteous and very slightly deferential to me, since I am 'well-spoken'. To the black woman who brought his cups of tea he was instantly near peremptory; to a surgeon he spoke as an NCO to a senior officer. A small, talkative man in a bed opposite deferred slightly to him; the deference was accepted. The small man's deference to the doctors and consultants was greater. Even for some of us who have moved from the working to the professional classes, it can be quite difficult to lose altogether that deference, towards consultants, at least. Class differences are kept up as much by the happily subservient as by the defensively secure; some afterglow is felt to fall on them both.

The working and middle class are divided not only by the tongue, as Orwell said; they are divided also by the stomach. There is a minor belief that if 'management' and employees share a canteen, a blow will have been struck against the sense of class division. Perhaps, and that is tried in some institutions. Look at the menus and you will see other divisions. There is, nowadays, food for vegetarians, of course, and 'light diet' salads for the professional women. For those on the shop floor, the fry-up will dominate, as the chip-pan does in the home. If working-class people really begin to merge with others, their love of the frying pan will be one of the last exemplary elements to go.

In some members of the English upper class, the sense of their own status is still stronger than their ability to 'place' others outside their usual circles. A personal example may be allowed here; it is funny, and typical of some in the uppermost echelons.

Christopher Soames, when ambassador in Paris, saw a Conservative Cabinet Minister talking during a reception at the embassy to an unknown someone who, he seemed to have assumed, was ignorable, deaf or perhaps monolingual in Urdu. He approached and asked in a loud voice, over the head of the unknown man: 'Do you want rescuing, David?' With that kind of grandee (to paraphrase Dickens) 'the voices alone are enough'; they bay and hoot. They can also be, to recall a Hunslet phrase towards those suspected of overt snobbery, 'Very vulgar'. Lord Eccles had the grace to indicate he was content with his lot. So he should have been, since he had specifically asked me to go across Paris to the embassy affair to help him on a tricky Anglo–French matter: on whether the French could safely be allowed to borrow the Rosetta Stone.

Other images are less off-putting and, like eighteenth-century salon portraits, capture an age and a system. A couple of years ago, I was for the first time (and after several refusals) at Buckingham Palace; there had been a ceremony in Westminster Hall followed by a large reception, both in honour of the United Nations system. My eye was caught by a group of three brigadiers talking together, all fresh from distinguished service in Bosnia. Full dress uniforms; tight-fitting black trousers outlining the calves; black, equally tight-fitting jackets, flared below so as to give, unexpectedly, a dancing-master effect. Epaulettes, medals, tassles over shoulders. Legs elegantly crossed as they stood, and spines so straight as almost to lean backward. Very healthy-looking, no spare flesh; mid-to-late forties. Destined to move even further upwards.

Constant smiles; entirely at ease with themselves; culturally at home. Plainly, overwhelmingly, this was what it was all about and to which all had so far led. From the right prep and public schools, to one of the top officer-training establishments, to drinks at Buck House. No questioning or disturbing thoughts? This world taken as manifestly right in all its main particulars and parts and especially in its structures of responsibility and power. The sense was of having arrived at the best of all possible worlds. They did not exude what Palewski calls the 'cultural imperialism of the French', the assumption of possessing 'the domain of values' in a more than national sense. But they knew where they were and found it good, were secure in their sense of its rightness. Not unpleasant-looking, though.

But enough of all this. It will go on but will change, though slowly. It is still a most fertile ground for English anecdotage and fiction.

At this time we should be thinking much more about that increasing and neglected bottom 10 per cent or so of English society. These people have effectively fallen out of any community: are ill-fed, ill-educated, often in one-parent families which have lost or are losing any sense of the sustaining texture a secure family and decent neighbourhood may give, beset by the constant need for palliatives: booze, drugs, fags, incest, violence; with hardly the energy or the public nous even to say: 'They ought to do this or that for us:' (Nick Danziger's *A Journey to the Edge* documents all this, as does Nick Davies's *Dark Heart: The Shocking Truth About Hidden Britain*.) These are people often consigned to what some local authorities call their 'sink estates'. These are the largely hidden casualties of the otherwise prosperous commodity culture, the worst costs of that culture, the untouchables; a new class about which the bulk of the old-style pre-war 'working class' would have been both shocked and, often, pitying.

'Culture saves nothing and nobody, nor does it justify. But it is a product of man: he projects himself through it and recognises himself in it; this critical mirror alone shows him his image.'

Sartre

'Civilisation exists precisely so that there may be no masses but rather men alert enough never to constitute masses.'

Bernanos

Sartre and Bernanos nicely complement each other there. But, first, it should go without saying, but isn't sufficiently said, especially by those among us who criticise a great deal in society today: in some ways most of us are far better off than any of our predecessors. We are generally in better health, live longer, do not want for food, are better housed, have been released from excessive toil, have money to spend and spare time in which to spend it. Advances in such related sciences as genetics, molecular biology and biochemistry promise even more remarkable movements towards better physical lives.

Less tangible, but at least as important: though the sense of status may be succeeding that of class, most people feel less deferential, less as though they are being 'kept in their place', the 'us' who are always to be below the 'them', free-er. Publicly available social justice for all has increased. That, as we have already seen, some of the manifestations of this new liberty seem ill-advised, instances of exploitation by the greedy and ill judgement by their targets, is true, but they point to the main need. The right democratic countervailing forces, of which the pre-eminent is education, have not kept pace with the changes, not adequately reassessed their roles. Most of us are still kept in our place not by the rigidities of poverty but by the invisible silken cords of institutionalised, consumer-directed flattery.

A response such as: 'But what about Waterstone's?' is inadequate. It is good that a chain of more or less serious bookshops should appear and succeed. It is necessary to recognise that they cater for the new, well-educated, professional meritocrats; they are enclosed, that 10 to 20 per cent; the rest pass by, unaffected, heading for their glossy and rubbishy diet. The newer divisions widen and harden.

The best change of the last half-century has been another entry: 'the gradual entry of women into society'. The 'glass ceiling' remains in many places but is cracked if not shattered in others, especially among some professional groups. Self-conscious quotas are increasingly out-of-date; the proof of equal competence is there – as one may see in any public committee, broadcasting organisation, publishing house, and so on. Further down, change is mixed; in almost all classes, unprecedented numbers of women are going out to work. Yet in many working-class areas in and above the underclass, women are still regarded and treated as subordinate. That is changing and will change even more. The main agent of change is what can fairly be called the sexual revolution and the freedom for women it can bring; with it comes the acceptance, even across 'respectable' council estates, that one doesn't simply have to 'get a man' and be married. The common choice of partnership rather than marriage in such places is a critical indicator of a greater sense of self-determination and self-worth, and it has become more widespread, more quickly, than might have been expected.*

So: in some respects we have advanced considerably. In

cultural matters – in Sartre's and Bernanos's larger senses quoted above – we have not. In these respects, especially in comparison with what might have been, we are where we always were or have gone backward – after a hundred years of declared universal literacy. We ignore engagements with moral questions as they now emerge, often in new and unsuspected forms. Our technological achievements, whatever benefits they may have brought, have in some ways and to some degree paved the way for those losses. That we publish more than a hundred thousand books a year is a technical, not an intellectual, achievement or indicator. Imaginative creativity of all kinds has not 'progressed' over the centuries. Why should it? Similarly, the larger part of all our experience is the rediscovery of old truths and the committing of old errors.

It is, at bottom, as hard as it has ever been to live together and with ourselves. Such engagements have to be fought by each of us in each generation. Here, we do not necessarily 'progress', no matter how many complex instruments of modern communications we may have in our homes.

Peculiar, to feel increasingly almost a stranger in one's own land. An effect of old age? Or is the prevailing culture changing so much and so rapidly that we can no longer take for granted, even among well-educated people, that some things are commonly valued more than others. Not the everyday things which are still part of our common culture. To add to an earlier list of those: family outings, high tea, toasted teacakes, the garden, the best things on television. All such things and many others that they stand for are still widely enjoyed. But what of 'Culture [as] a pursuit of our total perfection by means of getting to know, on all the matters which most concern us, the best which has been thought and said in the world'. Elsewhere, Arnold continues: 'And thus with the [best in the] history of the human spirit'. With great books, music, painting and sculpture, the Authorised

*For qualifications here see *The New Feminism* by Natasha Walter.

Version, the continuing, serious and civil quarrel of this society with itself.

Matthew Arnold's prose was meant to be 'uplifting' and causes amusement today. We could do with more of it: 'The pursuit of perfection, then, is the pursuit of sweetness and light.' The sense of the past, of connections back over generations, of a relationship with those who went before, of a continuous, absorbing, though not necessarily successful, path – that sense, even for some of the few who are still aware of it, usually goes no further back than Shakespeare. For most, it goes back only to grandparents, if that far. And most of Europe is where one passes through on the way to the sun.

Few physical heirlooms or treasured oral memories or written records remain for most families; will film and video and their successors compensate, or will those records deteriorate as they lie unrecalled in cupboards? A world of the continuous present, with virtually no looking back. Once, every family seemed to have its oral historian, often only partially literate, yet the one who kept the collective memory by names and dates, events, family tales. Some survive; I know two in our own extended family; both literate, of course, though not scholars, but in close, fascinated, admiring and continuous contact with our family's past.

All this may always have been kept alive by only a few. But not an entirely enclosed few. There were always the thoughtful Common Readers, to whom I constantly refer, in admiration; not those usually or necessarily to be found in the great centres of power, but in schools, colleges, universities, neighbourhoods, voluntary bodies and societies, local government, private houses; all having some civilising effect, however small. It is easy to ignore them. The railway booking clerk may be just a head and shoulders behind protective glass, until you meet him on a late train coming back to Farnham from London, reading his Promenade concert programme. They all in some ways echo my own and other's aspirations and experience, except that they have not had as many leg-ups on the way as we have had.

On the other hand, few 'highly educated' people in all areas of life and work today, especially those under forty, feel the need for access to, say, the previously assumed corpus of at least European intellectual and artistic culture. One has to conclude that these people, though often sophisticated and intelligent, are 'acculturated' in a different way from that expected only fifty years ago; the criteria have changed and largely cut them off from their predecessors.

What is left if one does not try to value 'civilisation' in the senses insisted on by Arnold, if one does not try to assess and maintain the slow achievements of humanity as it has emerged from the primitive? This movement can seem, especially to agnostics and atheists, the most important initial value, the foundation for the rest of human achievements, as it was for the unbeliever Bertrand Russell: 'I don't live for human happiness but for some kind of struggling emergence of mind.' Sometimes, it is plain, the 'struggling emergence' marks time; only material gains can be counted on our scales.

Looking back over the last century and a half, Gertrude Himmelfarb makes a useful distinction between Victorian 'virtues' and modern 'values'. Her historical comparisons have been severely criticised. Detached from those, the contrast is handy in relation to attitudes today. A 'value', she argues, may change; it is likely to be personally chosen and adopted, though probably from a box of acceptable 'values' offered by the culture of the day; a choice has been made by an individual.*

A 'virtue' can stand outside, has social links, is not made to measure for the needs of each of us; it demands to be generally recognised and honoured, detached from individual taste. This is a time of 'values' at the expense of 'virtues'.

Publicly, that is; it is comforting to see how many people, apparently followers of current 'values', in times of great trouble

---

*The Demoralization of Society, From Victorian Virtues to Modern Values, Gertrude Himmelfarb (Knopf, 1995). There are interesting similarities in Richard Sennett's The Corosion of Character (Norton, 1998).

draw on deeper wells of compassion and commitment, on older 'virtues'.

The main agents of change in this whole process are, as was noted earlier, the communication industries themselves; and within those the ever-increasing body of people who man the public relations and advertising agencies. Even after many years, I find it difficult to be restrained when writing about those professions. These people deal in half-truths at best, in lies more often. Advertising copywriting is corrupt fiction; public-relations prose is distorted truth, as in 'Care in the Community'. Its authors will say what they can get away with so as to promote their boss's goods or services, and will be paid handsomely, so far as they succeed. They are parasites who work against the arrival at a literate democracy, and particularly exploit the weaknesses of those many by whom adequate literacy has not so far been gained.

The most typical of those who become long-term professionals are immoral in senses they can hardly be expected themselves to recognise. They will play on decent sentiment among not very sophisticated people without apparent thought or care that this might be an exploitation of private feeling and even of grief.

Sophisticated observers, anxious not to appear spoilsports, will say of an especially popular advertisement: 'I rather liked that. Terribly well made. And very witty.' That was most recently said to me by an Oxford lecturer in classics; the divided society. Television-advertisement makers do not lack for cash or therefore talent. Most makers of such concoctions must surely know, deep down, that they are playing on intimate sentiments, but do not mind. There is always a false logical/false semantic excuse to invoke. This is not an argument the Advertising Standards Authority could come to grips with – too subjective. Generally, the profession is defended by its spokesmen on the grounds that such criticism threatens to infringe the adman's freedom. And this is accepted unquestioningly by many outsiders. This argument is invoked as an excuse by, for instance, more and more headteachers so that, in exchange for cash, they willingly let their school walls be used for advertising, aimed of course at children; as are the slot machines for soft drinks in the corridors. This is known, once again and so predictably, as recognising that they live in 'the real world'.

The actors who take part in these 'creations' are usually excused, if indeed many of them feel the need for an excuse, on the grounds that their profession is precarious and long terms of unemployment frequent. Not an apt excuse, since most of the more elaborate advertisements employ, for huge fees, actors at the top of their profession and rarely out of work. I have met only two, and those not making much money, who refuse such offers.

The climate of the time makes any suggestion that there might be a question of professional integrity here look beside the point. Has the executive committee of Equity ever debated the issue? These members are being very well paid to tell lies or near-lies: about products which in almost all instances they do not themselves use, through excessive claims they could not verify. They are misapplying their well-known voices and personalities. They are joined by that more ephemeral race, the Puffball Personalities of Television; and now, increasingly, by famous sportsmen and women. It is, and the phrase is not excessive, a shameful, inexcusable practice. They are all exercising aural prostitution of the personality instead of physical prostitution of the body.

One could go on: about the frenzied attention to young people, about the spiralling downwards of the tabloid press, about the degradation of much television in its pursuit of 'the competitive edge', mass audiences. The BBC can be regarded as one of the worst offenders here, precisely because we have the right to expect better; still, others are in fact worse.

For someone such as myself, who has for decades admired the very concept of a public-service broadcasting organisation, it is painful to criticise it now. It is almost certain that some at its helm today do their best to make sure the organisation does as much as they conceive possible to swim against the tide, to retain their brief as public-service broadcasters; and sometimes they partially succeed. I would have left for other work; but that tells more about me than about others. They may be right, in the circumstances, to battle on, against, let us say, *Who Wants to Be a Millionaire* – the pre-eminent example so far of dumbed-down TV, financially and programmatically questionable and clearly contemptuous of its targeted audience.

Some who work in television now do not, of course, recognise a dilemma. Incidentally, those of us who still make occasional more or less serious broadcasts note that our payment has for years remained derisory; we do not have the 'clout' of the mass-commercial agents and so can be ignored, as one producer told me, without embarrassment.

Sometimes, though, we are still given better. An American professor on a spell in Britain with his family found much television at first disconcerting. Then they all began to enjoy it. 'Our family stopped "watching television" and started "viewing programmes".' 'Watching television' is to be part of a block audience continuously and unselectively looking at the screen. 'Viewing programmes' is to act as individuals or, as in his experience, part of a family group choosing particular programmes for particular, interested attention.*

The worst example of this whole process is the National Lottery. It is established that the people who spend relatively most on it are those who can least afford to. Understandably: it feeds their hopes of a big break, a release from the grim round from which there seems no other than this almost chimerical hope of escape.

For those who want the high arts to flourish within an active democracy, it is ironic that much money assigned from the Lottery to good public causes should go to those arts, such as opera, to which – given our inadequate education, and class-bound cultural myopia – most of those who contribute to the Lottery do not yet have or wish access.

---

*See *Desperately Seeking the Audience*, L. Ang (Routledge, 1991).

The poorest should be as free as others to gamble. But the founding and encouragement of a Lottery by a government itself is democracy subverted into populism.

I have written elsewhere about an important but relatively neglected subject: how changes in language reflect and are inspired by changes in culture. New examples appear each year. Recently we have had an increasing religiosity: as in the 'Mission Statements' instead of 'Aims' in the literature of higher education (they have now arrived in university publicity), 'Dedicated Service' is promised in anything from undertaking to airport business-class lounges, and 'awesome' is applied to anything from a good goal in football to a fast car. *Pilgrim's Progress* has an unending life in the Anglo-Saxon consciousness, even when trivialised.

Directly opposed to those uses is the popularity of 'Attitude' as an end in itself, as in 'She's got attitude . . .', but towards what we are not expected to ask. That would be to imply the possibility of judgement.

'Transparent', which has been in fashion for about two years, seems a better word. It may be a reaction to so much in public speech which is evasive, trying to hide what is really being said: 'I see through you.' 'You are transparent' could then be a step forward.

Two men were talking on an Inter-City train bound for Leeds. They sounded like middle-range officials of an educational agency, on their way to inspect a branch office. They were discussing a colleague, who needed 'a salutary lesson . . . [was] not in touch with reality . . . [but] extremely adept in his field . . . [yet] should be marginalised, left on the outside . . . but at the same sort of level . . . he personalises everything . . . refers everything back to himself . . . [of course] he is quite well-heeled. Literally. But something about him . . . I think he's overreached himself . . . he's negative . . . monomaniac'.

A hopping from one cliché to another; placing familiar plastic counters in an equally well-known pattern within the controlled conversation space on their linguistic draughts board. The language was early twentieth century, middle-class office gossip mixed with late-twentieth-century computerised technologese, but the interaction was centuries old: the creation of an enclosed, warm, near-conspiratorial world. There was safety in criticising a third party in that isolated, sealed-off place. It was a less dramatic, English version of George Orwell's conversation on an overnight train to Mandalay.

Some useful phrases survive for centuries. Such as the English professionals' well-oiled preamble to disagreement: 'With respect, I do wonder whether . . .'. Pascal noted it in his countrymen three-and-a-half centuries ago.

Last, a touching example of language both private and public, in its phrasing and in the occasion which evoked it. The late Cardinal Hume at the burial of a murdered headteacher; impressive even to those who could not share his faith were his assured, heartening, mellifluous, middle-class tones and language of praise: 'He will now be appearing before our God, who will say: "Well done!" . . .'. God as a kindly, Catholic, public-school headteacher.

Sixty years ago, in *The Dog Beneath the Skin*, Auden and Isherwood predicted our emerging condition. In Act III scene ii, during a cabaret at the Nineveh Hotel, Destructive Desmond ('A stocky, middle-aged man, with an inflamed, pugnacious face' – his grandsons now appear on television most nights) invites his audience to vote on whether a painting by Rembrandt, which he exhibits and derides, or a cheap, sentimental print, shall be destroyed. The Rembrandt is destroyed there and then. 'Democracy' has triumphed.

That was a theatrical symbol. It is often evident in real life. Not long ago, during a 'chat' show, one of the participants announced that Mary Warnock had just published a book whose title was: *An Intelligent Person's Guide to Ethics*. An odd announcement on a lightweight talk programme. But it was made the occasion for silly giggles by the company; that was all.

On a BBC Radio Four arts programme in mid-1998, the presenter announced: 'The author Octavio Paz has died. And if you haven't heard of him, whose fault is that, yours or his?' Market-obsessed literary journalism. Yet some academics belong to the same world of false conjunctions: 'Historically, popular culture will be seen as more important than two World Wars.'

Worse: on the proposal to establish a museum to the Holocaust in Britain, a well-regarded BBC reporter put this kind of question to the proposer: 'But what is the relevance of the Holocaust to us today?' Almost incredibly shallow historical sense, or a foolish attempt to provoke a vigorous rejoinder?

The world of the closed mind is also that of the endlessly open mind, closed because it does not want to reconsider any of its attitudes, held open in case someone hurtfully accuses you of censorship because you criticise the goods or ideas they are selling. As so often, Samuel Butler had a dry observation: 'An open mind is all very well in its way, but it ought not to be so open that there is no keeping anything in or out of it. It should be capable of shutting its doors sometimes, or it may be found a little drafty.'

Is all this expecting too much too soon, and overstating the likely effects of current trends? Perhaps. But overstressing would be less of a mistake than denying the evidence all around. It is itself part of the sickness of the culture that even intelligent people shy away from consideration of likely effects. That would be too divisive, too élitist and judgemental, too much to bear individually, and to act on. It is easier to persuade a crude commercial film-maker to appear on television and firmly deny that his kind of work has any effect on the disposition to violence than to persuade someone to make the opposite tentative case. That would appear less robust, more 'do-gooding'. Television discussions are inherently one-sided; they highlight the brusquely assertive as against the most quietly qualified.

It is right to object in principle to the labelling of most of us as 'the masses'. One can say with Raymond Williams: 'There are no masses; there are only ways of seeing people as masses.' Yet though that may be corrective, it is a half-truth. Virtually all of us, from all classes and levels of intelligence, are persuaded from time to time to become parts of differently sized masses; look at the broadsheets' Sunday colour supplements. Those masses may overlap, dissolve and constantly reform; but they do their work. A harder truth: some of us are more often than others persuaded to be parts of near-permanent masses; we connive at our own deluding.

Samuel Butler again: 'The public buys its opinions as it buys its milk, on the principle that it is cheaper to do this than keep a cow. So it is, but the milk is more likely to be watered.'

H. G. Wells had a bleaker vision: 'In a flash I perceived that all had the same form of costume [the costumes of the mind] . . . in costume and in all the differences of texture and bearing that now mark off the sexes from one another, these people of the future were alike . . . a queer thing I soon discovered about my little hosts, and that was their lack of interest. They would come to me with eager cries of astonishment, like children, but like children they would soon stop examining me and wander away after some other toy.'

Yet there are various brakes on the process as a whole. Beginning with inertia (which begins to seem a positive if accidental value), it can move out to a habitual suspicion of anything, no matter how attractive, when it is offered by a smart aleck. Then, bloody-mindedness: a useful, if limited and sometimes obtuse, expression of 'common sense'; and traditional mickey-taking, a popular form of cynicism. More important is the capacity in some people to put experience into different compartments – as in buying no newspapers except one of the most popular tabloids, but taking their presentation of politics with a few grains of salt. Added to all those are the better aspects of the sense of neighbourliness, which may resist publicly stressed, massed and even insistent peer-group pressures; and the still strong hold, in many, of the sense of family and continuity.

If it were not for all these resistances, and others which I have no doubt forgotten, the invitations to live in a cocoon – of the conventional, the self-indulgent, the half-blind – would increase even more rapidly.

And the remedies? None are quick and easy, least of all in a society which likes to call itself an open democracy. We have to accept that Hardy's 'way to the better' will be slow and hard. The best weapon is, yet again, a serious and active commitment to education, especially to an education which encourages *critical* literacy. Seasoned with mockery, irony and contempt.

———

Albert Camus defined an intellectual as someone whose mind watches itself. Good; a neat, severe, French image. It makes a fine partner to Chesterfield's agreement with a judgement of Cardinal de Retz. In Chesterfield's hands it becomes not only patrician, but very English and very concrete. The fussy Cardinal Chigi is being dismissed as intellectually petty ('anal retentive', in today's jargon): 'Cardinal de Retz very sagaciously marked out Cardinal Chigi for a little mind, from the moment that he told him he had wrote three years with the same pen, and that it was an excellent good one still.' The aristocrat as intellectual.

G. M. Trevelyan died two decades after the end of the last war, but sounds nearer to Coleridge on the importance and place of intellectual life than to a writer of the present day when he declares that disinterested intellectual curiosity is 'the life-blood of real civilisation'. Such opinions and such language do not slide down easily now; they sound too directional, polysyllabic versions of that 'giving people what others think is good for them rather than what they like' with which populist journalists and broadcasters try to frighten their audiences away from 'do-gooders' – earnest people acting out of the highest motives, no doubt, but inevitably 'bossy'.

We don't like self-awarded titles and roles, least of all about 'brains'. Typically, 'clerks' and, even less, 'clerisy' have not lasted here, though they have occasional and respectable antecedents from Chaucer to Auden. 'Intelligentsia' evokes pre-Revolutionary Russia and their special political contestations. We don't seem greatly to want a word for this condition of mind, in the way that many here do not want a Bill of Rights. We can't define these things. We leave that to foreigners; but, we say, 'we know them when we see them' – intellectual power, the stout defence of individual human rights, artistic genius – by instinct as it were, and believe we know how to respect and practise them. We will just, though slightly uneasily, put up with 'intellectual', chiefly as a label others might perhaps pin on us, not as a way of describing ourselves. Far too self-important, that. It is more common to hear: 'Speaking as an artist/writer . . .' (unattractive as even those labels are when self-attributed) than: 'Speaking as an intellectual . . .'.

Some British writers, and more French, have aimed to capture the qualities of the intellectual, though the British use the actual word less. Pascal remarked that man is only a reed, but a thinking reed. That might seem to cover all mankind; but Pascal, I assume, meant to indicate that what distinguishes man from the rest of the created world is his ability and disposition, if he wishes, to use his mind hard and honestly, free from self-regard and self-interest, and that an intellectual should exercise this ability.

Much before, Socrates put the intellectual-moral position more directly: 'The unexamined life is not worth living'; the fundamental motto for intellectuals. As we saw above, Camus, as so often true to his nationality, used the direct title.

Hofstadter made useful distinctions between a person of intelligence and an intellectual. A highly intelligent person can outpace most others in seeing into processes, problem-solving and much else; his paradigm is the superlative chess player; but he may never 'watch' himself, may never 'examine life'.

Intelligent, rather than intellectual, people are commonly found in a band running from favoured radio and television interviewers to barristers. The former accept all the pseudo-intellectual assumptions of the day about personality, society, politics, the arts, and meet every challenge with: 'But surely we all nowadays . . . [share this or that apparently self-evident assurance].' Such as: 'But surely if people have only two weeks on the

Costa Brava a year, that will gradually make them more cosmo-
politan and internationally minded.' And: '"Pavarotti in the
Park" will lead on to a well-nourished love of classical music.'
Those myths are widely shared, certainly, but that doesn't make
them true. 'Professionals' here must not step out of line. They
leave that to Germaine Greer, the most effective of permitted
loose cannons. The barristers practise their law entirely as it
embodies the conventional sureties of the time, except for a few
of them, who are predictably known as the radical fringe.

Here we come back once more to Cardinal Newman's distinction between the once-born and the twice-born, between
those who are steady and unquestioning in religious belief
throughout their lives and those who, doubting or losing faith,
have to make an effort if they seek to return to it. It would be
foolish to say that none of the once-born ever prove to be intellectuals, or that all the twice-born are intellectuals. It seems
likely that a higher proportion of twice-borns than of once-borns
may be intellectuals, that their holding religious doubts may be
an indication of that sort of mind. I suspect there are more intelligent people than intellectuals. The limits of my own early
background ensured that – apart from one at Leeds University,
and he had more of a poet's than an intellectual's mind – I did
not meet any manifest intellectuals of my own generation until I
was in the Army (two of them at almost the same time) in Italy,
in 1943; an odd but nice paradox, that the Army should be the
unwitting go-between. Both, it so happened, were from
Hungarian-Jewish refugee families. Being intellectually uncertain, I was greatly impressed. A remnant of that attitude is
that, even today, if I see into something quite subtle, I tend
thereupon to downgrade it, assuming: 'Even I knew that, so it
can't be all that subtle.'

Intellectuality is not necessarily related to shrewdness, the
ability to estimate, to calculate. Such qualities belong more to
intelligence. 'Shrewdness' is assumed to be related to world-
liness, weighing things up; this may be done for respectable
reasons or for self-aggrandisement. It is not necessarily related to

wisdom. Nor is intellectuality; a mind may be greatly intellectual, fascinated with 'examining life', may even 'watch itself'. Yet we may, when they are under pressure, recognise in such persons a lack of wisdom, of the capacity to subdue the personality so as to learn from experience, which is the primal source of wisdom. The 'watching of self' can be purely aesthetic, or ideology-led, as with Sartre's early admiration of the Soviet Union. To his credit, he finally reversed his opinion.

Voltaire's absolute distinction – 'The best is the enemy of the good' – sounds close to the ever-hopeful 'We needs must love the highest when we see it'; but they are widely apart. The 'best' can have many forms other than those of virtue; it can be a superb demonstration of skill or craft, for example. The 'highest' is aiming at a clear moral or virtuous distinction. We noted earlier that many an intellectual mind sees no grounds for unease about unfettered advertising in a free society, or the unregulated commercial sponsorship of sport, or accepting money from the tobacco industry for one's university, or the production of violent images aimed at children. There are good arguments, as well as instinctive suspicion, for feeling uneasy about all such activities. My definition of 'intellectual' being more than aesthetic, I would be doubtful about the depth of 'intellectuality' of someone who saw no grounds at all for at least questioning them. Intellectuals should by their very nature question, challenge, 'take nothing at second-hand' as my professor at Leeds used to say. This is what Trilling called 'the opposing self . . . an intense and adverse imagination' turned on the culture in which one has one's being. To do all that, we must, I go on hoping, have criteria beyond the aesthetically self-contained.

So am I saying that intellectuality should be related to morality? Or, at the minimum, should have lively feelers – whose reactions may or may not be acted upon? Is it then proper to relate intellectuality not to the practice of virtue but only to the perception of where moral questions arise, no more?

There is an echo here of the argument hinted at earlier and likely to recur later, about the relations, if any, between the possession of great gifts as a writer, gifts 'to look right into the human soul', and such a writer's behaviour in private life. Similarly, we do tend to hope that one who practises that most freely intellectual of pursuits, philosophy, and in that practice explores questions of moral behaviour, will sooner or later come to exhibit good behaviour – another mistaken connection, as any collection of philosophers may show. A philosopher may, brilliant or not, be as unpleasantly self-regarding as an illiterate brute, and at bottom in similar ways, though the actual manners may be 'gentrified'. Or the immensely well-read literary man with a magisterial lecturing style will react like a petulant child if he finds his well-received lecture followed by an even more engrossing one from a colleague. Like many of us, philosophers (and writers) can be small-mindedly unkind to their partners and friends. Susan Sontag, writing on the death of Paul Goodman, soberly and humanely captured this: 'I suspect there was a nobler human being in his books than in his life.' Perhaps sometimes, but more rarely, the truth lies the other way.

My inclination to assume such connections took a small blow on the train some months ago. A man near me, respectably dressed, in his late thirties or early forties, put his muddy shoes up on the seat opposite. 'What an uncivilised yobbo', I thought. He was reading a paperback; no doubt a cheap and nasty thriller. He got up to go, putting *Great Expectations* into his jacket pocket. No connection.

From one angle, the birthmark of an intellectual is a disposition to *play* with ideas in the purest ways, just as one mark of a fine scholar is the ability to marshal a large range of complex ideas, to see hitherto unsuspected connections, and degrees of relative importance to this or that outcome. But the playfulness alone, and the mastery of the great scholar alone, may leave us unwilling to say, finally, not only: 'What a remarkable mind', but: 'What a true intellectual.' Even as one writes that, one realises it proposes a special and by no means universally agreed definition of such a person.

Having just read in typescript the partial autobiography of a

117

French friend who came first in his, as always, very gifted year at the École Normale, I am impressed again by the seriousness with which the French approach intellectual life. At about the same time I came across a comment, made in an English newspaper article, by Thomas Mann: 'Every intellectual attitude is latently political.' Not very English, either of those.

In such discussions, some, but too few in Britain, insist that one job of 'the intellectuals' in a democracy is, until more people are prepared to assume this role as a part of their citizenship, to stand up for the rights of all, and to be prepared, by public action, persuasion and education, to widen the number who assert those rights. It would be sensible not to expect this of every intellectual at any time; not all are called; some do their best work entirely enclosed, as do some academics; and in any event, some such people might not be effective in public activity.

In the nineteenth century, the belief in moving outside the walls inspired some of the best English intellects. It prompted some in the ancient universities, uncharacteristically, to promote the education of 'the unprivileged', for as many of those as could be persuaded to recognise their need. That Great Tradition in adult education (the old title is not excessively grand), especially as it expressed itself, in the early years of this century, through the three-year tutorial class initiated by Tawney, is an insufficiently recognised achievement. Few such classes can be found today; if you do come across one you are likely to be surprised at the high level of serious and sustained thinking demonstrated by laymen and women, so unfashionable is the activity; it makes even the broadsheet newspapers sound lightweight.

Those are the self-selected, to be admired and helped. At the same time, we need to recall two injunctions which strike deeper. Bishop Wilson: 'The number of those who need to be awakened is far greater than that of those who need comfort'; and Gotthold Lessing: 'We must not accept the wantlessness of the poor'; he meant of course spiritual, not material, wantlessness. I do not apologise for quoting those in at least three earlier books; they are benchmarks, as much for today as when they were first spoken.

The autodidact has an honoured place in English educational writing, a less honoured place in intellectual thinking. Perhaps it is so in France; Bourdieu, surprisingly, reduces the autodidact, but probably for culturally different reasons from those which affect his English counterparts. It is a symptom of the late-twentieth-century mood in Britain that few of those publicly recognised as intellectuals feel the need to be involved with adult education for a democracy. Indeed, insofar as they think of the subject, it is often to feel superior to it – as worthy, no doubt, but dull, a killing combination; the earnest study through NHS spectacles of T. S. Eliot's *Four Quartets*, in cramped schoolroom desks. Writers who take an active interest in the good health of that other highly intelligent British invention of the mid-nineteenth century, the public library, are not common. This at a time when the libraries are suffering from undervaluing and so underfunding.

Insofar as some writers do engage in public matters, many show less interest in the slow and grinding processes of democracy in Britain than in more dramatic causes elsewhere – torture by dictators in distant lands rather than the appalling unexpectancy, illiteracy and readiness to perpetrate vandalism of many unemployed teenagers in large British cities. Both foreign and domestic activities are worthwhile, of course, but a fair balance is not always struck. Above all, this British democracy, whilst it has recognised the need for basic literacy, for functional literacy and for vocational literacy, has scarcely grasped the fundamental need for that critical literacy I have already flagged; and who better to engage in that than intellectuals and other intelligent citizens?

Another test, a sort of litmus paper of the imagination, which many who today might think of themselves as intellectuals fail to pass, is the need to distinguish between 'sentiment' and 'sentimentality'. It is easy to find words to express that distinction, such as that sentimentality is an indulging in the expression of emotions for their own sake, sentiment a true and consonant response to the claims of feeling. The escape from overt emotion currently so widespread has made recognition of the differences between sentiment and sentimentality (or wit and whimsy) – in action, in speech or on the page – uncertain, unwillingly honoured. Television reviewers are often affected in this way, and take refuge in snide dismissals, as do some successful literary reviewers.

Still another sign of the current lack of public intellectual – that is, questioning – energy can be found in the universities. One may expect and should not object to arguments against the claim that a function of the universities is, amending Arnold, to throw a fresh stream of thought and feeling on the society we live in, to provide a critical centre. At all times some people have denied that that is the duty of universities, but the argument has nevertheless been sometimes engaged. The sustained force of its most recent proponent, the late Dr Leavis of the English faculty at Cambridge, seems now a faint echo. There have long been powerful voices in the United States – among my own late acquaintances were Charles Frankel of Columbia and Irving Howe, and in this decade alone several other powerful advocates have appeared, arguing the need for universities to stand for, assert the importance of, 'the examined life'.

Read the promotional literature which streams out of many universities today, not only, but most evidently, from some which were polytechnics, often with a technological bent, and which have a special urge to assert their new standing. There is behind much of the publicity the assumption that 'whatever is' in society is right, so long as it offers a donation; that this is (as in the convictions of most of those recently in power, whether in government or industry or commerce) the best or the only feasible form of society, today and perhaps henceforward. Society is not to be fundamentally questioned, least of all by those who seek more industrial and commercial funding; but who have a ground base of government funds, which we used quaintly to think would ensure free, not contingent, thinking.

'Professionals' (in this context a safer word than 'intellectuals')
is misinterpreted here as meaning those with a commitment to
serve society as it is at present and as defined by those who are
required to make major decisions and, presumably, 'know
better'.

It may be that those of us – and we are many – who graduated, climbed to, the life of the mind from unpromising
backgrounds, admire it too much and tend to put too much
moral weight on it. We got out and, we believe in an important
but not socially defined sense, 'up'; we might have headed for
commerce and perhaps greater prosperity. That would not do.
Our circumstances, if ill-nourished in worldly ways, were probably Protestant and puritanical; we learned to mistrust the
go-getters and sharpers. These things we were taught by home
and Sunday school, by grammar school and university. Like
homing pigeons, to a loft we knew only from hearsay, we headed
for the humanities and, above all, for literature.

We noted for ourselves the degree to which those around us,
in our native districts, were exploited by that race of conmen-
to-the-working-class described earlier, and how nowadays the
same people are kept in place by 'Them' above and outside,
not by forms of force but by soft and flattering persuasions. For
us, the capacity to think for ourselves, not so as to make money
but to stand on our own critical feet, became a dominant
impulse.

Some working-class habits survive, such as the disinclination
to argue, to quarrel, to fall out about those ideas we had been
introduced to. We listened in surprise and unease to the more
combative habits of those from backgrounds where intellectual
dispute was part of the culture. One result of our early environment has been the tendency still, even when someone is arguing
a case with which we greatly disagree, not to express our disagreement strongly enough, to muffle it, at the extreme to
demur too gently. Class habits can be hard to break, for the
newly arrived intellectual as much as for anyone else. I learned
this most directly and sharply from those Hungarian-Jewish

refugees from Hitler, met on gun sites in Italy, and generally, more from Jews than from any others.

One of the gains from entry to the intellectual life is, in the initial stages, to learn to mistrust 'commonsense': 'To break down the self-assurance of commonsense, to undermine the sinister confidence in the power and language of facts, to demonstrate that unfreedom is so much at the core of things that the development of their internal contradictions leads necessarily to qualitative change: the explosion and catastrophe of the established state of affairs.' The linguistic and mental aggression of that passage by Marcuse, even more than its obvious Marxist elements, mark it as continental European not English. A tonic from another society.

So is Julia Kristeva, demonstrating the French intellectual at unabashed and explicit odds with the received opinions of French society: 'How can one avoid sinking into the mire of commonsense, if not by becoming a stranger to one's own country, language, sex and identity.' The title, though, is unexpected – 'A New Type of Intellectual: The Dissident'. Is 'the dissident intellectual' really new to French society? The rejection is, again, inspiriting, in a way we have long imported from over the Channel.

'Breaking down the assurance of commonsense', refusing to 'sink into its mire' are admirable and absolute necessities for the intellectual, especially for budding intellectuals. Calling upon 'commonsense' can be justification not for sense presumed to be demonstrated abundantly by the common man, but for taking refuge when intellectually challenged and shaken in the most basic of received opinions (not thought, not 'sense'). Its favourite motto is: 'It stands to reason', which means: 'It is the universal, unchallenged and unconsidered assumption in these parts, and so must be right.'

That misuse of 'commonsense' being recognised, one has also to recognise Dr Johnson's 'good sense' when, to refute Bishop Berkeley's theory of the non-existence of matter, he struck his foot against a large stone until it rebounded: 'I refute it thus.' He was in part playing the no-nonsense Englishman who gives things their proper names. He was also, and this is the useful English pragmatism, refusing to be influenced by what he mistrusted as untethered theorising. He may have seemed slightly obtuse, but he knew what he was about.

Rochefoucauld has a gritty observation about the intellectual life: 'Intellectual blemishes, like facial ones, grow more prominent with age.' One then sticks more rigidly to intellectual manners about which one was more flexible earlier. As in the obsessive follower of intellectual fashions; adopted fashions change, but the desperation to follow each one does not weaken. So it is with the multiple applications of the phrase 'postmodernism' used in the last few years. There is no way in which they could all be brought into harmony or agreement. In some hands, the phrase is a mixture of mantra and ducdame (Shakespeare's 'cry to call fools into a circle'). It would be better not to label some attitudes 'post-modernist'. The coin has been used so often recently that it is worn almost blank. The phenomenon, which is worth sharper definition and application, has been reduced. It has been fitted into an assumed diachronic progression (and will be succeeded in turn). By being thrown around so often and unclearly it implies a control and understanding many of its users do not have.

An intellectually weaker version is face-saving, coat-tail-holding. By which hardly a sentence can be written, an opinion given, without external, and meant to be impressive, references for corroboration. 'As Shuckleburgh says' . . . or 'rightly says' or even 'justly and memorably says'. Sometimes what Shuckleburgh says is obvious and his way of putting it not especially clarifying. But the coat-tails are hung on to, as a raft in a shark-infested sea of other critics. This might be thought, and is, a weakness in young scholars; the evidence is all around that some do not grow out of second-hand holding-on, and sometimes are elevated into chairs.

Worse is the habit of the intellectual who hones a special way of looking at life and writing about it, and holds on for decades, sometimes through shortage of ideas, sometimes because the imagination is centripetal, sometimes from near obsession; most often because of the power of an external ideology which is, again, a scaffolding only. It results in the prior assurance that when you look at a piece of writing by such an author, you know that, whatever the subject, it will be put through the same old five-ideas, two-dimensional, intellectual mincer or waffle-iron, and so sound like all its predecessors. There can be intellectual timidity behind the rolling abstractions. I am prone to something of this kind of repetition but not, I hope, of abstractionism. I like to tell myself that I hammer on about a few themes because so few people seem to have seen their importance, and should once again be urged to listen.

One of the regrettable assumptions among British intellectuals (and academics, not all of whom are intellectuals) is that public service, especially committee work, is to be avoided, will damage your status as a free professional, and anyway is always of little use. There are honourable exceptions; some do serve on carefully chosen committees. But as to most, if you by choice or chance spend some time in dreaded 'administration' (in charge of a college, on secondment to no matter how demanding and worthwhile an executive post), you will be assumed to have irreparably damaged your standing as an intellectual and academic. You will be thereafter labelled 'a committee man' and that is rather like developing intellectual AIDS. I once worked on a committee brilliantly led by its chairman into the exploration of an important public issue. I wrote that it had been 'lovely' to experience the sense of working effectively to a useful end. I do not defend the word 'lovely', but it was pointing to an unusual and admirable quality. A literary reviewer, not unsympathetic to the particular book as a whole, professed himself astonished and amused that an academic could call any committee 'lovely'. One could hear the foolish assenting laughter all round his Oxford Senior Common Room.

Yet, when some who have scorned such work are finally invited to take it on for a while, the more observant among them realise that a special kind of courage can be needed, especially from the civil servants in attendance, for such work to be well done.

In committees, some people are natural conciliators, bonders. It can be educative to see them at work. Others are firecrackers, indulgent or valuable; some are natural scouts, frontrunners for the committee's intellectual work as a whole. Best of all, and almost unknown to the typical British intellectual, is the truly professional person. Not an exploiter or manipulator, but someone who has absorbed the nature and value of his profession – academic life and objectivity, broadcasting in the public interest, the civil service and impartiality – if left to find its own best ways. Watching such people in action is to admire them and, even more, to recognise the limitations of many intellectuals' habitual writing-down of 'the committee man' or 'the professional administrator'. It should be commonly recognised that there is need for a better bridge between the two worlds.

In writing the last few pages I now realise again how English I am in some ways. In asking intellectuals to be more politically and socially involved I immediately fear even the idea that they might seem to be being invited to set themselves up as a clerisy, as Platonic guides and mentors. I wouldn't trust them in that role, but I believe they could have more to contribute than is evident today. But not alone, not as members of a philosophical samurai caste, but working more directly and widely through those organs of communication in which they have voices; and, if they can bear it, in getting their hands dirty on the ground (or on committees).

We need involvements far broader than those. The central tap root must obviously be in education, education much more focused on the understanding of where we are as a society going badly wrong. Public-service broadcasting, though now under threat, has been and could be once again a major force here also.

Then there are the quite large numbers of intelligent laymen and women I have mentioned more than once. It is a shame that the links between them and most recognised 'intellectuals' are feeble. It's the wire-rimmed glasses, small school desks and earnestness stereotype getting in the way again.

Yet the very large numbers who attend the multiplying literary festivals all over the country give a clue. Many of them are over-intent on attracting the fashionable best-selling writers of the day, the TV Personalities of the Year, the current major actor and actress. They should become more intellectual and cultural as well as literary festivals, and their speakers chosen accordingly, soberly and, if necessary, unfashionably. I do not think their attendances would greatly fall off.

We have an extraordinary large number of voluntary bodies which in all sorts of ways try to work on behalf of fellow citizens. Anthony Giddens* notes that there were 160,000 charitable groups in Britain in 1991 and that nearly 20 per cent of the population engages in some voluntary work over the course of a year. Astonishing figures; astonishing levels of energy, much if not most of it directed at doing good for the community, to the support of civil society. Many are almost hermetic, concentrated on their particular areas of interest.

Under all that is the extended sense that one should go out and do something for others. They, too, could be invited to become more widely engaged. We have to learn to *speak to each other*, to talk more about what sort of good society we want beyond all the hype which thinks only about what other people decide we want in their pursuit of profits. We will not be destroyed by dictators; by synthetic cheerleaders, rather. This is a job for far more than recognised 'intellectuals', but they should help more by coming out of their habitual lairs and joining in more freely. We have several good, recent initiatives to call in aid: Amnesty International, Greenpeace, Charter 88, PEN and other anti-censorship bodies.

Alasdair MacIntyre is unusual among British philosophers in recognising this, and especially the relations between strenuous

The Third Way (Polity Press, 1998).

activity of the mind, a high professionalism and the demands of daily life, of everyday belonging. Virtue, he argues, lies in our relations with others in the maintenance of our shared professional practices as in our communal recognitions. This is an essential part of our 'moral particularity'. That kind of play between the pure and the pragmatic, that sense of belonging to one's place and time, and yet the awareness of the need also to pay proper dues to both historical debts and one's own intellectual journeys, is rare. It is good to hear it from a Briton – even if he long ago left for the United States.

PART THREE

ON THE SENSES:
An Earthy Interlude

> Be patient, solemn nose
> Serve in a world of prose
>   . . .
> Be modest, lively ears,
>
>   . . .
> Look, naked eyes, look straight
> At all eyes but your own
>   . . .
> Be happy, precious five,
> So long as I'm alive.

Time to be even more down-to-earth than in the two previous chapters. Auden's late and happy celebration of his senses makes a good title. Others, such as Swift (and one of my aunts), were shocked by the low, creaturely aspects of life. Even my most intellectual and physically hearty of friends thought it 'a poor joke of God's to put the hole for shitting and that for the pleasures of sex next to each other'. Most of us take the paradox, if paradox it is, for granted and get on with our ordinary daily work, in which there may occasionally be time for the attempt at a few High Thoughts. In general, of course, our days – work apart, and sometimes even in the course of that – are almost unconsciously passed in a succession of sensuous experiences: of sights, sounds, smells, tastes and touchings.

5

'Be Happy, Precious Five'

MONTAIGNE, TO WHOM I have come with astonishment and delight in these later years, talked lyrically about the language of our hands, head, eyebrows, shoulders. He would have appreciated Erving Goffman. Goffman no doubt recognised from Montaigne this simple truth: though later theories order, illuminate and develop our understanding, some of the insights within those theories were expressed demotically long before others saw, elaborated, and passed them from hand to specialist hand.

Most gestures of hands and arms, angles of feet and legs, are conventional, custom- and profession-bound, and fairly easy to construe: pullovered lecturers reaching for precision of thought with the help of pipe-stabbing waves of the arm; would-be important processions of Orangemen; or of City bowler hats with pin-striped trousers, heavily striped suits and shirts (as boring an outfit as could be conceived – the professional gent as Secretary Bird – but still clinging to the sacred objects). More exotic, a Guards officer of any rank and after no more than his first three months: the ankles almost entwined like those of the brigadiers met earlier; polite, stork-like inclinations of the head. The style is the man as he has merged into, been moulded by, the profession; these do not change, they are more likely to set, gel, over many generations.

More difficult are multiple gestures defined by sex, age, class, nationality and personality. As in a middle-aged, lower-middle-class housewife, long married in England but of southern Italian origin, talking to a neighbour in our local Sainsbury's. The hands turned from the wrists and made arcs; the upper eyelids had a recurrent life of their own; the *moues* and the lilt of the rapid voice were the central indicators, to which the rest provided a visual chorus. The listener had only to contribute a sequence of acknowledgements, chiefly by slight, rapid nods; that was sufficient background orchestration.

The dramatic anecdotalist is a near relative. Fast talking, with little connectors – of words or mere vowels, usually from the back of the throat – between each paragraph so that the speaker doesn't lose your attention to the claims of someone else, or yield to you. The eyes hold you throughout but especially at those paragraph changes; reinforcing the connective words or connecting sounds not just with the compelling stare of the eyes, but with them raised to heaven and even slightly rolled on the way there. Mesmerising; snake-charming. At the peaks the head swings away, arms and hands up and back in concert. The hardest part for this histrionic performer is to dare a theatrical silence, a stillness, whilst yet holding the audience. The experts do it confidently. Less practised performers bridge the gap with an intake of breath like a continuous but slightly slack high wire, and then a 'Well, anyway . . .' on a rising note which also suggests: 'Don't interrupt. Just wait for this.' Recollected in tranquillity, it may seem to have been an ordinary anecdote; but well packaged and presented. I have only once, for a dare with myself, managed to cut in.

A black nurse in the Whittington Hospital, North London, where I landed for eight days after breaking a leg in those parts, was more physically comprehensive. Fortyish, not pretty, but vitally alive. Dressed as though a clothes horse had come to life and grabbed what was to hand. Shapeless yet lithe, so that she seemed multiple-jointed, as though she could have walked on her hands as easily as on her feet. She was another type of compelling, frequent talker, more animated than most of the white nurses. She had created a face, a posture, a whole personality which overrode the rest. Yet it was not compensatory; instead secure, successful, undaunted.

The language of the eyes, much used by novelists, is harder to read than that of limbs. We are accustomed, over-accustomed, to 'cold' eyes, 'cruel' eyes, 'sparkling' eyes, 'thoughtful' eyes, 'watchful' eyes. That keyboard is a little worn and yellowed, even though we at once recognise the attributions; they still hit more or less the right notes. Yet we have become too much used to assuming eyes are clear indicators of character. Beerbohm called them 'the windows of the soul'. They are not so transparent; they can lie, though not as much as smiles. Proust was another who trusted eyes; he believed they revealed the degree of intelligence, but that the nose indicated the level of stupidity. Odd, that; I think some noses can suggest a questing intelligence, like that of a truffle-hunting dog. Old axioms tell us the nose does not, at least, deceive: 'as plain as the nose on my face'. *Pinocchio* succeeds on a similar conceit, the extending nose as lie indicator, and Cyrano de Bergerac charms many.

The language of the nose is certainly odd; an inch less of Cleopatra's nose, mused Pascal, and the whole history of the world might have been different; an inch or two more and the nose risks becoming a joke, like protruding ears. Big ears and a big nose on the same face need huge compensating from, for instance, gentle eyes and a mobile mouth, and may then become lovely-ugly, *jolie-laide*.

The mouth has long been a favoured and slightly sophisticated source of clichés, as in 'a generous mouth'. It suggests one of more than usual width and with full lips. That it indicates a ready sexuality is a common deduction among 'blokes'. 'Thin lips' we can all read – meanness, though not so forbidding as 'tight' lips. The woman in the house three doors down may have 'thin' lips, and their message may be borne out by her actions. She may have tight lips too, but tight lips can be harder, more calculating. One might talk of a tight-lipped rather than a thin-lipped commercial operator. Thin lips can be natural and do not always indicate an unpleasant character; tight lips are cultural and usually nasty. Chins are harder to read or even to identify. The Bertie Wooster chin is by now unusable except as a comic echo; an 'indecisive' chin is still fair currency, as is the meaningless identification of a dimpled chin with good nature. Why do so many Australians seem, at least to the English, to have nutcracker mouths and chins? Biological? An exported caricature? A distorted generalisation on our part, inspired by our wish to see Australians as 'rough cuts'? The image does seem to signify the slightly raucous. Perhaps the sound preceded the sight, the accent the required visual accompaniment.

Voices are altogether trickier, an instrument we are more conscious of using and one we play with subtlety; theirs is an almost universal register. At their simplest, they run on firm tramlines. Lively cartoon figures of young girls from which there issue booming bass voices always prompt uneasy laughter. The well-known stairway has cracked and collapsed under our feet. The expected response is dislocated, thrown out of gear; as it also is in the reverse of the picture above, when from the face and figure of an old-style, mill-owning 'master of men', there might come the voice of a forty-year-old Oxbridge intellectual woman novelist, precise, discriminating, suggesting sophisticated relationships, a world of the mind and of minutely and subtly weighed tastes and judgements.

Probably that was why, though this was three quarters of a century ago, parts of the London literary community found J. B. Priestley hard to assimilate, even to take seriously, to 'place'. Faced with literary London as a young man and to some extent out of cussedness, he had reacted into a more firm commitment to his Bradford flat vowels and locutions. Even late in life one expected him to drop on occasions into: 'Ah'm a plain, blunt-spoken man. An' Ah call a spade a spade.' He was too sensible for that; he left such tropes to a few Members of Parliament and stand-up comics. But once, in our house, rebuking me for criticising as self-indulgent one of his sentences, he dropped into mill-owner mode; as if ticking off a callow apprentice.

Eyes and mouth are the prime elements in composing the face: the main visual clues. By which we mean, in all its complexity, the 'expression'. 'I don't like your expression' is compact and easily translatable. Near to that, but richer, is: 'I don't like your tone of voice.' A screw tighter, because usually spoken to a particular person and probably class- or family-related, is: 'Don't use *that* tone of voice with *me*.'

One observer claimed to be able to read character from the size of the eyebrows.

The face taken as a whole, which includes but is not wholly contained by the 'expression', poses the main paradox in all such readings. 'You're lying to me. I can tell by your face', is a common everyday challenge. A Goldsmith character asks 'Am I in face today?', which sounds very eighteenth-century, pomaded middle class. Montaigne came in characteristically shrewdly: 'There are quantities of human beings, but there are many more faces, for each person has several.' Yet are they all equally convincing, or some more 'true' than others? I suspect the latter.

Macbeth has a gallery of faces. 'Your face, my thane, is as a book where men/May read strange matters.' Like so many of Lady Macbeth's utterances (the right word for her forms of speech), that announcement is heavy, pithy; an inescapable, not easily evaded, summing-up of the state of things at that moment. She knew her man.

Aphorisms about the face tend to be short, sharp and shocking. I wrote something about faces in an earlier book, but the theme is worth developing and varying here. A most important shock for most of us, though it does not usually appear until at least early middle age, is the realisation, as one day we look in the glass, that we all make our own faces, that we have now made ours, that it is older than we have been used to thinking, and the story it tells probably not altogether to our taste. Our life so far shows there, a record of what it has offered us and how we have treated what we have been offered. If this is an index to character, one which has just become clearer to us,

135

what have all our acquaintances been thinking of us, probably for some years?

'We make our own faces': that is the common judgement. Obvious, but not often taken further. Most judgements are depressed. As is Camus's: 'After a certain age each man is responsible for his face.' Orwell's form was harsher: 'At fifty, every man has the face he deserves.' Auden read nervy, bored unexpectancy into typical, bar-haunting, New York faces; lost and fearful.

Yet he celebrated the beautiful language of life inscribed on, sculpted on, the face of an old woman; who must be happy and at ease within herself because when you are very old, 'Even a teeny-weeny bit of greed/Makes one very ill indeed,/And a touch of despair is instantaneously fatal.'

By that point in our lives, our faces have been shaped by those attitudes, those responses, those thoughts, those demands daily made on us by others or by ourselves, which we have become most used to meeting, willingly or fearfully. We are constantly preparing 'a face to meet the faces that we meet'. The faces of the successful are, must be, more effectively than most, 'fronts' before the world. They can seem double: on top, the mask of successful arrival; just below, the cost of getting there.

We make our changing faces like blind men kneading dough in our sleep. If the sudden realisation on that middle-aged morning is not pleasant, that is due to the revelation that we have acquired lines from experiences some of which we do not remember having; we had not realised they had by now made our faces into 'an open book', a record of successes as well as failures, inevitable sadnesses, even grief, the realisation that the face says: 'Things have not made out as well as I would have wished.' There are also faces which say to the wearer and the world, often with unappetising cocky assurance, sometimes with due hesitation: 'You've done very well indeed. Congratulations.'

But for many, this is a moment of less happy revelation; the truth then is that, try as we will and with the best intentions, the road of life has tripped and worn us. The dead are not yet, by early middle age, all around us; but the walking wounded are, and we are of their number. What may save us, if we are lucky, and open enough to appreciate the realisation, is love, the idea of love, the proof that love exists, the surprise that it has reached out to us, and remains. These evidences may be assimilated as supports and comforts, after the initial shock of the first middle-aged, true, but now to be adjusted, sighting.

Conversely, one of the most touching of all faces is that of a young girl joyously and nervously expectant before life; even more when she has for the first time fallen in love and feels herself loved. Henry James has a wondering and wonderful remark about the typical American girl, perhaps visiting Europe for the first time: she has a permanent exclamation mark between her eyebrows. *Portrait of a Young Lady.*

Even after that first shock of early middle age, and after we have made slight adjustments so that the new face now fits not too uncomfortably, we go on deceiving ourselves, discounting further signs of ageing, staying in our mind's eye as we finally realised we had appeared at forty-five, even until we are sixty. We are endless and recurring cheats about our own physical selves, resetting the clock like a dodgy used-car dealer. At seventy-five we kid ourselves we look sixty-five, and are by then ready to be satisfied with that. Unless a sudden grave illness intervenes, the shutter clicks over at roughly ten- to fifteen-year intervals. Serious illness usually pushes on the clock so that it skips at least one whole interval.

We have to try to live with our real, our undisguised faces at each phase, increasingly difficult though that may be. Some faces may be better lived with if we are not conscious of the message they carry. Such as those of two middle-aged spinsters I knew when a boy, 'lady' assistants who passed their adult lives in the ladies departments of large, 'good' stores, who saw over the years a procession of married women go in and out with money and years to spare, probably sure of affection, not alone. Even if such well-heeled women did not patronise, the assistants found it hard not to hate them. No future, no likely change; no longer much interest even in the flickerings of fashion. For one, a small and lonely flat to go back to; for the other, an ageing mother. They tended to have a fixedly affronted air, as if from the reaction to an outrageous proposition or horrible smell. Several Hunslet women who had struggled, unmarried and in their late thirties, from being simply seamstresses, basic workers on the conveyor line in huge clothing factories, into the senior, 'passers' (of others' work) group, had that air too; sadder in the end than that of the seamstresses.

They have their male counterparts, some much less attractive because their expression has been imposed over the years. Prison life is inherently ugly and full of strain, for prisoners as for warders. As a profession it may have in the beginning attracted the latter for good or bad reasons. Over the years it imposes on most the marks of its pressures; sour eyes and tight mouths, the expression which signals in advance as a pre-emptive strike: 'Don't try to monkey about with me, lad, or else . . .'. The grating, inhumane voice can go with all the other signals of a refusal to be humane because the job won't allow it or from a natural inability to express charity; left with 'nothing but a jailor's voice and face'. Recently I came face to face with a warder unloading remand prisoners outside Farnham Magistrates' Court. He looked, sounded and acted as though he was well past the point at which he could entertain much compassion. You can see those faces in the streets too, not only in the more likely professions, but in all sorts of people for all sorts of reasons. Experience is infinitely varied, but particularly leads to certain bold templates of expression, especially under stress.

How did the grandmother we saw, sitting in the middle of a plainly middle-class family waiting for the plane to Menorca, grow to look like a cartoon from working-class life by Giles: hat squashed on and held with a large pin; legs protectively tight at the knees; hatchet-like, suspicious-looking face; glaring out as though convinced that she is about to be 'done', and won't have it?

'The old plain men have rosy faces', said Stevenson. Going through the Polish countryside, I was touched by the lined, but seemingly open, face of an elderly peasant from whom we asked the way; a face heavily scored by time and labour, but apparently innocent of guile. Apparently; he may have driven hard bargains over corn or cattle. Or there are the faces of some devoted scholars; a different kind of innocence there, about things of the world. The faces of some other scholars, set-lipped and usually looking over rimless glasses, sure that their work has not been given the admiration it deserves, suggest they are expecting to be offered suspect material by one of those jumped-up young graduates who rise by flashy work.

At some moments, in quite young people, you may catch a line near the mouth which at present only comes and goes, or a flickering shadow under the eyes, which projects the face forward to that of the fifty-five-year-old-to-be. The reverse is the slightly worn face of a fifty-five-year-old woman which yet retains, like a sketched hint below the surface, something of her earlier beauty of bone sculpture, eyes and complexion. It is often a peculiarly poignant face, as if she were silently saying: 'Ah, but you should have seen me thirty years ago. What beauty I had then!' Being even older yourself, you feel like saying: 'You still have.'

Valéry has a good, in-depth, double exposure: 'It is the child one must detect in the intimidating man with his long beard, bristling eyebrows, heavy moustache, and weighty look – a captain. Even he conceals, and not at all deep down, the youngster, the booby, the little rascal, out of whom age has made this powerful monster.' One of the English tycoons I have met fits that description. On first meeting him, one instantly felt like mischievously using his Christian name in a friendly manner; calling him 'Bobby', say, though that might have been taken amiss. Another also still has a young man's open and agreeable face. Is that the triumph of decency over dubious pressures, or one of the kind Henry Adams noted (quoted a few chapters back), that of a man entirely caught up in and obedient to the questionable but unquestioned demands of his society?

There are the simulacra, the faces which try hard to have a certain kind of false meaning. They can deceive the observer for a while and may deceive their owners as they look into the glass. They are the facial equivalents of highly deceptive artificial fabrics. Yet, though they are overreaching faces, they may well be true to their owner's experience. A man may be no more than a minor boss in a minor public service, have reached his limit there. The effort, with the addition of a certain conceit and failure of imagination, has given him the face of a commander of men. So in one sense, the face may be called a simulacrum; in another, it is true to itself.

Like many novelists, Tolstoy could see this phenomenon from several angles, especially both the generalised and the particular. At one point he notes that, for all Karenin's air of consequence, you realised, on watching him closely, that he had reached his professional ceiling, which was not as high as his bearing might at first have suggested, might be proposing for itself. Was there, behind the apparently confident glance, the only half-hidden realisation of a degree of failure, a dead end, the buffers? Anna may have recognised that; it may have contributed to her loss of affection.

We do not need to have those intellectual 'i's and 't's crossed. What Tolstoy tells us is that Anna suddenly realised how much she disliked the hairs in Karenin's ears; they had mobilised her distaste, her half-submerged disenchantment. Tolstoy didn't, she didn't, and we don't, need the generalisation.

'Happy the man who never puts on a face, but receives every visitor with that countenance he has on'; Emerson's flat but strong down-to-earthness. How few of us match the image. There are faces that look happy and unambiguous and full of probity which, when in repose, not on parade, settle back into suggesting a deep, continuous good nature. Those, too, cover a fairly wide band. Some are at bottom artificial, the faces of unrelaxed, hard-pressed but wooing salesmen, or of a congenital, 'don't attack me' nervousness, weak behind the forced smiles; some signal an insensitivity to what is really going on.

Some, and one admires them from first meeting, are entirely true to themselves. As in Blackpool rock, the stamp of the undisguised character runs right through. These are not the faces of people 'to whom nothing has happened', or who have been incapable of recognising the weight, perhaps the awful weight, of events they have known. These are the faces of people to whom much may have happened; but who have, as we poetically say, 'faced' it, surmounted it. One may expect to meet a few such in a lifetime.

In all observing, and no matter how much one tries to avoid it, one is led – there is indeed no escape unless every face is unique in every particular, which from one perspective they are – into a sort of typecasting. The novel rests on two assumptions: that this is so, but also that it must be resisted, is a lie; that all generalisations, though they may throw shafts of light, end as reductions. Schopenhauer grimly observed: 'A person of any sensibility hardly ever sees a new face without a sensation akin to shock at encountering a new and surprising combination of unedifying elements.' The novelist might aim to show this, charitably or cynically; the academic social scientist might not feel free to make such an external, 'unedifying' value judgement; the philosopher inhabits or seeks to inhabit a freer area between the two.

Few can escape some broad-brush generalisations; they are in some senses true to most. There are other faces much harder to read. Their lines have been scored by the winds of another world. Their pressures have not been those of family life and other relationships, or of getting and spending, of ambition and competition, of the desire for friends or at least for wide and warm, 'supportive' relationships. They have listened to another music. You cannot call them 'good-natured' because good nature has to be directed at another or other persons; for the same reason you cannot call them 'mean-natured'. You 'know' them in the usual limited sense, and you know it is advisable not to come too close, that they are engaged in a silent dialogue, hearing a language to which you do not have access. They are the saints or the absolutists.

'A good face is a letter of recommendation.' That old proverb is characteristically firm and assured. We would all like it to be true. Firmness is all; we say, firmly again, as though that indicates our perspicacity: 'I never forget a face.' Of course not; faces are usually memorable. We remember faces easily, but more often than not and increasingly cannot put names to them. Nor can we find all faces easily readable; our vocabulary is always restricted, and not as complex as is needed.

Faces can seem elemental, mystical, dramatic masks, as they did to Hardy: 'I am the family face;/Flesh perishes, I live on . . .'. We relate them metaphorically to failure, courage, death: 'I am afraid of losing face'; 'I feel ready to face the world' (or 'the music'); 'He turned his face to the wall'. And we relate them to the expression of love. Hamlet remembered that his father so loved his wife that he wished 'the winds of heaven [not to] visit her face too roughly'.

So writers are at odds about the meanings of faces; or are wise in their day and way about their contradictory meanings. Shakespeare can write: 'They are the lords and owners of their faces'; and we recognise people of whom that may be true. Like all good dramatists, only more so, Shakespeare through his characters uttered hundreds of aphorisms and their opposites, all as truth; all true in the context of the character and the drama, and often in life.

On the 'faces speak truth' side there is, among the earlier examples, Sir Thomas Browne: 'There are mystically in our faces certain characters which carry in them the motto of our souls, wherein he that cannot read ABC may read our natures.' Yes, but only to a certain level.

The opposite opinion, that faces as often as not lie, is more frequently asserted. Even if we cannot take the utterances of different characters in a play as opinions of the author, the recurrence of certain themes may tell us something about the author's engrossing interests at that time, about the insights, questions, which were preoccupying him. *Macbeth* refers to 'faces' more than once. A few pages back, Lady Macbeth was quoted stating that she could read her husband's expression 'like a book'. We also hear there: 'False face must hide what the false heart doth know'; that has its place in the play's dramatic movement, and more widely. More powerful, more epigrammatic, more reflectively detached, is: 'There's no art to find the mind's construction in the face'. True: but we all have to make an informed guess sometimes.

Montaigne produces one of his troubling *obiter dicta*: 'Age imprints more wrinkles in the mind than it does on the face.' That calls for more rolling round the head than most such brief utterances; it is the kind of remark which makes Montaigne stay with us.

Edwin Muir was the least expectant of all: 'The features of men tell us less than they should . . . The faces of the worst murderers can be paralleled in ugliness by the faces of the most blameless saints'; which seems to close the matter, until we have had a long think. In the course of which we realise that the sentence could be reversed, especially as to the difference between a face and an expression, and that both meanings are true much of the time. The endless inner process of self-justification can make most faces mean anything and nothing. I doubt, though, whether we would for long see in a murderer's face a deep saintliness.

The case is open. But still the faces stay in front of us. Auden's neatly, sharply transposing lines are apt again; we suspect and half-hope they can be applied to us: 'Private faces in public places/Are wiser and nicer/Than public faces in private places.'

The Victorians, the best of them more open to their emotions than we feel safe in being, loved faces and left some of the most evocative celebrations of them: 'He said, "She has a lovely face;/God in his mercy lend her grace,/The Lady of Shalott."' As so often with Tennyson, the rhythm picks us up and carries us along. Browning, less rhythmic, more thoughtful, has as much effect, though less music: 'A face to lose youth for, to occupy age/With the dream of, meet death with'.

Unsurprisingly, those are about women's faces. Rossetti's lines are about his own: 'I do not see them here; after death/God knows the faces I shall see,/Each one a murdered self, with low, last breath./I am thyself – what hast thou done to me?'. Which takes us all the way back to the continuing making of our own faces, and the realisation of that fact, probably in middle age, or even somewhat earlier.

'If a way to the better there be/It exacts a full look at the worst.' Hardy's lines, almost a motto for one of his deepest beliefs – and that face of his, formed by a habitual, unflinching look at the worst – emerge into our consciousness more often than we might wish; the old, resignedly engraved, unhopeful expression. His poems of remorse for his lost love are just as honest to the self, and unforgettably, etchingly telling: 'Your face, and the God-curst sun, and a tree/And a pond edged with grayish leaves'.

Last, another Emerson riddle, if only apparent: 'A cheerful, intelligent face is the end of culture.' It may indicate that nothing has happened to the bearer, that the joys and sadnesses of experience, of living within his culture and taking good stock of it, have all passed him by. Or such a face, no matter how intelligent its owner, may be a mask against depression, or an endless sense of insecurity.

—————

'The past is the only thing that smells sweet'; Edward Thomas had a sad nostalgic focus on the smells of early life. 'Childhood is measured out by sounds and smells'; Betjeman is nostalgic, too, but less sad. For good and ill, pleasure and distaste, smell is throughout life the most evident sense. Touch needs to be the most delicate, unless you are careless about doing damage to yourself; taste is usually the most enjoyable, seeing and hearing the most important. It would be difficult, had we to choose, to decide which of those last two to lose first; probably hearing, since something can be and more will be done to make up for that loss, but the loss of sight is as yet irreparable.

Smell is the most democratic sense, the most wilful, out of our control, anarchic; it comes upon us without our will; we can only evade it by pinching what then seems like our snout, or moving away. Only a few writers give smell its demotic, pandemic place; most concentrate on the two main gates, sight and hearing, those two being much the most used, and civilised.

We can, more or less all the time, control our use of the taste-buds. Most of us are less responsive, remarkably unresponsive, to the complexities and pleasures of touch. From Henry Moore to the carpenter up the local alley, craftsmen live by and revere touch; but they are a minority. Most of us are unconscious of the importance of our own sense of touch much of the time; except as babies, towards babies, when in love or if we are burnt. Then it can be insistent, overwhelming. Having been badly burnt during the war, I still flinch at a sudden flash, even of a cigarette lighter; it is indelibly connected with the agony of burning flesh.

Apart from the hands, those multi-purpose tools, the Swiss Army knives of the human body, which serve many purposes other than touch alone or than any other sense, the nose is our most evident agent of the senses. It pushes itself forward, like a radar antenna; it is cheeky, obtrusive – a characteristic which, as we recalled earlier, writers have occasionally celebrated.

Hands are everyday tools, ears can have jewels hung from them, the eyes can sport designer sunglasses, we use our mouths for talking as well as tasting. Except for the current exceptional fashion in the West of hanging safety pins and the like from it, and similar cultural traditions among some tribes of Asia and Africa, the nose has no dual use; though a few noses tempt you to try hanging your hat on them. Noses chiefly cause experiences to come upon us, nice or nasty.

We recall scenes by seeing them again, looking at paintings or photographs or in the mind's eye; they are relatively easy to conjure up in words. We are sophisticated at calling up sounds, even if we are entirely unmusical. For its sound alone, the collared dove is a welcome immigrant to English gardens; by contrast, the cuckoo, though its call is superficially like the dove's, sounds as though it is aggressively, impatiently, banging to gain entrance. Touch is almost insensitive to memory recall (though it may be that craftsmen, again, have a subtle language for that).

Smell excepted, taste is the most directly evocative sense. It can recall scenes and sounds of all kinds from party conversations over canapés to the sound of massed guns ahead as you eat your dawn rations; and it appropriates, as a major element in its complex work, smell. Proust's aunt's madeleine is the instant and whole gateway to his childhood world and so to his later years, which live within the evocation of that memory of taste and perfume. Taste and smell are married to a degree the other three are not; those are tacked on, separate instruments, not half-assimilated like these two.

Smell calls up memory in a multi-dimensional way to an extent the others cannot encompass. During the war, I did not have much close experience of battle. But there was, and is, the smell of the dead from a night tank battle which set off the final assault from the West on Tunis (we were 'standing to' as anti-tank gunners two fields further back in case of a breakthrough). At dawn, the dead were spread across the fields and small hills, already stripped and rotting as the hot North African sun came up. With that went the acrid smell of cordite from the barrage of a few hours before. Those sensory memories survive powerfully over more than fifty years and I know they will never go away. 'Nothing awakes reminiscence like a smell'; Hugo was there pointing to one aspect of his novelist's trade; his keyboard, to borrow an image from another sense.

We all have our anthologies of smell-memories from childhood, and many of us are almost haunted by them; some recall sadnesses, some are pleasant, some confusing, worrying, even at this date bittersweet. For me, the smell of pee from the long black dress of a relative come on a Sunday visit, at a time when you hardly reached to her knees; the smell of working-class poverty in the 1930s, when we were all crushed on the lower deck of a Leeds tram on a rainy day (the great social historian, H. L. Beales, when he suspected that at one point I was underestimating the improvements in working-class life, counselled me to remember that particular smell); warm oven-cake; the unbathed elementary schoolmates' stale sweat after the gym session (no changing rooms, no showers); carbolic soap; the pungency of fried onions in every English fairground, fast-food shop, Truckers' café and almost all homes; the sharp, almond-essencey smell of nasturtiums in a window-box (the working-class companion to geraniums in tightly organised municipal flower-beds, and as ubiquitous); the smell of melting tar rising from the cobbles, sure sign of 'a real heat-wave'.

The only food which unites – except for me and a few others – the working class through the lower middle class to the middle class is their passionate devotion to onions-with-and-in-everything. An Englishman waking up in heaven hungry, or ordering his last meal before execution, would think things had gone unacceptably wrong if the meal wasn't announced well before it reached him by the smell of those thick chunks. At such moments most English convicts would be descendants of Shakespeare's wilful prisoner Barnardine, only willing to come out for execution when good and ready; and full, I would bet – of onions. For onion devotees, the smell is, I suspect, as important as the texture.

Among the happier memories, some obvious, some not, are: certain flowers, especially those sharp and uncloying; new-mown damp grass; Irish stew and Lancashire hot-pot; bacon and eggs, again and inevitably; fresh toast; fish and chips; the warm rustic-brick-and-roses Lutyens-garden smell; rain on a sooty landscape; a popular French bourgeois restaurant at about eleven o'clock on a Sunday morning; home at the same time.

Sight and sound soon glide from the private experience to the public communion. Touch and taste are much more private. Smells, too, are public but also private, and that makes for much of their interest. They go from the public to the private, but not the other way. The 'smellies' which Aldous Huxley envisaged in his *Brave New World* – didn't the cinema industry try them years ago? – would have been a mistake; like, and the vulgar image comes to mind, farting in church.

I am above all aware of the sense of smell, the crude animality of it. Not as memorably as George Orwell; he was a smell master. If Pinocchio's nose lengthened when he lied, Orwell's did so when he smelled a moral issue. His was a conk of conscience, a puritan proboscis. Typically, he said in *The Road to Wigan Pier*, that it was 'a sort of duty' to get inside places as filthy as the Brookers' boarding house, and above all to smell them. Also typically, he added that it was best not to stay too long in such places. My Brookers' was a B&B in Harwich just before the war, where I arrived by bicycle from Leeds *en route* for the Continent. They charged a shilling a night and I shared a bed with a large, civil trucker. It wasn't worth a penny more. The smell was an immoral act; it spoke of a collapse of all decent domestic values.

That kind of smell assails you, is invasive; you feel it getting into your clothes; it is as penetratingly horrible as the touch of grease-coagulated fluff. A bad taste you can spit out, though it can be horrible while it is with you; you can close your eyes and ears; you don't have to touch something revolting (though when you do so by accident you can be surprised by its nastiness).

My relentlessly genteel Yorkshire spinster aunt Clara, who engaged in a lifelong war against 'nasty', 'awful' smells, was true to type. I wrote about her earlier but will approach her here almost entirely through her sense of smell. Except to repeat that I carry on what looks like a lifelong war with her memory – trying to let the tortured love underneath have its proper place against all the more grotesque memories.

For all senses she had her codes: in paintings, from the 'lovely picturesque' to the quite unattractive because baffling; in sounds, from the equally 'lovely' music of the Winter Gardens to the entirely unlovely 'caterwauling' of crooners. To touch, and even taste, she paid relatively little attention. Smell was her master-indicator, from the manifestly 'beautiful' smell of, above all, 'attar of roses' to the 'horrible stink' of a lavatory just used. 'I shouldn't go in there for a while if I were you', said as though it was the warning announcement of a dreadful situation, deeply embarrassing to have to make, but one which civilised behaviour demanded. The horrible God of Stinks had not yet cleared off.

She carried on a long guerrilla war, with her nose as the advance scout; the nose itself verged on the Punch-like; an unfortunate concurrence. Luckily, she seemed not to mind, or to be unaware of it.

In the lavatory, she tried single and multiple smell-disguisers, mostly synthetic flora. Just as chemically made extracts of fruits, handy for cake-baking, which never in the end taste right – taste artificial, cheap-shop-boughten – these 'fragrances' smelt as though bottles of a cloying perfume had been sprayed around. 'Cheap and nasty', not out of place but awfully in place, cloying. She then tried two such emitters at the same time, and that was overpowering. She hated smoking, not from hygienic or health considerations but because: 'I just don't like the *smell*.' In the end she had to yield if only to mute the odour of the dual chemical perfumes. She went so far as to put a packet of ten fags and a box of matches on the window ledge. 'I smoked like mad,' said one of her amused sisters, 'And the smell was *horrible*.' Farts, phulnana perfume, fags: thus far had her hatred of the worst smell of all, of bodily evacuation, taken her. 'Oh, dear,' she must have felt constantly and inwardly, 'does it *have* to be like this?' The thought of going into a lavatory not long after someone else had come out must have quite revolted her. Hardly any of us like that; for her, it must have seemed like going over the top during a gas attack, without a mask.

Her obsession against our animal stinks was an indication of the power of her puritanism, her fear of and disgust with the body. Her fear and mistrust, above all, of that dreadful conjunction by which we can all feel afflicted: those two holes whose propinquity displeased even my most intellectual friend. To persuade her to admit that the act of sex might yield natural pleasure would have been pointless, like asking an unflinchingly upright bishop to 'just try' a brothel. Had her face, I used to wonder, ever been attractive, with its own unique version of the bloom of youth, as almost all women's are at that time, no matter how briefly. She remained a spinster and for that there were many reasons – her large nose, her bossy appearance (her attitudes bore that out); she wanted to control and contain her world in all its aspects, never to be taken by surprise. She was angry inside herself about the maleness of men; part of her also found it attractive, so that she could on occasion be skittish; the other side revolted. Above all, she had a relentless rage to order, entirely to command and corral her world within her own narrow vision.

Surprisingly to me, Montaigne appeared to be uneasy about any smell: 'To smell, though well, is to stink.' If my aunt had been told that Napoleon sent a message to Josephine announcing his early return from battle and telling her not to wash before he was back, she would have been appalled, and reinforced in her deeply rooted suspicion of France and all its ways. Napoleon was no Plautus – 'a woman smells well when she smells of nothing'; he liked his woman's, his women's, body smells, their sweat; a powerful aphrodisiac. That is one of the reasons why we can be attracted to the French; not having had the Puritan revolution, they can be open and straightforward about the body and so about sex to a degree which at first shocks the English; then, eyes open, we can feel liberated, if we are willing to be – and perhaps recognise better our own often rough national sexual habits; as many Polish airmen from the last war will confirm.

It seems unlikely that Nelson would have written in that way to Lady Hamilton, but is not certain. The English upper class can be coarser, cruder in speech, than the middle or lower middle or respectable working class. Perhaps that goes with living on the land. They will say a young relative is 'in pig' when she is pregnant, perhaps partly enjoying the down-to-earthness, but not feeling greatly daring. The culture of horse-riding and horse-racing, that mixture of upper-crust and working-class rough physicality and sexuality, were well but nastily caught by a jockey's laconic comment on television only recently: 'Stable-girls are always in season.' Three centuries back, Jonathan Swift, Irish and a cleric, had what sounds like an instinctive aversion to the fact of evacuation but seems to have been unabashed about sex. 'I wish I had my hand on the warmest place about you', he wrote to Stella. I remember the surprise, almost shock, on reading that, as a twenty year old writing an M.A. thesis. I had had to ask permission to consult the letters in a closed library.

Others find neither 'honest sweat' nor 'fancy scents' attractive in lovers, or generally. For them a good bath with ordinary soap and water produces much the most attractive perfume; indeed, it would hardly be called even a perfume; it would seem 'natural'. Like our own 'Englishness', by which all other people are seen as 'ethnic', but we as normal, what we are: English.

Deeper down: a teasing biological fact which has its place in proverbs from more than one country, but would not be happily admitted by many people in many societies. It occurs, and this may be the earliest example, in Icelandic; it is well established in English: 'We all love the smell of our own farts.' Perhaps some people would reluctantly agree that our own farts are less unpleasant, more tolerable, than others'; many would not admit even that. From which it seems reasonable to infer that smell is the sense most directly and complicatedly bound up with our images of our self, biological or cultural. But if the old proverb speaks truly, why should that capacity, that olfactory distinction and assertion, exist? Why should the digesting of the same food by different people produce shit with different odours, each being more acceptable to its depositor than those of other people? Do individual glands work differently for different people whilst a meal is being internally processed? No doubt scientists know the answer. Better, and more to the point: the proverb is also, first and foremost, a sharp metaphor; about self-love, naturally.

The complex place occupied by the sense of smell in our imaginations leads us to use it frequently as a metaphor for something we do not like or trust, something which hits us nearly, is unpleasant and a threat. No image from sight or sound or touch or taste is so universally and instinctively used in these ways. 'I smell a rat'; 'I'm being led by the nose'; 'I'm paying through the nose'; 'They've put my nose to the grindstone'; 'That put his nose out of joint.' Where something which we cannot quite put our finger on worries us, we say: 'I can't at the moment explain why, but there's something about this [a commercial deal, a relationship, an argument] which doesn't smell quite right to me.' The atmosphere of that bar on 42nd Street, New York, in late 1939 didn't 'smell right' to Auden, and the resulting image is almost banal, so common is it: 'The unmentionable odour of death/Offends the September night'. Banal, but highly metaphoric. He wasn't yet actually smelling real smells of real deaths. It was the atmosphere of threat (Hitler having just invaded Poland) which could be said to smell of death.

'Stink' is the extreme near-synonym for 'smell', a very bad smell indeed. An emanation, as in 'You are a real stinker' – I smell the unpleasantness of your character coming off you. The reverse practice, of ourselves 'smelling things out', has its most cruel literary expression in *Lear*, when the blinded Gloucester is told to 'smell' his way to Dover.

We were driving across the dire agoraphobic wastes of Death Valley, California, at the turn into the 1990s. It grew dark as we reached the mid-point. We came upon a not-very-smart-looking motel plus restaurant, the only one for miles around. We had an immediate sense, on entering, that no one was going to put themselves out for the sake of travellers, even though they would compose virtually the only clients. An overweight young woman was unwelcoming behind the serving counter/bar, assisted by an uninterested young man who looked like a wanderer from job to

152

job. One hot dish only on offer ('Dish of the Day – Ellie's Own Desert Stew' – made of what? desert rats?), partnered by a disengaged refusal to suggest something else for a tourist who did not like that manifestly onion-laden dish. An air of unhelpfulness overall, an apparent lack of any sense of a common humanity. We retreated to an unkempt, chill cabin outside.

It would have been no more than slightly excessive to say that there was not only a smell of Ellie's stew but also a 'smell' of incompetence or even of squalor there. We looked, we heard, we did not touch or taste; smell both actual and metaphorical was the dominant way of apprehending the place.

PART FOUR

MAINSTAYS:
'Holdfast is the Only Dog'

An agnostic, trying to describe the things which seem above all else worth holding on to in this apparently meaningless world, must seem to believers – and sometimes to himself – like one who launches on the vast seas of experience with only a paper catamaran.

My twin hulls, it seems, are composed of the experience of family life on one side, and on the other the importance of the imagination at work, through art and primarily in literature. One we live with day to day, and can either find it trammelling or a main buttress, or something in between; the other is a unique way in which we try to body out and perhaps order and assess those and other experiences, within ourselves, in the home and in the world outside.

So there is the first difficulty; this effort seems like a finger in the dyke. 'Literature is not enough.' Yes: I can think of a better.

The greater difficulty concerns especially the sense of family. Put as simply as it is above, it sounds hermetic, even uxorious. It need not be. The emergence of an understanding of the nature of family relationships, that developing sense of belonging, of companionship and compassion, is the springboard from which we may move out to build wider and better relationships with others: in the neighbourhood, at work, in all the parts of civil society within which we move, obligatorily or voluntarily. From that perspective, the tests of family life are only a beginning, but fundamental.

I mention all this partly to give the case its proper dimension and also because of a strange experience. Some years ago I included in a book a few pages on family life, much smaller in scope than what now follows. Most reviewers took no exception to them. One out of about a score seemed anxious to consign those pages to the outer darkness.

To write positively about family life clearly angered the reviewer. Was this the contemporary fear of sentimentality rising again? The reading of sentiment as sentimentality? I do not know, but the irritation was out of proportion. The further pages in this chapter may go some way to satisfying that critic. Yet I am not sure they will.

My two mainstays are, naturally, earth-bound and finite. We die; they die. Except that, in a sense, we live on in our descendants and, if we are very lucky, in our writing. But those two are wasting assets. I can imagine no more; and accept that. As Carlyle is reputed to have responded when hearing that Margaret Fuller had announced that she 'accepted the universe': 'Gad! she'd better.'

6

On Neighbours and Family

'Pull not down your hedge.'

I HAVE PREVIOUSLY written much about working-class neighbourliness, often implying if not claiming that the sense of the neighbourly is particularly to be found in those districts – partly on the grounds that if you did not help one another there, you could not buy help; you had to stick together. I now know that neighbourliness is strong in the middle class. But the practices differ to some degree. It is time to adjust the balance.

Working-class neighbourliness of the older kind extends to only a few nearby streets and is tight; middle-class neighbourliness spreads wider and is more loosely articulated. Need and closeness, the lack of movement, have historically inspired the making friends of near neighbours among working-class people. A Scottish proverb is severely correct: 'We can live without our friends but not without our neighbours.'

Among the middle class, the children, rather than contiguity, are the chief creators of neighbourly relationships; their friendships at school radiate out to connections – occasions, trips – with friends' parents beyond the nearby avenues. That is all too neat a comparison; working-class children can provide, if a less inventive (inventiveness is lubricated by money), a similarly rich service to neighbourliness as can middle-class children. Middle-class parents do not habitually slip next door to borrow some sugar; their helpful interweavings (occasional baby-sitting, taking in parcels, feeding the cat when you are away, letting their daughter – your daughter's 'best friend' – 'sleep over' at your place) all are paying homage to the same idea.

What of professional people today and their double lives? On the one hand, there are their horizontal links with professionals of their kind across the world, or at least throughout Britain; on the other, the vertical, the traditional neighbourhood relationships – unless they have chosen to live in a more or less wholly 'executive' enclave, in which case the horizontal and vertical relationships become blurred but not inevitably destroyed. Executives can be neighbourly so long as their area is not too competitive about status: about the car with the latest registration letter, the second and third cars, the professionally tended garden, the 'best' local private school, the superior kitchen and all its gear.

Slightly askew are the increasing numbers of class-jumpers, especially those who have graduated from the old working class to the professional, who know the professional routines but are uneasy about adopting those of the traditional middle class. Slightly floating, slightly untethered; not a bad perch to settle on, so long as it does not produce compensatory aggression (or a defensive holding-on to a stubborn, flat form of speech) instead of a slight, observant, amused swinging from the perch – or chandeliers.

'Do not love your neighbour as yourself', said Shaw: 'If you are on good terms with yourself it is an impertinence; if on bad, an injury.' The sense and the practice of neighbourliness can sit easily with 'keeping yourself to yourself', with indicating that you do not wish to be subject to someone who is 'forever dropping in'. 'Good fences make good neighbours.' The sentiment of Robert Frost's line was preceded by many a proverbial saw; two will do. One is at the front of this chapter, on the value of hedges even if you love your neighbour; the other is not as dour, being slightly poetic: 'A hedge between keeps friendship green.' Come to think of it, working-class terrace houses did not have hedges or fences. The line was invisible, but there.

Neighbourliness is habitually, one could say instinctively, conservative, loving routines, anxious that the accepted order shall be maintained, not reflective or intellectual; a series of firm, if narrow and similar, cultures within a larger culture of greater complexity. Good neighbourliness is decent and helpful but can make a comparative stranger feel over-sophisticated, over-weathered; like Pater's Mona Lisa, older than the rocks among which she sits. Sticking together for warmth, not wishing to be challenged, afraid of solitude, its rages only forms of that 'rage for order' we met before; not the Maker's rage for order Whitman identified, but a bulwark against any threat to the pursuit of habitual and predominantly domestic practices.

Neighbourliness's better side is at least as important. Jane Jacobs caught this when she reflected that today, especially in large cities, life is more and more publicly planned, organised by a self-aware attempt to create public trust; and that neighbourliness by contrast is the place where we exercise *casual* public trust, and that that is more real than the publicly organised version.

Christopher Isherwood thought the finest single line in modern letters was from *A Streetcar Named Desire*: 'I have always depended upon the kindness of strangers.' The limits of neighbourliness: and demands beyond it.

Friends need not be neighbours; and vice versa. Friends are not dependent on nearness, though it can help. Neighbours become so by congruity; friends we choose for ourselves. There can be mutual links. Maintaining friendships needs work, and many of us will eventually not pay the price. Once we are fifty-odd, the friends left are likely to stay for good. Which is just as well since our capacity for forming new friendships deteriorates; we have less energy to meet their dues. Most friendships which simply fall away, rather than breaking up in a quarrel, do so not from positive disinclination but from inertia, unwillingness to put out the necessary hospitable effort. We may not by now respond readily to feelers for friendship from those who are at present good acquaintances. Acquaintances are easier to cope with but, especially if they emerge from mere propinquity, as at work, can become by that chance too close; bogus friendships.

————

Whenever I think about marriage, I remember a friend's wife. They were Roman Catholics with four children. After a good few years, the wife simply left home and thereafter lived alone up North, teaching. We did not know why.

Years later, the husband suggested they might divorce or at least formally separate. She was wide-eyed with astonishment: 'But I'm your wife!'

On first hearing, that might seem rigidly Catholic. It could also be interpreted as the expression of a sense of inalienable conviction, of innocent but unshakeable commitment, and in that sense having dignity.

My wife Mary was an only child, much loved in a secure home. She remembers deciding quite soon that she would herself want 'a proper family', since, even though greatly cared for, to be an only child is to miss a lot. I, too, had been a sort of only child, in a household of adult relatives, ranging in age from thirty-odd to seventy-odd.

Neither of us has regretted the decision to have a family. Many references to the family in literature might have made us at least slightly cautious. They tend to be guarded, if not positively chilly. They speak of constant troubles, spitefulness, harrowing incidents and horrible gatherings.

But not all. Surprisingly, given his own disordered life, Auden more than once paid homage to the English sense of family: 'The English have a greater talent than any other people for creating an agreeable family life.' Nice; but he was nodding there. Italians, Jews, Chinese and many other peoples value a close, warm family life at least as much as the English.

Blake was more severe, not male chauvinistic but realistic. He recognised, rather, that in hard times and easy, the wife has to work as stoutly as her husband at keeping things together; a joint operation, as often as not: 'When a man has married a wife, he finds out whether/Her knees and elbows are only glued together.'

That reduction is always easier than praise does not altogether explain the unflattering judgements on the married state. Montaigne declared that there was 'little less trouble in governing a private family than a whole kingdom'; but his private family was much larger than most we know.

Samuel Butler, the Victorian, snugly decided: 'More unhappiness comes from this source [the family] than from any other.' His bachelor life was cushy: the manservant Alfred attended to most of his needs; regular visits to his French prostitute cared for the carnal.

Add that, for many, family life especially in the early days and if you have no substantial aid to fall back on – from parents, say – can be at least mildly hag-ridden by money, the lack of it. I have mentioned this more than once in writing over the years; it is part of my childhood legacy and those of several now comfortably off colleagues from similar backgrounds; it sticks for decades, but can be shucked off eventually.

Worries about children are all too obviously many and varied. The most immediate and everyday are located there, in the wish to 'do right by them', and so to meet the increasing cost of everything, as they regularly grow out of clothes and shoes and all ancillaries. A banal attitude, but true.

Whenever an unmistakeable bill falls on the mat there is at least a slight shake of worry. Will this upset the monthly balance, make it more difficult to buy the children this and that, throw us into a small overdraft? An early-married world of repeated small calculations, with little 'play' or room for play (an exact word, that, but with a double and doubly exact meaning). Not a great worry, all this; just a silly recurrent tic.

One of the releases as the salary mounts, if you are lucky enough to be on an increasing scale, and most of all when the children at last leave home for good, is that you no longer have to calculate constantly, to 'scrimp' so as to make ends meet. It then seems a very long time since you heard one of your relatives envying someone who had just become 'a five-pound-a-week man'. You have entered the world of the nicely cushioned and do not 'want' (a routine verb) for anything you really need or even, with ever so slight a self-indulgence, would like to have. You join those who month by month give something to charities. You can buy, if not the best, then the near-best, not simply the cheapest. And hire craftsmen's help. They in turn may begin to see you not only as they do someone from nearby but as a money prospect from another class area. They look at the job, then at you, and decide how much you are 'good for'. The first time you realise this marks a small but discernible social shift. It seems hardly believable that we began family life after the war on £400 a year (£350 basic salary plus £50 more because, after hostilities ended and before demobilisation, I lectured a few times a week at the University of Naples).

You can take a sensuous pleasure in going round the shops. Those Bisto Kids no longer have their noses pressed to the windows; they have come inside. You wouldn't enter a shop clearly beyond your present range; but you can go relaxedly into most places and, though you may not buy anything, are repeatedly pleased to realise there are many things you could now afford, but don't want.

Again, a recurrent theme for many originally from the working class: bargain-hunting is for a long time an aboriginal near-obsession. Later, that is linked to a tendency to accumulate things beyond the point of need – little things, mainly, and just as easily given away. To grandchildren first, who are quite likely to look at the shiny notepad, or elaborate key-ring, or pencil holder, or other odd little objects and say: 'No, thank you.' Good.

There are unprompted, wave-like phases. For a long time, hardly consciously, you draw on the old fear of debt and buy no major items. Then relaxation sets in: in one month, pushed on by the fact that you bought most of them at the same time some years ago so that they have grown old together, you slaphappily renew not one but two or three of these: the living-room carpet, the television, the washing machine, the vacuum cleaner, the cooker. Then, slightly frightened at your own wantonness, you withdraw into the small fortress.

You discover in yourself an elaborate set of unexpectedly and perversely different scales. A book costing over £15 ought usually to be borrowed from the public library, but an item for the car at £50 is bought without a tremor. Books still belong to your first, adolescent phase of spending; the buying of cars, even if second-hand, inhabits another and more expansive landscape.

The children, once they are managing within their own families, are more relaxed. They will as a matter of course spend what seem large amounts on their children's recreations and holidays; take out a mortgage so big it almost alarms you; incur large credit-card debts from time to time.

Behind all, and in spite of the relaxations, the old niggles remain; the need to become secure up to the grave, and beyond, for the sake of the one who lasts longer; to save for the bad times which – 'you never know' – may be lurking ahead. Until you think better of it you will go round a couple of miles to save 3p a litre on petrol; a windfall arrives, but you feel uneasy if tempted to spend it on a liberal gesture. Yet you can easily flip over.

In all this you bear more tightly on yourself than on wife and family; your wife has a similar tendency. You can each urge the other to let you spend amounts on them which you would not easily spend on yourself. You always remember those days when a child's wish for some pleasant indulgence might produce from you the lowering 'that's a bit beyond us, love', and want to reduce the memory.

The habit of continuous calculation stubbornly stays. Not to slip up; not to throw away anything which 'might come in handy'. The obverse of that is, after all the arithmetic, to discover a capacity now and again to make one of those acts of liberation not only from the calculations but also from aggregations, hoardings: of, say, large used envelopes. Even more daring: almost to empty your wallet, occasionally to surprise yourself by a slightly alarming act of largesse.

———

Aphorisms about children are often as mildly depressing as those about the family. Many of us know Bacon's: 'He that hath wife and children hath given hostages to fortune' – enough to keep you awake occasionally in the small hours. Bacon could also qualify: 'The joys of parents are secret, and so are their griefs and fears.' Others have noted again and again our deep self-centredness as children, our narcissism and solipsism. All these things are true, often until well after adolescence. So are parents' joys and miseries, but they continue until the end.

It is painful to see the future shining from the children's eyes, their expectation of happiness. (Funny: I seem to recur to the power of eyes, even though I discounted it a while back.) The world is all before them. So that when, at three years old, our eldest child asked his mother: 'Shall I be happy all the days?', she could have wept (the poignancy made all the greater by the phrase 'all the days' instead of, for instance, the less haunting 'all my life').

She understood then, if not earlier, the pity which, before all else, Graham Greene felt for children. There will be disappointments, if not distress, to come, innocence lost, corrupted or let down, and we wish we could gather them up and hold them from all harm. But the road is theirs, without us. Birds learning to fly, they detach themselves at moments, quite early on, educating themselves to be without us, to be self-defining.

More happily, you begin to understand better Nietzsche's remark, echoing Schiller: 'To become mature is to recover that sense of seriousness which one had as a child at play.'

How much influence can we have on their inner growth, no matter how attentive we are? 'About as much as a brace on their teeth,' an American friend replied. A great deal, Camus thought:

'A child is nothing by himself. It is his parents who represent [define?] him'; and: 'It is through them that he defines himself, that he is defined in the eyes of the world.' They learn from us largely subconsciously: especially about reactions to stress and, if we can command that, calm. They learn these things even if they are half-consciously deciding not to be like us.

They learn more from their siblings and in different ways from each sibling (as in different ways from each parent). The sibling interconnections run in several directions, often between the same pair. But this is true of their parents' love for them. All are loved but not in the same ways (though with similar intensities); such particular differences of attachment last through life.

There is a shock, as from very cold water, when someone announces they have never liked this one or that of their siblings; there is slight admiration, too, for their frankness. For others, and these may be the majority, a brother or sister, even after their deaths, will retain something of the hold they had when they grew up together, or even if they were apart throughout that time.

A photograph of our sister at twenty falls out of an old envelope. I am moved by her beauty and the way she recalls our mother (who, I suspect, may only be remembered from a photograph): slim, with a finely boned face, self-possessed, keeping her self to herself, dressed within her own dignity. It all comes back as fresh as ever; or is that only a false memory, from that old photograph?

It is much the same with Tom, the brother who was older and is now dead. Tougher than I am, but with a courteous and well-guided gentleness, the admiration for which filled the huge parish church in Grantham for his funeral service. Our sister Molly loved us both, but looked up more to Tom and still does, to his memory. So do I.

Those old photographs lead me, momentarily, up a side alley. Some photos of Mary's parents, taken almost a century ago, bring memories of what has come to seem a distant land. Passing-out day at the Chester Church of England Teacher

Training College, just after the turn of the century; the upright world of James Kaye-Shuttleworth and his kind. A later photo is of both husband and wife looking like figures from not fifty but, again, a hundred years ago: the dress to the ankles, the permanent hat-with-pin; for him, the three-piece suit with tie, 'Hunter' watch and gold 'Albert' across the waistcoat. Sturdy, earnest, well disposed, unadventurous, George Herbert's people, the quiet but thorough sweepers of homely rooms. We remember, even now with a slight but pleased surprise, how our children leapt across the division of years and manners, to make immediate, very affectionate connections.

'My son's my son till he gets him a wife, / My daughter's my daughter all her life.' Too brisk and dismissive as to the son, that. There are many epigrams about sons but not many as strong as that one about the mother–daughter relationship; 'Like father, like son' is weaker. There is much popular sentiment, especially about father introducing son to manly pursuits. On the mother–daughter relationship the lines are more precise. A mother will usually refer to 'the children' or 'our children'. When she is alone in the hairdresser's chair, smiling to herself, she is likely to say: 'Had to come in today. My daughter's arriving tonight'. That bond has to be at bottom stronger than that between males. The mother has been more central from the start, and the mother-to-be will be. The man is a relatively secondary begetter. Even more quickly than the man, the mildest human mother, like the mildest-seeming animal, can be roused to self-disregarding fury if her young, male or female, are threatened. They have cost too much to come into the world. I wish I had been able to give birth; nothing in the man's experience can match that.

From the beginning, the memories accumulate and stay. The smell of milk on the baby newly released from the breast; its wondering and wavering glance of total trust in the first few months; the bird-like limbs of your eight-year-old daughter.

Looking back, you assess the rewards and sadnesses of the different phases. One we missed: the untrammelled few years before the children began to arrive. For us and for many in our cohort, five or six years of war service obliterated those. If forced to choose, we might say that the most pleasant years were when the children were still at school, cheerful and in good health, still closely tied to the home and family; a group, yet by then much aware of themselves and each other as individuals; bound also in membership of the whole. 'Especially at weekend family meals,' one of them recalls, 'we joked all the time.' You expand with pleasure when one of them, back from first term at university, remarks on how many of his friends 'slag off' their parents but adds: 'I don't do that. I love you two.' Even as I write that I anticipate a shrugging-off, probably a snide embarrassment in some readers. Uxoriousness again! Not at all. So it was.

You remember also the near-disasters, any one of which might have altered the terms of life for those who survived: that you managed to stop just in time before joining a multiple car crash; that two of the children escaped from motorcycle and car accidents; that your incompetence nearly caused a boating disaster; that a cancer in one of them was conquered as it wouldn't have been twenty years before; that on making an emergency landing on one engine at Ibadan, the two of us, on the way down, hurriedly and silently ran over the arrangements agreed for the three in case of such an emergency. Above all, we were lucky that no one had a lasting disablement from birth or after; if they had had, we would, like virtually everybody else, have unremittingly cared for them.

Occasionally, from the perspective of old age, you wonder how you found the courage to take it all on, this giving of hostages to fate and fortune. At the worst moments, when the burden seemed like becoming too much and you showed it, one of the children might say with a child's directness: 'We didn't ask you to have us, did we?' No, you didn't.

Then, one by one but surprisingly quickly, they have all left home. The easy commonplace suddenly acquires force: 'They have fled the nest.' But not before they have helped to enlarge and educate the heart. Summing up the whole experience, you may then remember Dr Johnson's deeply melancholic 'Marriage has many pains but celibacy has no pleasures', and wonder from what dread fate marriage has saved you; not the 'burning' threatened in Corinthians, but perhaps something fairly raddled and lonely and self-involved.

Meanwhile, home remains much as it always was: 'Shaped to the comfort of the last to go.' Larkin humanely adds half a dozen lines later that home 'started as,/A joyous shot at how things ought to be', a celebratory domestic note we do not usually expect from him. The acknowledgement from outside of the rightness of 'a sort of clowning'.

You are freer to go on holidays which aren't a compromise between competing wishes. You spend much time thinking of each child and their different families; when they are on holidays you follow their progress day by day, and in occasional low moments fear a call saying there has been an accident. In that sense, you are never off the hook and would not wish to be. You feel old, almost echoingly bereft, and quite ancient when your daughter says how much she misses her first-born, just gone to university.

These days, you can manage for money and can help them from time to time. But you have to become used to being on the sidelines, even though everyone works to retain the sense of a coherent family, and seems, all in all, to succeed. You can come near that, but it is not entirely possible. For one thing, and no matter how hard your children work to keep the links strong, you are now only one half of the family ties they have to honour.

The children have gone, but come back: to see you and to show their own children as they grow. They can be slightly miffed if you pay more attention to the children than to them. But if you venture even a mild critical question about the way the children behave, are being 'brought up', they can, whilst appearing to accept the comments reasonably, take slight umbrage. You are of a past generation and cannot understand the way the world has changed. Since each new generation believes this, it is all the more ironically surprising that so many aphorisms from centuries ago retain their full relevance.

Few lines in Shakespeare, few brief words in English literature – two single-syllabled words twice repeated – carry so strongly the sense of family attachment, of love: Lear, his mind wandering, is yet aware enough to ask Cordelia to forgive his treatment of her. She answers merely: 'No cause, no cause.' There is no more to be said. 'Forgiveness' would be out of place. He is her father. The ties bind, however irritating the old man may have become, no matter how far away the daughter has gone and whatever the strength of her new links; and so with sons and mothers.

One begins to see then, without patronage or any sense of familial superiority, how childless couples respond when they move into middle or old age. Some, usually well before then, drift apart. Passion or close mutual interests have gone, and there is now little to hold them together. Others seem to hold more closely than ever, are as interested and loving in old age as they were earlier, or even more attached; they do not need additional holds.

–––––

Anouilh goes to the heart of it: 'Love is, above all, the gift of oneself.' In one of his most direct, accessible and memorable lines, Blake is just as true but polysyllabically earthier in celebrating: 'The lineaments of gratified desire'.

To observe those lineaments semi-publicly is unusual, startling and disturbing. I remember a boy telling how he once, on a Sunday afternoon, called at a friend's house to ask if he wanted to play in the street. Eventually, the boy's mother answered the door in a quickly thrown-on dress. She had an air of fulfilled remoteness which disconcerted the caller, which he did not understand. Years later, I learned that Sunday afternoon among working-class couples had habitually been the favoured time for relaxed love-making.

Such things are not much talked about in England. Jewish people are more open. In 'Kangaroo', Lawrence, his image characteristically brilliant, wrote about their 'warm, physically warm love, that seems to make the corpuscles of the blood glow'. A Jewish wife, giving us supper in her Jerusalem home, mused on this and on its differences from English puritanical attitudes, on the duty of the husband and wife to make love on certain regular days, as a wholly welcome part and restatement of the continuing marriage relationship, not an obligation which might seem enforced. There was a quiet, candid beauty about this which our own upbringings had not offered us and which we for a moment found slightly embarrassing.

But not in the mind or imagination; more in the slight shock to our own conventional public definitions of married sexual practice. The practice many English people have actually arrived at may well be near enough to the Jewish, though less attentive to particular days and regularities, but hardly at all attentive to our Northern culture's assumed prohibitions and inhibitions. That culture does put its unmistakeable mark on some people, on the sour, bitten-in face of a woman of only thirty-five, say, with children; and you wonder how she managed to make herself physically available for that purpose. Did she ever know 'the lineaments of gratified desire', passion; or did she simply put up with it? If so, the door seems to have clanged shut years ago, the key thrown away; and her face gives that message.

Passion goes, must go. But its traces remain, always; its memories: the radiant, expectant faces as the train pulls in carrying one of you after a long absence; the half-smile as you each turn at last to sleep. Graham Greene, acute as ever, noted this tender survival. After no matter how many years, he said, and whatever space is now between you, you keep a special warmth of feeling for a woman with whom you have made love; if only once, long ago and far away. This is more than Yeats's 'Honey of generation', though one could argue that at bottom it is a transmuted form of that.

La Rochefoucauld said we could not 'fall in love' if we had not read about it (or seen it in films or on television, presumably). The matter is not as plain as it seems. One could more easily accept: 'One would not know how one is expected to act when one "falls in love" if one had not read about it, etc.'

One has to distinguish between 'falling in love', which is likely at the start to include passion, and 'being in love'. In arranged marriages in parts of Africa and Asia, the man and woman may not see each other until near or on the wedding day. Sometimes they do not greatly care for each other at the start, but will obviously have full sexual intercourse (a clumsy phrase, but I am avoiding 'will sleep together' as a foolish evasion. And 'will fuck' still seems coarse, even after all Lawrence's efforts). That would be normal, whether from the usual urges or to propagate a family and continue the line.

If passion is the overwhelming urge to come together with a specific person, with no necessary thought of propagation and in an emotional/sexual relationship which transcends animal rutting, then partners in an arranged marriage may know this quite suddenly. There is plenty of evidence that such partners can gradually feel love for each other, become 'in love' (which is rather different from 'falling in love' in the Western sense) and remain so. The 'falling in love' which La Rochefoucauld labels and reduces is one of the West's most evident individualistic attitudes; to grow into love is a different and more lasting matter, and of course can be, is, experienced by Western as much as by Eastern people. Love is different from passion and by chronology likely to succeed it. It is slightly odd but possible to 'be in love' (not 'fall in love') and feel passion later. Even if the falling in love took a long time, passion – if passion there is to be – will usually beat it by a short space.

Love knows and embraces the physical but is not dependent on or dominated by it. It always remembers physical passion with gratitude but its ways are more slow-burning and pre-occupying. Which is one reason why many men and women do not seek temporary partners: the passion of husband and wife is sufficient in the early days; it transmutes into lasting love for the longer haul without, as I've said, forgetting the force of passion. To embark on an affair can then involve too much fret and fuss

171

for the sake of some casual and short-lived excitement. On receiving an overture from the husband of a friend, a colleague's wife replied, only half-comically: 'No, thanks. I've enough drama in my life deciding whether we'll have broccoli or peas for supper, or both.'

Love is a process of growing into one another, of growing together like plants, of intertwining without entirely interlocking; and certainly without submerging. It can play to and fro within itself like the violin and piano, gently communing with each other, in the second movement of Beethoven's *Spring Sonata*. It builds up over decades, so that after many years it may seem not so much a coming together of two people as the emergence of a new third entity. One or both may say: 'I don't know how I could bear to go on without you.' Which is sincerely meant but usually mistaken; almost always the one left grieves deeply, and carries on. Sometimes their friends are surprised and slightly shocked when the survivor finds a new partner after no more than a year. A colleague had a striking answer: 'I found I could hardly sit in the evening without a woman opposite to talk to, to be affectionate towards and to feel affection returned. I think "X" would have understood.'

Love is quietly accommodating, ignoring recurrent bumps, allowing leeway for each other's weaknesses, ready to ignore some things, closing some doors but indicating that others are still open. It builds up over the years a range of unspoken but clear signals: changes of mood, getting out of the wrong side of the bed; or 'presenting', as animals do, though more subtly, giving little unspoken signals of amorousness which the other person as intimately recognises.

It can look enclosed and parochial and in some ways is. Observed from inside, it has its ordinary days and also the days when it suddenly glows. It is riddled with tender gestures and acts which go unremarked but are felt underneath. Among the passages I remember most often and warmly is that from 'Tintern Abbey' about the sustaining force of 'little, nameless, unremembered acts/Of kindness and of love'. It can be affectionately comical and slightly exasperated. A friend used to say of his wife: 'She's near stone deaf, old boy. But she goes on writing those bloody long novels.' At which point you realised how solid the marriage was; he was not to be carried off by any of the very attractive young women in his splendid personal office. You recognise the same when, across a public room, you see a married couple looking straight and fully and with open, secure affection at each other. Private faces in public places.

Love needs time to take root and must be treated patiently. If it is disturbed too often, especially in the early days, it will not settle; the ground is too shallow and not yet sufficiently nourishing. The plant has to bed itself in slowly so as to put out more and stronger roots.

Once settled and secure, it is unlikely to be free of squalls, of swayings backwards and forwards which nevertheless do not uproot. In some instances, one partner is over-dependent on the other, and that may be easily accepted or an irritant, especially if the stronger character is also habitually preoccupied, whether for admirable or selfish reasons. In a few marriages where circumstances are like this, one may occasionally see a dance of bad temper one day and then kindness, an attempt to make up, the next day. In unpleasantly extreme instances, the dominant partner may at intervals act so as to dissolve confidence and maintain in the other a baffled resentful subservience, and the next day balm is put on the wound; a refined cruelty. Like stretching an elastic band to near but not quite breaking point. Or the words may stay the same but the tone marks a distancing, cold reserve. You may notice this when not far into what promises to become a more-than-casual acquaintanceship with another couple, are always shocked, and suspect that there may soon be a coming apart for them.

Trollope accurately caught the hardest truth here: 'With people that are indifferent to him, no man is less exacting; but with those near to him in life he never bends, not an inch.' The modern version is: 'He is kinder to his secretary than to his wife.' Both can be easily answered by the accused. It is, he may say, because he is indifferent to outsiders that he would not bother to engage strongly with them; he expects and exacts and hopes for better from his nearest and dearest. That is so, but a face-saving excuse.

Montaigne dug further and was superbly, exhilaratingly frank: 'If anyone should think when he sees me sometimes look bleakly at my wife and sometimes lovingly that either emotion is put on, then he is daft.' Montaigne as a Yorkshireman.

The English, and no doubt others, have a sly line: 'Judge a man by the look of his wife.' True, but needs careful handling. Some wives and some husbands seem naturally placid, content, not easily rocked; internally plump. It doesn't sound as though Montaigne's wife had or was led to acquire that look, which does not make her less interesting; quite the opposite. Rather, someone we would greatly like to have known.

Growing into one another; being intertwined. A special place seems to be held by couples each of whom has been divorced so as to marry the other, with whom they have 'fallen passionately in love'. They may well have had reasonably contented marriages, children they love, comfortable homes. They have given up all that, caused great distress to their deserted wife or husband, to their children, and to themselves – as they realise how deeply they are missing the children and much else. But they felt at the time that they could not do otherwise. An exceptionally honest friend said, and was not rejecting his new marriage: 'If I had realised the agony it would all cause, I don't think I'd have had the courage to go through with it.'

Such a couple often seem peculiarly tender towards one another, as though the new relationship is fragile; as though they have been through a shipwreck, have to handle each other very carefully in case the new vessel too begins to show signs of being storm-tossed. They sometimes have a look which compounds fear with a sense of being wounded. Will the earth now remain firm beneath their feet? Two other frequent comments after separation or divorce sound like distant bells from different emotional parishes: 'The worst part was in the few months before we

174

decided it wasn't working' (bad, too, for the friends forced to watch the signs of growing rupture, and torn in two by them); and the late-compensatory: 'We are better friends now than when we were married', which can sound glib, or bittersweet.

Pascal muses on the force of habit in all our lives. The routines of habit come to seem like forces of nature and attract a hidden belief in the unexamined rightness of particular routines. You follow them as if half-awake. The phrase 'ingrained habit' is exact. Habits are scored on the character as if on marble. To an observer they can seem to have the permanence of lines in stone, or be like blue veins against the flesh, or canals made by the spirit's (not the 'mind's') tracks. Habit can be a form of laziness, and like the built-in memory of a computer – an almost automatic touch on one button releases the pre-set programme. They are known, usual, not surprising but essential; they tidy, partly control, the universe, unless some cataclysm makes them no longer able to be followed.

In some ways similar, in others different and not necessarily a form of laziness, though usually simple and even corny, are the routines built up in a long marriage. A winnowing, a fitting-in, an accommodating – in kinds of food and the way they are cooked, holidays, bedtime and getting-up time, friends. Most strengthen after the children have left home. Before then, habits, though at least as common as they are later, are compromises, determined mainly by convenience; with four, five, six to cater for, you must take the short cuts regular habits provide.

Habits acquired later can have a ritualistic, almost a symbolic quality, and certainly the air of mild lay celebrations. As with us – the Grade A boiled eggs over breakfast together every Sunday morning, but hardly at any other time; the good pork joint on Saturday or Sunday evening; reading the Sunday paper in bed, another sensuous experience; even the fish for Friday lunch – which is both a nod to a religious custom no longer felt to be in force, and a straightforward memory from childhood. Such habits are unspoken reiterations of a feeling of continuing belonging.

Invited to a small lunch party, we found there an elderly professional man and his wife. It was immediately clear that the wife
was in an advanced stage of senility. Her husband drew not the
slightest attention to this but throughout cared unremittingly
for her, as though she was a two year old whose behaviour need
not be remarked on and was taken for granted by the child herself. There was a purity of un-self-regarding devotion in the
quiet care he gave. The rest of us implicitly tried by our own
reactions or, more accurately, lack of reactions, to live up to his
example. She is dead now, died not long after we saw her. He is
dead too; the obituaries referred to him, not unkindly, as professionally a dry stick. There, he had acted with a beautiful love.

On an aircraft returning from the Balearics there sat near us a
very old man, probably well into his eighties. His eyes were
rheumy and his face and hands discoloured with the purply
tinges of advanced age. But well dressed and groomed. Being
unobtrusively looked after by a daughter or perhaps a much
younger second wife. He was taken to the lavatory, brought back
and carefully seated. The front of his fine-quality, neat, well-
pressed, pale-fawn gaberdine trousers bore a large wet stain,
which luckily he did not notice or took as a matter of course.
The chance indignities of old age; and the love.

Since men tend to die earlier than women, there are probably
more women looking after barely capable husbands than husbands looking after wives. That difference apart, the responses
are similar.

If one partner, for example, suffers a stroke in early middle
age, it is almost always taken for granted that the remaining
partner will attend devotedly until the end, which may be many
years away. They almost always do, though sometimes they rage
inwardly at the way their own lives have been reduced to attending to the needs of one who has now no needs except those of
physical care, very demanding needs indeed. When the invalid
dies the grief is genuine; and so is the submerged, hardly
acknowledged relief, which does nothing to reduce the long history of unquestioning devotion. The obituaries often record a

death 'after years of painful illness bravely borne'. Naturally, there is no need to add: 'and borne also by his devoted wife (or her devoted husband)'.

The earlier years of reciprocal love make the tie there. But so can sudden love; or why should a woman, in love again at forty, marry a man who is, she knows, inexorably going blind? Nowadays, Wordsworth's openness to overpowering feeling can embarrass us; a pity: 'There is a comfort in the strength of love;/'Twill make a thing endurable, which else/Would overset the brain; or break the heart'.

———

'The test of freedom.' Chesterton described the family as the test of freedom because it is chosen in freedom, self-made, self-selected, self-conducted. T. S. Eliot, slightly surprisingly, took that thought further than Chesterton; for him there could be no adequate vocabulary to describe the almost unconscious exercise of love within and across a family, a love which defines all else. There are other such statements, but not many. It is, again, an easily misunderstood and suspect sentiment. Chesterton and Eliot were both practising Christians. 'Now and forever we are not alone' is a Christian statement. An agnostic can, if lucky, adopt some such announcement when thinking of the meaning of the family, without trying to find a vocabulary for it.

A secure family is a creation, a hedge, a bulwark against the world outside, as I have been given the chance to learn so far as the will allows; to learn about good nature at the heart, about how not to bear grudges or utter malice. Those brought up in loving homes can be ill-prepared for much in the 'real world'. They may also have been given a sound preparation for that world, if they have learned also a determination to face its disappointments as much as its rewards. Then they may do more than simply survive.

Few sights are more attractive than that of an elderly couple at peace with themselves and one another; still seeing in each other the young faces which first drew them. They may have created simply – but it is not 'simple' – a prick-neat home, enjoy modest holidays, coffee mornings, pleasant rides out in the car. This can be the creaturely world of wealthier nations, very privileged: calm within itself if its inhabitants will have it so or imagine it is, or ought to be; and that it will remain so. Meanwhile, few tests of the deepest unity are stronger than the ability to watch your husband or wife entirely immersed in an occupation detached from you – without having the itch to interrupt, even with an anecdote.

Or walking out together. Many of us consistently distort the achievement of D. H. Lawrence; *Lady Chatterley's Lover* is put too much at the centre. We tend to forget the moments of acute homely perception, as here, in *Women in Love*: 'Their mother . . . dressed in a summer material of black and purple stripes, and wearing a hat of purple straw, was setting forth . . . beside her husband, who, as usual, looked rather crumpled in his best suit, as if he were the father of a young family, and had been holding the baby whilst his wife got dressed.'

We came upon an elderly Frenchman in the park of a quiet hotel in the Auvergne, looking at a small grassy mound. 'My wife's grave,' he volunteered, without drama. 'We came here for our honeymoon and many times afterwards. She died four years ago. I come back each year. Life is not the same.' One could easily imagine the wife, above all her deeply loving good nature; and his continuing sense of loss.

So: a family can give us unique access to our own emotions, can constantly open the heart; if we will let it.

When Sir Toby Belch boasts to the rather ludicrous Sir Andrew Aguecheek that Maria, who has just left them, 'adores' him, we know that is a philanderer's lightweight use of the verb.

Sir Andrew responds simply: 'I was adored once too.' His 'adored' stretches itself out, has enormous, pathetic, lonely, transforming length and weight; it transforms the sad knight into a person no longer of comedy, and demanding more than pity. Sympathy and respect, rather.

7

On Words, Books, Reading and Readers

FOR MANY PEOPLE, T. S. Eliot gravely observed, literature is a substitute for religion, and added: so is their religion. It will be plain, I hope, that neither substitution applies to me. I value literature so highly because it is the best creative activity – the making of things outside ourselves – that I can imagine, discover and respond to. If I had a religion, literature would be happily made into a side-support. More: literature, words, language are my second prop; face-to-face relationships are the first.

It is easy to see some reasons, though they are not comprehensive, why things have turned out in this way. They include, first, the use of language as a way of climbing out of Hunslet, and second, the instinct from adolescence to know better how to see into experience; that turned me on to books, not priests. Things might have gone the other way, but didn't; for reasons I am still not clear about.

———

Yeats's celebrated line – 'words alone are certain good' – is dangerously attractive, even compelling. One wants entirely to believe in it, and can in some senses do so. But not to give entire belief. In the end the goodness of people – some people – will triumph over the 'goodness' of language.

The first word I remember being caught by was 'drizzle'. Very much an English word, probably not common in California;

beautifully onomatopoeic and perfectly fitting our weather. 'Oh, dear, it's *drizzling* again.' Recently, supermarket shelves have exhibited 'Lemon zest drizzle cake'; worth trying for the name alone.

For some children from bookless homes, the sense of language, often inspired by teachers of English, was and may still be the first way out; language for its own sake, not for the entry to something grander, such as 'the exploration of life' and 'the mirror of cultural change'.

I was well into adolescence before I began to respond in that second way. Earlier there was, for me as for many another, the headiness of language as a sort of drug, through finding the poems of Swinburne, at eleven or twelve, in the public library. Was that entirely an accident, or had someone casually mentioned him, a teacher or a more widely read classmate? Swinburne was a good discovery at that stage since he was, as compared with the great novelists, more in love with words than intellectually interested in life; so was I, then.

More sophisticated, but no less gripping, there came later poems such as Melville's 'The Maldive Shark':

> About the shark, phlegmatical one
> Pale sot of the Maldive sea
> The sleek little pilot fish
> Azure and slim,
> How alert in attendance be.

Melville moves straight off, as if in mid-description, and the movement then recreates the smooth, assured glidings of the little fish around the huge shark. Yet that language is also echoing with cultural styles and placings: 'phlegmatic . . . sot . . . sleek . . . alert . . . in attendance'. An exceptional interplaying and hard to absorb for anyone under about fourteen.

For most and perhaps all of us, the affair was both physical – sensuous, on the pulses – and an introduction to possible exactness of thought. An agent of the imagination and the intellect, both at once; and as a way of 'speaking to each other'. The links of language with logic are often played down nowadays. Even very simple logical distinctions within language, such as between 'few' and 'less', are discarded as unnecessary or even as meaningless. It is pointless to grumble at this late stage about the misuse of 'hopefully'. But both these misapplications cause a blur, small enough perhaps, but a blur in thought and so a loss of clarity.

There has always been, for me, the sense of a possible audience, of someone out there. 'Whom do you think you're writing for?', I am sometimes asked, now and again with near-truculence. 'Who makes up the "we" you invoke often and with some apparent confidence? Haven't you realised that your supposed habitual audiences, "the saving remnant", have all but disappeared or been, through professional training, dispersed beyond reach; that most stick to their own specialised professional reading nowadays?'

Certainly public voices, especially when they dilate on how we live now, have lost many of their traditional and easily identifiable readers. Most intellectuals tend to address known circles of their own kind; and, of these, academics are among the worst. All this is partly true; and the broadsheet newspapers are under such pressure to compete that they no longer give as much time and space as they once did to slower and more considered work.

> This is undoubtedly the age of humanity – so far, at least, as England is concerned. A man who beats his wife is shocking to us, and a colonel who can't manage his soldiers without having them beaten is almost equally so . . .

One recalls such Victorian voices – this is Meredith, beginning *The Bertrams* – assured of certain certainties but also welcoming change. Were their usual confident tones well founded? What intimacy, what similarity of responses, ideas, prejudices, notions, thoughts, beliefs – about individuality, family, marriage, class, nation – they assume; in their readers, at least. They are so confident in tone that they can sometimes adopt a rococo,

181

rhetorical, high-level, ironic and complicit knowingness, which we would not dare.

Look again at *Beauchamp's Career*. Meredith is not much read today, is regarded as out-of-date, often pompous and mannered. Push through all that and you are impressed by the sureness in his analysis of Victorian attitudes: about people and their relationships (which he does not romanticise), about the politics of both Houses of Parliament (on which he is, like Trollope, well informed), about 'abroad . . . overseas . . . Empire' (all taken confidently, not insecurely or always critically); about, of course, the solidity of land and birth and class and marriage. No franchise for women; they have to make do with marriage, childbirth, loyalty to husband and family, strength in adversity, friendships with their own sex; and are then the recipients of an often romantic chauvinism.

Ann Veronica may be about to peer from the next corner, but her head is still hardly showing. There are dismissals, sometimes roaring dismissals, of the increasing political pretensions of 'the people'. The peerage sits on top of society, immutable. Whatever one's qualifications about the longueurs in reading Meredith, one admires an author who has a great peer dismiss his new neighbour Dr Shrapnel with the unshakeable lordliness of: 'They are people who have tea in their gardens.' It's the plural that does it. 'Garden' would have been lower-middle to middle class, pre-Betjemanesque; 'gardens' lifts it into the truly, blindly contemptuous-aristocratic. Strange, again, to think that book was written just before the end of the century: Wells, Shaw, Temple, Tawney, the Webbs were already at the gates of 'the gardens'.

I do not mean to imply that Meredith himself shared the conventional assumptions described above. He need not have; indeed, we know from the memoirs of at least one very good acquaintance, Lady Butcher, that he was, for example, concerned about the secondary place assigned to women. Like any good novelist, he reflected and, if he wished, implicitly or explicitly criticised the assumptions of his time, did not necessarily approve of all of them.

Stranger still, on the matter of tone of voice, is to realise afresh and through comparisons how markedly – decades earlier – Dickens, though he wrote for a similar audience to his coevals, had his own voice. Of course, he sought the middle class and knew their vocabulary and tones. In a deeper sense, he does not consistently give the impression that his voice and stance and outlook have been *determined* by the social milieux of the core of those who read him. He achieved his wide readership more by his range of outlook, linguistic genius, wit, ability to tell a story, and many other gifts than by a socially restricted tone of voice.

Later, roughly about Meredith's time, Hardy, too, did not share, or at least exhibit, that enclosed and sure sense of a particular audience. He confessed engagingly to modelling his style to some degree on *The Times* leaders. Or was it the second leaders? Or the third? More often he wrote as if for himself, but with a grave courtesy which seems to imply that he who would run is welcome to read.

Though the old certainties about the existence of an identifiable group of readers have been badly shaken, some of us are still unwilling to give up the hope. Perhaps those readers are less class-identifiable today and not embarrassed by that. Perhaps they are more melded together, most of them recipients of some form of higher education; even meritocrats, a group not quite so easily serviced by the advertisers as the rest of us, a group roughly within socio-economic group B and a bit above. Still, as we have seen, most are also – to some degree and often without knowing it – caught by the advertisers, who have by now identified each particular group's and sub-group's tastes. If people in a part of group B become your central readership, does that mean that you and they have become an element in a small section of commodity culture? Probably, to some extent. Another example of something not at all hoped for when the literate society was looked forward to.

So it remains difficult for some kinds of writer, myself included, not to believe they are writing for a group out there, of people who to some extent share their views, or – perhaps better – their general outlook on experience: individuals, but in this at least grouped. Their readers are expected to be rather more than commonly literate and able to scoff at all the right things. And admire the right things? No such author would dream of explicitly 'rejoicing to concur' with the views of his hoped-for readers; but some wish they could. Perhaps to some degree we can, can believe they still exist, and compose a small but worthwhile audience. My own postbag suggests this is so, slightly. In addition to general letters of comment, I receive at least half a dozen unsolicited autobiographies in typescript each year, for critical reading.

None of those considerations will come near to satisfying or even interesting many writers. They know they write because they have to, that it is a deep-seated and long-standing impulse, like wanting to have a baby, babies; or a mildly grumbling appendix, or a medium bout of indigestion. That is roughly how it can feel metaphorically, but the images do nothing to explain *why* it feels like that to the authors. They may then say, though feeling slightly sophistical, that at bottom they write for themselves, about what seems most worthwhile, or simply interesting, or amusing. More choose to give bluntly disguising answers – starting with 'I do it for the money' – and seem unwilling to tell others or even seriously to ask themselves why they write. Perhaps that might be too unsettling.

For Flaubert, writing was a dog's life, but the only one worth living. Graham Greene saw writing as escape from horrors even greater than Flaubert suggested: 'Writing is a form of therapy; sometimes I wonder how all those who do not write, compose or paint can manage to escape the madness, the melancholia, the panic fear which is inherent in a human situation.'

Tchekov is a good model in a quite different sense. Even in translation he appears to be at ease, speaking to us humanely, honestly, without pretension, as one human being to others. He was certainly not writing in a democracy, but he makes us believe that in any halfway-working civil society some writers should be able to find an audience of concerned intelligent lay readers. That is an essential ingredient of such a democracy: not the audience only of intellectuals or even of 'highbrows', but that of the common readers – who are never really *commonly* to be found, but who even now are more widespread than many of today's literary people seem to assume.

———

'"A book cannot take the place of the world" . . . One of the problems that calcifies the contemporary stand-off between the average book-lover and the proponent of the bright technological future is the former's invariable descent into misty-eyed humanism, a sort of escapism by default that nearly always antagonises any non-bookish person . . . Regarding the book as a moral penicillin . . . won't do now, and if we want the book to hold its own against the VCR and the Information Superhighway, one of the first things we should do is to treat it with a little less reverence.'

What dreadful, smarty-pants stuff, and so typical of much in present-day intellectual journalism. Flirting with information technology and careless of the relations, if any, of all that with meaning, belief, meditated action. The muddled language is matched by the muddled thought. Flaubert and Camus are preferable: the one with 'Read in order to live', the other with 'To write is to become disinterested. There is a certain renunciation in art.'

If only for a multitude of practical daily purposes, reading is essential. Or has been; the almost unbelievable increases in the range and power of electronic means of communication are likely to make most utilitarian, day-to-day reading obsolete. Little electronic things in the pocket, in touch with thousands of other electronic things in the world outside, will bring that about.

It would be a pity if these developments inclined young people today not to bother with the 'obsoletes', with, let's say: Borges and many another Latin American, African, Asian or Caribbean author, Chaucer, Fielding, Smollett, Joyce, Lawrence, Pasternak, Solzhenitsyn, Mann, Scott Fitzgerald, Hemingway, Proust, Leopardi, Cervantes. The confident lack of cultivated literacy in many glad embracers of the new communications world has to be quietly but very firmly deflated.

More widespread and important, because less technological and striking deeper, is the assumption that reading in its less obvious senses – not just for 'informatics' and perhaps knowledge, but for reflection on life, on society and personality, for hard meetings with other minds, most of them superior to our own, for a special sort of relationship with 'the best that has been thought and said' and for special pleasures – will, chiefly under the pressures of a general, 'post-modern' relativism, also become obsolete.

The rejection can be a double one: first, of the belief that it is good to meet minds better than our own – the concept of 'better' minds may be accepted grudgingly and partially, if at all; second, that the process at its best, its most effective, is solitary. Steiner is almost poetic here: 'To learn by heart, to transcribe faithfully, to read fully is to be silent and within silence.' This willed detachment from a group may seem at first an error, but so it must be in the beginning. We are free to come back to the group at any time and there to compare and question. We may be helped to read well by conversation with others; we may usefully discuss what we have read. Yet essentially the act of reading is private; we must at some point come to it on our own. Even more, we must come to it in our heads, silently, absorbing the words through our eyes into our brain, intellect, imagination, and at our own changing pace. Which means also that any audio tape, no matter how well read by no matter how practised a reader, is partial, cannot give a full, internal experience.

Which may help to explain why wealthy entrepreneurs (collectors of incunabulae included; incunabulae can then become predominantly visual objects of possession) acquire visual art rather than literature. Visual art can be regarded as a range of commodities, of visual commodities – even if the collector keeps them locked away for his eyes only – high-flying instances of commodity culture. Reading is an *experience*; books have to be internalised by each of us, with effort by us in response to the degree of challenge from the book. The jump from buying expensive incunabulae to settling down and reading any of them is great.

Other defenders of reading have their own firmly held but sometimes questionable convictions. Which begin with the assurance that any sort of reading is worthwhile. Until we have reached, let us say, ten or twelve years of age, that may just be credible. At about that time, for those who will go further, some degree of discrimination sets in. Long ago, we may have begun, as convention says, by spelling out the labels on sauce bottles (like many others, I still remember the incomprehensible French of the labels on HP sauce bottles. '*Cette sauce de première qualité . . .*'), then 'gone on' to 'comics' and on again to all kinds of boys' or girls' authors; which we need not, when we are adults, make fun of, but which no longer satisfy us.

Most people do not go through that progression. The 'any sort of reading is good' argument is at best a statement of a temporary condition for some (those who do go on), and wishful thinking about what happens to many others (they stay where they are). For luckier people to be willing to settle for that barrier in relation to others can be one more of today's forms of unacknowledged condescension.

Brighter children may be, to a great extent, left to look after themselves. They will read virtually anything at the start, because virtually anything can engage their imaginations, their emerging love of words and situations. They will soon set off on that almost involuntary learning by heart of passages which grip them; this lasts and accumulates throughout life. They will be luckier still if their parents read to them; read books which, even if aimed at 'their level', do not talk down. By the age of eight or nine, there are a lot of good books especially written for children, and many children will find their way to them, for the time being.

'Write for children as you do for adults'; that, surprisingly and engagingly, is attributed to Maxim Gorky. Sooner rather than later, parents will do well to choose an 'adult' book (one not directed at a particular age) which they themselves admire and which a reading by them to their children can make open. It will surprise no wide reader that much of Dickens is ideal for this. Those teachers who argue that children must be left entirely alone to 'find their own level' – and even that it is 'bourgeois élitism' on the part of parents to read to their children books they themselves admire – such people are misled, as usual by good intentions. Our daughter, now just in her fifties, still remembers with pleasure our reading *Great Expectations* to her well before her teens. All parents should read to their children. It is plainly wrong, a confused egalitarianism, to argue that because many do not, parents who wish to do so should forbear.

Which throws the onus all the more on the teachers. Here, as in many other ways, one of their main roles is to compensate for the inadequacies of some – well, not to be mealy-mouthed, many, perhaps in some places most – homes. If a teacher has been affected by the critical ideas just mentioned, the children will be doubly ill-served. This is not in any way a world in which we are left alone to find the best for ourselves; too much presses in other directions. We all need help and some more than others. Without that kind of help from the school, many children will not come near meeting the better, let alone the best.

The school must compensate. If it does not, brighter children, even those whose parents give them no help, will have yet another advantage; they will graduate to the more intelligent in their group who, sometimes being cleverer than they are and perhaps all of a year older, will tell these newcomers where they have become stuck. We will have prepared the rest for an adult life of repetitive trash.

This is not to forget the reminder by C. S. Lewis and George Orwell. Bad literature may evoke good impulses. A bad book may have been well-intentioned, as Aldous Huxley remarked: 'A bad book is as much a labour to write as a good one; it comes as sincerely from the author's soul.' Those observations are about popular literature of a more innocent time and kind. Oscar Wilde was sharper when he said that all bad poetry is sincere. Most modern mass-produced 'reading matter', 'print product', shows few good impulses and little sincerity.

Luckily, the atmosphere seems to be showing a few signs of changing; some better counsels have recently emerged in schools and colleges. Already some spokesmen and women for the populist phase have begun to speak differently, to talk of 'quality', to recognise that to 'share' with their pupils a reading of teenage girls' favourite magazines does not mean you have to discourage access to Charlotte Brontë; that is at least undemocratic, at worst an unconscious reducing of their pupils' imaginative human rights. 'All good books give me an existence as wide as man'; Emerson on the birthright of us all.

'The appetite grows by what it feeds on'.* Shakespeare was right, commonsensically correct. Most of us are not natural climbers. If we have had few opportunities to acquire sensible discriminations at home, if we have been discouraged at school from any kind of 'going onwards and upwards', and of realising the pleasures of that progress, then we are as we leave school pre-prepared human packages (like shoddily prepared semi-frozen foods) ready for the entrepreneurial exploiters, who will profit from our condition of dead-end near-literacy. They will continue to provide us, aggressively and wooingly at the same time, with the sort of rubbish which produces most profit. The net has closed. We go round and round on the same carousel.

Does this simple fact need repeating? Certainly. If, at a serious conference on the subject, you are moved to say what is said immediately above, you will be at once challenged. A well-respected author, looking at you as though you have been guilty of intellectual snobbery but responding more in sorrow than anger, will tell the grateful audience that reading of any kind can, most often does, lead onwards and upwards, that an adolescent

---

*Rabelais said: 'Appetite comes with eating.'

reading of stereotyped sex-and-violence, say, or crime fiction –
Mickey Spillane and his contemporary counterparts – will lead
on to Graham Greene and then to Joseph Conrad. It would be
interesting to have more than exceptional instances of that excellent march.

The belief is a triumph of ill-founded hope over unwelcome
reality. It accepts and encourages reinforcement, not change,
living within received prejudices rather than aspiration – hardly
a sustaining web of educative aims. Tastes then either go round
and round at the same level, or drift down to find a lower and
even more congenial point of rest.

Also to be questioned, indeed challenged, is a related myth:
that television adaptations of the classics can greatly encourage
the onwards-and-upwards progress in reading. This happens
rarely, no matter how many copies of a book, in its original
written form, have been sold. Most are not read. The 'book
of the film', abridged and simplified, will be more accessible;
but it is a cheat.

The television experience is different in kind from the experience of reading a good book (second-rate novels may adapt
more faithfully; they give the producer more room for visual
manoeuvre, and distortion is less important). We may watch
the television version of *Pride and Prejudice* or the even more
impressive adaptation of *Persuasion* with enjoyment, but without coming to terms with many essential qualities – the
subtle, ironic authorial voice, and much else.

The achievement of any sort of stretching upwards is the right
of all, but never easy. George Bernard Shaw, very good at com-
pressed truths, asserted that to understand a printed page is a
phenomenal achievement.

That is a more complex statement, an implied definition of
'reading', than it may at first appear. It means very much more
than a five year old's: 'Mummy, I can read. Listen.' Within a very
few years that child will begin to understand much more from
what people say or from what is overheard within the family, very
much more than can at that stage be put into its own words, be

190

'understood' in the sense of unconsciously analysed, translated into tone, its sometimes contradictory messages construed, behind the straightforward words and sentences. Shaw was stressing how remarkable an achievement it is to be able to understand speech beyond the functional level. Reading, responding to words on the page, he goes on to say, is even more difficult, is 'a stupendous feat of sheer learning', this arrival at the ability to 'understand' not only conversation but, in these deeper senses, a printed page.

Clearly, we are in another region altogether from that occupied, honourably, by initial literacy, primary literacy, functional literacy. We are in a much more demanding area of the mind. Shaw is deliberately indicating the greater complexity of a full, a mature, 'reading' than is indicated by that child's: 'I can read now.'

All of which may sound difficult and unappealing. It can certainly be difficult, a continuous effort, and few of us at any time fully meet it except with encouragement. What a deprivation that can be. Imagine not having read some at least of the range of authors mentioned earlier. But some who have not had that experience do not miss it; that slightly finger-wagging phrase 'You don't know what you're missing' means nothing to them; it is a statement of loss, but comes out as a disconnected truism. There are several unacknowledged but handy continuations of such challenges. The best known is a form of: 'How do you know what you are missing till you see what you can have?', which is also the best rejoinder to those providers (especially in broadcasting) who do not see the need, the democratic need, to offer opportunities to broaden taste.

On the other hand, and indisputably, some bookless, 'unprivileged' people arrive at wisdom, by native observation and thought. It really would be a form of cultural snobbery not to recognise this. Yet it is false patronage to say that there is no need to offer anyone the chance to broaden their tastes, the range of things they enjoy. That is the blind, 'stay as sweet as you are' attitude.

One can get well along the way to becoming a good reader without suffering unduly. There are crutches, qualifications, mediations, sensible rules of thumb, which a variety of authors have gladly indicated.

In his essay on 'Studies', Francis Bacon recommended skipping some books, even recognised several levels of attention and time which one might give to different books according to their intrinsic worth. That in itself shows the courage and good sense of an already well-stocked mind.

Dr Johnson doubted whether one had to read all books from beginning to end. He also recommended reading any book only as inclination leads. Others, among them Rilke, invoked the same rule: we had best only turn to certain books, no matter how well recommended, when we sense we are ready for them. Forster said much the same but extended the point: 'The only books that influence us are those for which we are ready, and which have gone a little farther down our particular path than we have yet gone ourselves.' A moment comes when a certain book has to be read, a certain author really known; at that moment they may be said to choose us.

The witnesses increase. Cecil Day Lewis told me he had long kept away from the thirteen volumes of *Remembrance of Things Past*. Until one Friday, when he felt ready for Proust; he went to Chatto's storeroom (he was their chief editor) and took the lot to the West Country for the weekend. His intimations of advanced pregnancy were genuine; he read them all, over that weekend. There may have been some exaggeration there, or some misremembering by me; but the general point is sound.

There are some authors with whose books we never feel quite at home, try as we will. Their minds seem to work in a different way from ours. Santayana is an instance for me. He produces, so far as I understand him, feelings of respect and admiration. He uses everyday words, not jargon. He employs what one might call 'ordinary abstractions', ordinary words for subtle and elusive qualities, or unfamiliar qualities; and loses some of us. Which is no doubt our loss. This almost natural process works the other way, too; we know instinctively, on an early reading, that some authors' writings (not necessarily their personalities) are 'our own'; a process which Bonamy Dobrée, my professor at Leeds, consistently promoted. That makes them neither better nor worse, just intellectually and artistically more quickly available; they meet peculiarly strongly an inner need.

So it is wise, except in rare cases, not to read books out of duty, or in response to that talk of the day which is meant to induce nervy insecurity, the feeling that not already to have read such and such a book is to be partially cultivated. (What a relief, to escape that social threat!) A year's moratorium on the reading of almost all new books is bracing. And think of the time saved – for reading classics.

'To read well.' Such a phrase holds complex meanings. It includes, is bedded in, the idea that to read well should mean initially and before all else to read openly and as if disinterestedly. Which is more difficult than most of us at first assume. To say to an author: 'I read your book and did not agree with your remarks about so-and-so' may not be an instance of deconstructionism, another proof that we reconstruct texts, that there is no text 'in itself'. It may be an honest judgement. Or it may be an instance of careless reading. The reader has not necessarily reconstituted the text to suit his own present needs, though that often happens; he may have read sloppily. Or he may be right; he may have understood, and disagreed.

Reading matters because literature matters. Eliot's 'the intolerable wrestle with words and meanings' starts with the author, who offers the reader the opportunity to share that struggle. Not to do so is not to 'read well', with all that can mean of experiences missed.

John Stuart Mill said that Wordsworth's poetry expressed for him: 'The very culture of the feelings'. I quote that passage often, perhaps too often; but it captures a sense of our likely loss, linguistically and intellectually.

Much of all this I myself learned from words, from books, from authors; and from teachers, in that Hunslet school and onwards; not from being read to by relatives (it would almost have had to be the other way round), but by beginning with reading, at eleven, the grammar school's 'set books' for the public examinations and other recommended books, at the living-room table. Such things opened the doors of the world, of an immensely wider world than I or people like me had so far envisaged.

———

'The function of poetry [and of literature of all kinds] is to upset the simple platitudes by which men live, to reveal the essential chaos in which human life must be led . . .'

Disturbing, that dictum of T. S. Eliot, for the writer and the reader, but genuine; and unprovable, as are all such marmoreal testimonies about the uses of literature.

It gives plangent force to Auden's poem on Herman Melville, whom he greatly admired. Melville's 'terror' of many things in his tormented experience, said Auden, had to 'blow itself quite out' through his writings; from *Typee* through *Moby Dick* to *Billy Budd*. So that: 'Towards the end he sailed into an extraordinary mildness/And anchored in his home and reached his wife,/and rode within the harbour of her hand . . ./Goodness existed: that was the new knowledge . . ./the truth was simple . . ./Evil is unspectacular and always human,/And shares our bread and eats at our own table,/And we are introduced to Goodness every day.'

That fully drawn-out 'extraordinary' above is another example of how a poet can give fresh life to a tired word; and a small and homely image – 'and rode within the harbour of her hand' – confidently invokes the sense of loving, married, redemptive security.

The claim recurs: that literature *matters*, matters first and above all because it begins by recognising our littleness and inadequacy. It brings us up sharp, offers the opportunity to face things better. And yet, without proof, it assumes our significance; here, or perhaps somewhere beyond. At this point, leaving aside the defence of intuition against objectivity, Auden, a guilt-ridden believer, says simply: 'Every poem is rooted in imaginative awe.'

Music is often rated more highly than literature. Forster thought it was the queen of all the arts, and one sees why he says that. More authors have written more rhetorically about music than about literature. Carlyle: 'Who is there that, in logical words, can express the effect music has on us? A kind of inarticulate, unfathomable, speech, which leads us to the edge of the Infinite . . . [and so on]'. Pater famously claimed that: 'All art constantly aspires towards the condition of music.' Auden was perceptive as ever: 'A verbal art like poetry is reflective; it stops to think (so does prose even more). Music is immediate, it goes on to become . . .'.

I can in a certain sense accept all those affidavits. As I do so, my mind fills with arias from Mozart, symphonies from Beethoven, songs of Schubert. I listen to music every day. But I believe that, objectively, music itself *tells* us nothing; but it moves us, to the bottom of our beings; we make our own dreams from it, as Forster so lovingly did with Beethoven's Fifth, in *Howards End* (some musical experts sniffed at this). In a sense, we *use* it. When I first, as an adolescent, heard that superb aria 'La Ci Darem La Mano' from *Don Giovanni*, I was swept away by what I thought was its convincing expression of the power of love. Within the drama it is, of course, bogus, a cynical pretence of love. I can detach it, place it back where I first found it, and say that even a hypocritical hymn to love merely distorts for its own purposes but does not destroy a wonderful truth about human experience; it destroys the credibility of the character, but not the music; the music does not mock itself. So there can, except technically (and some people gain their greatest pleasure from appreciating supreme technical virtuosity in music), be no final, *literal* interpretation of a particular piece of music. One has to say either: music can be all things to all people; or it urges us towards what cannot be expressed in language; or both. That is not to diminish music or claim less for it than those quoted above have done – that would be foolish; it is simply to distinguish music from literature.

195

A slight diversion, on language set to music. No doubt there are many studies of this. I am glad to have found one exceptional example for myself. A marvellous marriage, it seems to me, is consummated in Verdi's *Macbeth* where Macbeth's soliloquy on the loss of 'Honour, love, obedience, troops of friends . . .' is given a musical life which perfectly bodies out the extreme pathos of the words.

To return to literature. It demands that we see, and recognise the words for seeing. It can be slackly misread, or made the subject of a theory which hands to readers powers to make of it what they will; but those are distortions of a truth and can be corrected, in words. Literature requires us to take it straight, in the end to take what it says directly; even if we have to find our way through irony, cynicism, obliquity or surrealism. It's gotta used words when it talks to us. It explicitly faces experience and tries to put it into some kinds of words so that we too may face it.

The testimonies march increasingly through the last two centuries and more. Nietzsche: 'We have art that we may not perish from the truth.' Kafka: 'A book must be an ice-axe to break the frozen sea within us.' Emerson, on the way a book 'builds a road into chaos and old night'. He might have added what he also believed, and as Dr Johnson in similar terms asserted, that in doing this it creates its own kind of comfort and delight. But, again, are they all cries into the wind; or into chaos and old night?

Samuel Butler, of *Erewhon*, not a greatly rhetorical author and one to whose poetry we do not often turn these days, may have almost the last word: 'Yet meet we shall, and part, and meet again/Where dead men meet on lips of living men.' Writers will be talked about, will be remembered. But there is more to it than that sort of hope. They trust they will be talked about, or silently appreciated, as among those who looked into the terms of our lives and tried to 'speak truth' about them through their writings; authors publicly and seriously presenting themselves in straight philosophical guise are usually but not always unattractive figures; they have as much right to try as any of us, and perhaps more.

Books matter also because they may, as may music, last after we have gone. Time will pardon authors 'for writing well' (not for being virtuous). They stand as witnesses that we were here, and loved and wept and laughed, were weak and brave and all the rest, and tried to see into the heart of life, to 'make sense' of it. 'Reading is what is left of us.' Much more remains in books than the captains and the kings have left behind or will leave. Books reduce Hitler and Stalin and all their predecessors to the status of examples; bad examples, usually.

So we go on saying, from within the bosom of Western culture. But the doubts persist, especially today. Forster may have been remarkably prescient: 'It is a mistake to think that books have come to stay. The human race did without them for thousands of years and may decide to do without them again.' I believe – I trust – that Forster was mistaken. Yet by now, for many people, books are beginning to seem archaic, left on the roadside. Strange that we have been brought to asking: who will go on reading? Who will retain the memories? Even stranger that people such as I, hoisted by books into a deeper and richer world than I could in childhood ever have imagined, may now be looking at a depopulating landscape. But I cannot really bring myself to believe that. The gain has been too great, for me as for so many.

The last two chapters here are largely of memories and reflections, on the approach to the end of life; not sad, I hope, but a modest gathering together. We have done with the manifestos, the hammerings-on about a few main themes; rather, I want to make a grateful recognition of what has been, often without my knowledge at the time, given to me. From almost a standing start.

PART FIVE

ACCOMPANIED BAGGAGE

'Everyman, I will go with thee,
And be thy Guide
In thy most need
To go by thy side'

Bunyan was affirming the ever-present succour of God. I adopt it, gratefully, for those things which seem likely to go with me to the end.

There is a further, nice, relevance. Those lines of Bunyan appeared at the front of each of Dent's Everyman Books. Before cheap paperbacks appeared in the 1930s, that collection was one of the main gateways – very wide and built with serious judgement – to English writing as a whole. All common readers were deeply in their debt.

So: time to make in these last two chapters the all but final stocktaking.

8

The Landscapes of Memory

Memory Rules

Memories are not ordered by time but rather by importance; their importance is revealed to us over time, not decided by us. So they constantly reassemble themselves, like packs of cards being shuffled by unseen hands. Most writers, and it is surprising how many are teased by the ways it works, mistrust the powers of memory. No doubt we try altogether to forget some things because to retain the memory of them would be too much to bear ('Some things are best not remembered', many people observe in dour moments). Yet they remain, even if very far back, independent of our conscious or unconscious wills; they remain and recur even though we wish they would not and try to shrug them away. Altogether to forget is difficult.

Sainte Beuve observed an odd quality in some: 'There are people whose watch stops at a certain hour and who remain permanently at that age.' Who can defy time and dislocate memory, or thinks they do? Some widows and widowers? Or those who, like characters in Scott Fitzgerald, can never shake off but try to recreate the pleasures of their youth? Or those who simply feel psychologically at ease in one particular decade?

Shakespeare was more concise; memory is 'the warder of the brain'; for 'warder' one might substitute 'conscience'. Montaigne added stern codas to that: 'Unless a man has a good enough memory, he should never venture to lie', and, even stronger, 'The importance of living is to be able to face one's memories when one is old.'

In my available memory bank the only hopeful remark is from de Quincey: 'It is notorious that the memory strengthens as you lay burdens upon it, and becomes trustworthy as you trust it.' He certainly did not speak for all.

As we grow older, and whatever we might wish, the claims of memory become more insistent, if no more under our control. When we are young we can be cavalier; there will be world enough, and time. From middle age and onwards, memory is more peremptory and engrossing. It shocks us by revealing, usually on a prompting by someone else, how much we completely forget. Not the necessarily central things, but chiefly those from the second outer circle of meaning in our lives: that we do not, until reminded, at all recall meeting so-and-so on a boat to France; or even going to dinner at someone's grand house (we do remember the aristocratic host who served minute sherries; one each). We often want to deny that those forgotten events happened, especially if they are rather unpleasant; but we know at bottom we cannot.

The Fluidity of Personal and Social Memories

Memories are fluid; they dissolve and re-form in the mind according to which emotional angle we are looking from, have been pushed towards. They can be made and remade into different shapes, like a constructional toy of malleable plastic. Yes, all time is eternally present, in individual lives. Eliot also thought that was true in the life of the race. But that second form might be only partial and patchy; the memory of the race could then be said to be held by only a few people. Or perhaps Eliot meant a sort of Jungian memory, which we all have and carry, unconsciously. I have always thought that might be true and, if true, exceptionally important.

Or one could claim – or hope – that the past of the race will survive so long as only one woman or man remembers some special features. Imagine being among the last few people on earth to know the smell of a Cox's Orange Pippin; then, when they and it have gone, a smell-less or unsmelled blank?

Ernst Renan was more accessible, historically neat. He argued that communities are defined by the memories they keep and by those they collectively forget.

Our individual memories, as we advance further into old age, run more often backward, drawn from our earlier lives; a to-and-fro process – forward on the feet, backward with the head. The head seems more and more stuffed with older and older memories, which can appear to become increasingly sharp and accurate. That may be a deception. The nineteenth-century psychologist Ribot gave his name to a law: that early memories become sharper with age. I am told Ribot's Law is now discredited. A pity; it was mildly warming. But one has only to hear a married couple at the dinner table, say, disagreeing sharply about the details of an experience they shared thirty years ago, to accept Ribot's fall. One of my own sharpest memories and one which will remain is also one of the most recent: looking for the grave.

Short, Long-Term and Inconscient Memories

The day-by-day memory of the present, the short-term memory, loses its force, slips and glides. Does that mean we are no longer storing memories but that, like groceries past their sell-by date, events increasingly rapidly slip off the shelf of memory, now after no more than two or three weeks? Few seem likely, even if we live for another ten years, to remain, to become part of our longer-term memory store. Pelmanism, a fragment of which I was introduced to as a child, can still be a small crutch; and sometimes instantly lost thoughts of only two minutes ago float back as I rinse my face after shaving.

Perhaps there is a more subtle process at work. Perhaps we

have unconsciously become more selective, learned to drop the short-term memories which do not seem worth keeping, whereas in youth we seemed easily to retain almost all, important or interesting, or just things that happened. The brain then had apparently endless storing capacity, was an almost bottomless cistern. One of Borges' characters unashamedly threw up his hands: 'My memory, Sir, is like a garbage disposal' – it takes any and everything and makes a mush of it. The memory in old age may have become more choosy, have learned to dispose of useless baggage, while holding on to some incidents, important to our sense of ourselves, which do not embarrass or hurt. In that, we may have some power of choice.

Milton, I remember reading long ago, was said to enlist his daughters to take down thoughts, lines of poetry, amendments, which came to him in the night. In his prime? Most of us have thoughts in the night, in sleep or in those twilight times before and immediately after sleep, and in interim periods of wakefulness. Until we are old, we have the confidence that they will be recovered in the morning, brought out from the left-luggage locker at the back of the head where they have been securely held until we could turn the key and attend to them. Perhaps Milton continued to have far too many thoughts for even his exceptional brain to hold until he woke.

As to us, we know as we age that we will wake teased by the memory that we had a thought, thoughts, which we valued but cannot now remember. Sometimes we have in an unoccupied moment two thoughts, then a third. We turn to write them into the little notebook at the bedside and find the third has already pushed the first into vacancy. This is the super-short short-term memory, not simply an unconscious device for off-loading useless stuff, but a by now congenital slippage of that part of the mind, so that it forgets things about which we only remember that we hoped to remember them. They just go, inconsequentially, like Sunday newspapers the family dog drops a few yards after leaving the shop. The handy notebook can help to recover some thoughts, and I understand that this is standard psycho-

...e size of a world they cannot now manage. No more setting
...ut, brightly, yet with that ball of reliable mental cord still con-
...ecting us with a settled place and time, and with at least the
...immediately preceding generation, or two.

...There can be a danger in recalling too often and too closely
...ose memories of childhood which so held poets such as
...etjeman and Edward Thomas. Conrad, introducing *The Arrow*
...*Gold*, had a warning to all would-be exponents of recovered
...emory: 'In plucking the fruit of memory one runs the risk of
...oiling the bloom, especially if it has got to be carried into the
...arket-place.' 'Spoiling the bloom' must mean editing, distort-
...g, censoring or inflating.

...The sharp memories of childhood cover all senses, but not
...th equal strength; the verbal (mainly memories of favoured
...rases of the district and day), the visual (of course – the
...erest lies in just which pictures are remembered), and
...ose of taste and smell and touch. To try to put them in order
...y be to learn more about the shape of childhood and the
...otional clutter carried along.

...The exemplary sights, for me, include not only that cramped
...ze of back-to-back streets, and the 'living rooms' which now
...k so small; just as strongly recur pictures of the rural heritage
...entioned earlier, the great spaces outside Leeds: the lime-
...ne caverns, dry stone walls, curlews and peewits; long but
...der domestic rivers; spring-loaded, thyme-perfumed grass
...the caressingly windy Northern uplands. And the aromatic
...p Hopkins loved; its hold, discovered in late adolescence,
...ke immediately to me:

> What would the world be, once bereft
> Of wet and of wildness? Let them be left
> O let them be left, wildness and wet;
> Long live the weeds and the wilderness yet.

... Mexico is wonderfully tonic, but how boring to live there
...manently. All these experiences were and are the greatest

analytic practice. I would need much training. I can rarely read
my night-time notes the following morning. That verges on a
folk tale; a message on which much may depend but which the
gods make indecipherable when the central character awakes
and needs it.

Long-term memory is bitty in a different way; like a large
jigsaw with parts missing. I have 'recognised' as an acquaintance
from thirty years ago someone going quickly through the barrier
at Waterloo – a former student. I recalled her face and its expression, her way of walking, details from the period I knew her, and
especially fragments to do with her problems and the people
associated. I remembered her sitting in my room in distress and
what I did to try to help. I had forgotten her name and those of
others. They were not people without qualities but complexes of
qualities without names. It follows that I have also forgotten the
names of those to whom, so far as I know, nothing particular
happened in the years I knew them. But I would probably
'recognise' them on sight.

So it is with places. Why do certain places, of no identifiable
importance to the conscious mind, stay in the memory: roads,
villages, shops? That halt at traffic lights in a little French town?
I can understand why a glimpse of a small and comely Auvergne
neighbourhood clustered on a gently sloping hill above and
across a river in the early September evening is captured by
memory. It looks like the land of lost content which I have,
underneath and unknowing, always looked for.

But why does that odd moment stopped at the traffic lights in
an undistinguished place remain, why is it unforgettable? Is it
tied with an emotion, a thought, a sense of time held but passing
which I had at that moment; jolted to the front by that external
public injunction? The motorways will ensure that such small
revelations happen less often. Even the service stations are as
predictable and interchangeable as plastic supermarket bags,
forgotten even if I had to change a tyre there. I would not have
forgotten if one of the children was temporarily lost there; that
would have joined the indelible.

There will remain other snitches in the memory; recalled because of especially compelling sights, stinks, culture shocks, tastes-and-smells, taken on board together: a square in Avignon which was the epitome of all coherent small-town centres; a broken-down *gîte* in Burgundy which stank like the farmyards of a long-ago English childhood; an over-genteel Virginian bed-and-breakfast place which encapsulated some of the best and worst of American generosity and hospitality; a late, rushed meal in a Cologne basement restaurant at a time when some cloud hung over us. With an effort I can 'read' the hold of some, of others not. Perhaps looked at all together they would gradually reveal a coherence of the imagination. This is a murky area; Chesterton's 'landscape of our dreams' again. What decides the landscapes? And 'dreams' must mean more than pleasant dreams, or aspirations.

Still, the Past Holds Us

Do individuals in all generations and places increasingly look to the past as age advances? That seems likely (and this is not to try to reinstate Ribot but to approach the subject from a different angle), as does the fact that the pasts we look back to must differ. Obviously; though many groups of them must have thematic similarities. Nostalgia may be a constituent part of the universal memory store, particularly when it dwells on loss brought about by a failure of the will, the occasionally but recurrently realised wearing-down of character and hope; or for that matter on things enjoyed and done well – but one is cautious of dwelling too much on those; the Protestant conscience supervenes. Warmth towards the self can be self-indulgence and may tempt the Furies.

The public components of that nostalgia or regret or much else could certainly have a lot in common. The mood for many people at the end of the twentieth century is defined by the increasing speed of change; by the growing sense that we cannot

easily find a human scale in experience; that the more complex and puzzling than in childhood imagined, endlessly fluid, endlessly taking by su

Television alone could have accelerated that, not alone, but is one of the most insistent fact endless and successive changes, with which we keep up. Why do so many of us feel incomplet 'kept up with' the day's news, in the press and br relief is amazing if we will ourselves to have a f treadmill. Paradoxically, television is also stat each day it packages the news in the same way the sense of change, is predictable. The signing a Radio Four news programme in the middle that's the news at one o'clock' – is on the one overstatement (do you mean that that little, s cornered package 'mirrors the world'?) and on perfect summary indication of the daily chewe

Increasingly, in the world outside, the pr markers, the trusted stage props, are bein embracing swirl. We go to historical-environ covering several acres so as to see those ma recreated; it is a partial and temporary comfo not need that comfort, being apparently u change; they simply and smoothly ride u successive 3-inch waves.

The physical are followed by the moral ma of how we should best manage our liv 'Authorities' exist no longer, it is more than make up one's own mind. Old working-class still congenitally say: 'I wonder what me made of this', meaning: 'I wish I could have more securely and self-congratulatory, as assumed the discarded chief shepherd's m like me mother every day.' That is usually oral historian.

Older people often look back to an Eden

release and comfort to those who live in the big cities, most of which have countryside not far away. Roundhay, the largest of the Leeds public parks and one of the earliest in Britain, was the bridge to the discovery of the outer areas; the 'three-speed bike' for £4.19 was, for me at sixteen, the main releasing agent.

Even inside the cities there was a surprising variety of natural things: sooty Ragged Robin, sparrows, spiders, sticklebacks and tadpoles in jam jars on the kitchen window-ledge, dock leaves, large aspidistras, rank rhubarb, rabbits, guinea pigs and pigeons in the occasional backyards, bluebells in grimy woods just past the tram terminus.

Bachelors still living at home and probably 'bookish', their parents uncomprehending but – especially the mother – 'fond'; thought a bit odd, 'a bit of a mother's boy' but not assumed to be 'queer'; timid, rather (I heard about homosexuality only when at university, and as a dirty joke); reluctant to go out and find himself a wife? Spinster daughters ploughed a harder furrow; they had to wait to be asked. Elderly aunts who crossed their legs so that their laps could hold the 'best' handbag; and showed voluminous '*Directoire*' knickers of 'crêpe-de-chine' (that last name redolent of a way of life now gone, its limits, its economics, its hint of the ever so slightly sexy-exotic, its inhibitions, its imperialist echoes).

I am tempted to go on; that would be very easy. I will make do for now with only three taste-memories: vanilla slices, Tizer the Appetiser and the sharp taste of a young privet leaf (the old brown ones held tiny, white, wriggling grubs).

A visual memory. Humbug-sucking, soft-seeming old men; often whippet-like, whistling as they spoke through pre-NHS gnashers or unfilled gaps. Did they really emerge over the decades from the rough, tough adolescents of those streets? They did. A fat and bald, rather than lean, old man accosted me in a Hunslet working-men's club in the late 1980s, where we were making a film. He was affronted that I didn't immediately remember him from elementary school sixty years before. 'Sat right behind you, I did,' he said, in a hurt and resentful/aggressive way. Then I remembered him; his pencil jabbing my back meant he wanted help.

There were small myths, though some may have been true; such as: 'If you work at so-and-so's sweets factory you can eat as much as you like. But after a couple of weeks you can't abide them.' The cant phrases of adolescent sexual gossip from one, boldest and first of his group, who has launched into taking a girl for a walk, or up the nearest back alley: 'Did you get a feel?'; 'Did you get her down?'. Told to me to try to elicit a vicarious thrill in one whom they regarded as a sort of monk.

Then – to a much older and more sophisticated ear – a surprising range of favourite songs. Not only the obvious romantic songs from the working-men's clubs, or the Palm Courts which a few patronised on holiday; but, thanks to the regular visits of the Carl Rosa Opera Company, the best-known arias from what we always called '*Grand* Opera'. Many in the respectable working class of Leeds would have been puzzled to hear opera dismissed, as it is so often and callowly today (most often by middle-class intellectuals desperate to be populist), as bougeois-élitist, highbrow, for the nobs and snobs. They admired it and naturally gave it a high place among such musical achievements as they knew about.

The explosion of a drunken fight between husband and wife over booze-spending or adultery. The tight, mean voices of some minor officials and the feeling that some day you would 'get your own back'. But 'when it came to it' you 'couldn't be bothered', though you find it hard to lose the memory.

Medicaments in a small side cupboard: Andrew's Liver Salts, Beecham's Pills, Owbridge's Cough Medicine (or was it 'Lung Tonic'?), Bile Beans, Slippery Elm. All of them 'sworn by'. The spoiled priest in Graham Greene's *The Power and the Glory*, on the run in the Central American wilderness, comes across a bungalow now deserted by its English occupiers; and is surprised by the cupboard full of medicaments. They must have been very ill, he muses, to need so many. Not at all; if that were so, even today more than half the population of England would analytic practice. I would need much training. I can rarely read my night-time notes the following morning. That verges on a folk tale; a message on which much may depend but which the gods make indecipherable when the central character awakes and needs it.

Long-term memory is bitty in a different way; like a large jigsaw with parts missing. I have 'recognised' as an acquaintance from thirty years ago someone going quickly through the barrier at Waterloo – a former student. I recalled her face and its expression, her way of walking, details from the period I knew her, and especially fragments to do with her problems and the people associated. I remembered her sitting in my room in distress and what I did to try to help. I had forgotten her name and those of others. They were not people without qualities but complexes of qualities without names. It follows that I have also forgotten the names of those to whom, so far as I know, nothing particular happened in the years I knew them. But I would probably 'recognise' them on sight.

So it is with places. Why do certain places, of no identifiable importance to the conscious mind, stay in the memory: roads, villages, shops? That halt at traffic lights in a little French town? I can understand why a glimpse of a small and comely Auvergne neighbourhood clustered on a gently sloping hill above and across a river in the early September evening is captured by memory. It looks like the land of lost content which I have, underneath and unknowing, always looked for.

But why does that odd moment stopped at the traffic lights in an undistinguished place remain, why is it unforgettable? Is it tied with an emotion, a thought, a sense of time held but passing which I had at that moment; jolted to the front by that external public injunction? The motorways will ensure that such small revelations happen less often. Even the service stations are as predictable and interchangeable as plastic supermarket bags, forgotten even if I had to change a tyre there. I would not have forgotten if one of the children was temporarily lost there; that would have joined the indelible.

There will remain other snitches in the memory; recalled because of especially compelling sights, stinks, culture shocks, tastes-and-smells, taken on board together: a square in Avignon which was the epitome of all coherent small-town centres; a broken-down *gîte* in Burgundy which stank like the farmyards of a long-ago English childhood; an over-genteel Virginian bed-and-breakfast place which encapsulated some of the best and worst of American generosity and hospitality; a late, rushed meal in a Cologne basement restaurant at a time when some cloud hung over us. With an effort I can 'read' the hold of some, of others not. Perhaps looked at all together they would gradually reveal a coherence of the imagination. This is a murky area; Chesterton's 'landscape of our dreams' again. What decides the landscapes? And 'dreams' must mean more than pleasant dreams, or aspirations.

Still, the Past Holds Us

Do individuals in all generations and places increasingly look to the past as age advances? That seems likely (and this is not to try to reinstate Ribot but to approach the subject from a different angle), as does the fact that the pasts we look back to must differ. Obviously; though many groups of them must have thematic similarities. Nostalgia may be a constituent part of the universal memory store, particularly when it dwells on loss brought about by a failure of the will, the occasionally but recurrently realised wearing-down of character and hope; or for that matter on things enjoyed and done well – but one is cautious of dwelling too much on those; the Protestant conscience supervenes. Warmth towards the self can be self-indulgence and may tempt the Furies.

The public components of that nostalgia or regret or much else could certainly have a lot in common. The mood for many people at the end of the twentieth century is defined by the increasing speed of change; by the growing sense that we cannot easily find a human scale in experience; that the world is wider, more complex and puzzling than in childhood we could have imagined, endlessly fluid, endlessly taking by surprise.

Television alone could have accelerated that, and television is not alone, but is one of the most insistent factors. It suggests endless and successive changes, with which we are required to keep up. Why do so many of us feel incomplete if we have not 'kept up with' the day's news, in the press and broadcasting? The relief is amazing if we will ourselves to have a few days off that treadmill. Paradoxically, television is also static, unchanging; each day it packages the news in the same way, and so reduces the sense of change, is predictable. The signing-off soundbite of a Radio Four news programme in the middle of the day – 'And that's the news at one o'clock' – is on the one hand a grotesque overstatement (do you mean that that little, selective, smooth-cornered package 'mirrors the world'?) and on the other hand a perfect summary indication of the daily chewed-up pabulum.

Increasingly, in the world outside, the prominent physical markers, the trusted stage props, are being lost in the all-embracing swirl. We go to historical-environmental museums covering several acres so as to see those markers idiomatically recreated; it is a partial and temporary comfort. Many others do not need that comfort, being apparently unaware of secular change; they simply and smoothly ride upon the present's successive 3-inch waves.

The physical are followed by the moral markers, the definers of how we should best manage our lives. Now that the 'Authorities' exist no longer, it is more than usually difficult to make up one's own mind. Old working-class people in Yorkshire still congenitally say: 'I wonder what me mother would have made of this', meaning: 'I wish I could have a sign.' Or, perhaps more securely and self-congratulatory, as though they have assumed the discarded chief shepherd's mantle: 'I grow more like me mother every day.' That is usually said by the family's oral historian.

Older people often look back to an Eden that never was, fear the size of a world they cannot now manage. No more setting out, brightly, yet with that ball of reliable mental cord still connecting us with a settled place and time, and with at least the immediately preceding generation, or two.

There can be a danger in recalling too often and too closely those memories of childhood which so held poets such as Betjeman and Edward Thomas. Conrad, introducing *The Arrow of Gold*, had a warning to all would-be exponents of recovered memory: 'In plucking the fruit of memory one runs the risk of spoiling the bloom, especially if it has got to be carried into the market-place.' 'Spoiling the bloom' must mean editing, distorting, censoring or inflating.

The sharp memories of childhood cover all senses, but not with equal strength; the verbal (mainly memories of favoured phrases of the district and day), the visual (of course – the interest lies in just which pictures are remembered), and those of taste and smell and touch. To try to put them in order may be to learn more about the shape of childhood and the emotional clutter carried along.

The exemplary sights, for me, include not only that cramped maze of back-to-back streets, and the 'living rooms' which now look so small; just as strongly recur pictures of the rural heritage I mentioned earlier, the great spaces outside Leeds: the limestone caverns, dry stone walls, curlews and peewits; long but slender domestic rivers; spring-loaded, thyme-perfumed grass on the caressingly windy Northern uplands. And the aromatic damp Hopkins loved; its hold, discovered in late adolescence, spoke immediately to me:

> What would the world be, once bereft
> Of wet and of wildness? Let them be left
> O let them be left, wildness and wet;
> Long live the weeds and the wilderness yet.

New Mexico is wonderfully tonic, but how boring to live there permanently. All these experiences were and are the greatest release and comfort to those who live in the big cities, most of which have countryside not far away. Roundhay, the largest of the Leeds public parks and one of the earliest in Britain, was the bridge to the discovery of the outer areas; the 'three-speed bike' for £4.19 was, for me at sixteen, the main releasing agent.

Even inside the cities there was a surprising variety of natural things: sooty Ragged Robin, sparrows, spiders, sticklebacks and tadpoles in jam jars on the kitchen window-ledge, dock leaves, large aspidistras, rank rhubarb, rabbits, guinea pigs and pigeons in the occasional backyards, bluebells in grimy woods just past the tram terminus.

Bachelors still living at home and probably 'bookish', their parents uncomprehending but – especially the mother – 'fond'; thought a bit odd, 'a bit of a mother's boy' but not assumed to be 'queer'; timid, rather (I heard about homosexuality only when at university, and as a dirty joke); reluctant to go out and find himself a wife? Spinster daughters ploughed a harder furrow; they had to wait to be asked. Elderly aunts who crossed their legs so that their laps could hold the 'best' handbag; and showed voluminous '*Directoire*' knickers of 'crêpe-de-chine' (that last name redolent of a way of life now gone, its limits, its economics, its hint of the ever so slightly sexy-exotic, its inhibitions, its imperialist echoes).

I am tempted to go on; that would be very easy. I will make do for now with only three taste-memories: vanilla slices, Tizer the Appetiser and the sharp taste of a young privet leaf (the old brown ones held tiny, white, wriggling grubs).

A visual memory. Humbug-sucking, soft-seeming old men; often whippet-like, whistling as they spoke through pre-NHS gnashers or unfilled gaps. Did they really emerge over the decades from the rough, tough adolescents of those streets? They did. A fat and bald, rather than lean, old man accosted me in a Hunslet working-men's club in the late 1980s, where we were making a film. He was affronted that I didn't immediately remember him from elementary school sixty years before. 'Sat right behind you, I did,' he said, in a hurt and resentful/aggressive way. Then I remembered him; his pencil jabbing my back meant he wanted help.

There were small myths, though some may have been true; such as: 'If you work at so-and-so's sweets factory you can eat as much as you like. But after a couple of weeks you can't abide them.' The cant phrases of adolescent sexual gossip from one, boldest and first of his group, who has launched into taking a girl for a walk, or up the nearest back alley: 'Did you get a feel?'; 'Did you get her down?'. Told to me to try to elicit a vicarious thrill in one whom they regarded as a sort of monk.

Then – to a much older and more sophisticated ear – a surprising range of favourite songs. Not only the obvious romantic songs from the working-men's clubs, or the Palm Courts which a few patronised on holiday; but, thanks to the regular visits of the Carl Rosa Opera Company, the best-known arias from what we always called '*Grand* Opera'. Many in the respectable working class of Leeds would have been puzzled to hear opera dismissed, as it is so often and callowly today (most often by middle-class intellectuals desperate to be populist), as bougeois-élitist, highbrow, for the nobs and snobs. They admired it and naturally gave it a high place among such musical achievements as they knew about.

The explosion of a drunken fight between husband and wife over booze-spending or adultery. The tight, mean voices of some minor officials and the feeling that some day you would 'get your own back'. But 'when it came to it' you 'couldn't be bothered', though you find it hard to lose the memory.

Medicaments in a small side cupboard: Andrew's Liver Salts, Beecham's Pills, Owbridge's Cough Medicine (or was it 'Lung Tonic'?), Bile Beans, Slippery Elm. All of them 'sworn by'. The spoiled priest in Graham Greene's *The Power and the Glory*, on the run in the Central American wilderness, comes across a bungalow now deserted by its English occupiers; and is surprised by the cupboard full of medicaments. They must have been very ill, he muses, to need so many. Not at all; if that were so, even today more than half the population of England would be very poorly indeed. Boots the Chemists would easily survive even if it chose not to diversify into the drugstore's equivalent of haberdashery.

A Sensible Shape

That kind of cataloguing soon becomes an indulgence and one to which I am prone. Why does it have such a hold on me – and on many people who may not write about it themselves, but do write to me because they are responding to echoes in the lists of someone else? I suspect one part of the answer is simple: never, in later years, do we have such an omnivorous appetite for the sensuous clutter of life, and forever after we are trying to make sense of an even more complicated chaos, against newer pressures to order; 'to make sense' (what a giveaway) of adult life and its responsibilities.

It is difficult to make a more 'sensible' shape out of all this, to assess what deep impulses caused some habits to be firmly carried over. Some have at least become clearer to me, in this and earlier writings. Such as the realisation, noted earlier, that I could never vote Conservative, because to do so would go against the whole weight and flow of regained, held, memory; and the realisation that so many on the Tory side did not and still do not understand the lives of most of those I knew, do not try to understand and so do not learn. Odder carried-over habits include what might be called, pseudo-theoretically, 'The Liberated-Bisto-Kid Syndrome': that love of shopping described earlier, whether for necessities or, better, non-necessities, the proof to myself that I now have, if not money to burn, then money in my pocket, enough and to spare.

How does one explain also, given the close-together, gim-crack backstreets, the love by the more than usually literate among working-class people of the English rustic style in architecture? Not only the thatched cottages on cheap birthday and Christmas cards – that seems an obvious romantic longing for a rural life – but for places such as Kelmscott Manor, Lutyens' houses and Gertrude Jekyll's gardens. The attraction may have had to do with the style of life imagined in those places, not ostentatious but felt to be eased with a certain gentleness. It came also from the history books we found for ourselves or were introduced to by those fairly common autodidacts and by grammar-school masters, who were themselves sometimes escapees from similarly restricted backgrounds, and from the several well-thumbed volumes of Arthur Mee. This attraction may seem related to that compelling love of the Yorkshire moors and their villages; but the relation between the two is slight and different. One attraction comes at second hand, from the guidance of others and from reading; the other is deeper and started the first time we left the outer tram terminus and started walking; it was directly felt on the pulses. Literary memories have by now merged into and with actual memories of events and places.

A composite of false, often mistaken memories? I doubt that; there could have been, as Orwell said, many worse ways of life than the culture of these streets and the pull of the hinterland. Older now and more experienced, I recognise in some of the more drab and destitute, poverty-stricken and malnourished areas of Eastern Europe visual echoes of our life of the 1930s. Thin echoes. Very few of us were as hard up as that, and we did usually have sustaining elements; it was in part a strongly supporting culture. Which has now gone in those most deprived parts of Britain mentioned earlier. The underclass in the sink estates are at least as deprived as those in the slums of Eastern Europe.

So we go on trying to find a pattern in a long life brought back by the memories, moments, we may recognise as marking the end of one stage and the beginning of another. Though why one should seek that sort of dividing is puzzling; it may be related to the act of making art itself, to finding an order in the disorder, if not the chaos. What if we had taken that road rather than this; that would have led to other, multiple choices, each moving away and in a new direction, so that not much later we were miles away from our starting point; Robert Frost's 'The

Road Not Taken' draws the exact pictorial image here. Whatever branchings away we took, or were unconsciously led to take, the tendency is to tell ourselves, as we pause to look back from time to time, that all turned out for the good in the end.

The phases do not match a division by decades, even though we all tend to cling in our more public, popular style of thinking, to the notion of decades as natural markers. More likely is the division: childhood, adolescence, marriage and family, the point at which all the children had finally left what had been home and would no longer be called 'home' except in moments of inattention or through the jolt of a sad event. Then the Indian summer of early middle age, and the onset of old age itself and the realisation that the curtain could come down at any minute. 'Come in, number 27, your time's up'; the old municipal park boating-lake call which induced temporary deafness. That's no longer possible. An obvious pattern, this, but not less true. Each part has its representative pictures.

It becomes more interesting when we ask ourselves from this very late perspective, as I did in the chapter on family life, which of all those stages was the happiest not just for you but for you and your partner. Not necessarily the first flush of love, exceptional though that was. More likely, I decided earlier, is that middle period when we were all in good health, together in the home; family holidays; the children growing into independence but still deeply attached to us, as we to them; that would be difficult to beat. A closer look would fill in the light and shade at all times and reveal all aspects as unlikely to be entirely forgotten; in the end, as I said at the very opening of this chapter, memory will not be cheated.

There are the phases as marked by places and by work: for us, Hull, Leicester, Birmingham, Paris, London . . . and so out to grass. And the markers of each: friends; those who never quite became friends but were influences; the books of the times; the incidents and accidents; from time to time the revelations, sustaining or depressing, about ourselves or others; the losses of all kinds; the gains carried over.

You could follow another, less chronological, more thematic line. Are there recurrent, symptomatic incidents in your life? I find that at crucial stages all the way along until I floated off on my own – and became able to offer a push along to others younger than myself – I was given free, disinterested lifts to the next stage towards the open sea. I named those way back, in Chapter Two. Schoolmasters are good at that; teachers of English seem particularly alert, perhaps because they are trying to make direct contact with our imaginations, our burgeoning responses to the life of the emotions as enhanced by literature. Then you remember, indeed never forget, the unending, strong support of one particular person; and realise, perhaps now with even more than usual force, how essential that has been since the relationship was first formed; and you hope the support has been reciprocal. You remember also the steady kindness of some older people, almost all by now probably dead and not all sufficiently thanked.

Or you recognise, again for the first time, the disparity between what to the world would seem important phases and others which seemed shadowy and humdrum. The test here is how often memory brings some of them back, and with what strength. The large public passages, if some there be, may be called up rarely; memory may linger on the smaller, unremarked days and phases, with greater warmth and, occasionally, longing. Or you look back on a period in which your job demanded all the energy and commitment you could collect. It is now some years past, and not only others who were on that march, but you, too, seem simply and with hardly a jolt of memory to have absorbed it, taken it for granted, given it no special niche, on the whole forgotten it. That is uncomforting, but salutary.

Certain incidents which clutch more than others, happy and unhappy, stay hidden in the mind, but in their time – some, often – come back to consciousness. Oddly and luckily, the happier ones, especially when connected with children, are almost all near the surface, no matter how old we are: the warm biscuity smell of babies, wrapped ready for the pram; the

214

overwhelmingly full, open light in a young child's eyes as you are seen after an absence, and the rush towards you; the toothless grin of a six-month-old baby at the breast as, walking in, you are perhaps for the first time recognised; the unabashed familial welcome, the collective babbling rush to open the front door, when you come home after a trip. These are moments unpopular to write about; the chasm of 'sentimentality' yawns. They are valued by the memory, whether we will or no, and we do wrong not to accept them as fully as we can. No greater grief than the remembrance of things past – Dante's line can seem to run against such particular experiences, though it has its force. Yet, recollected, many memories produce not grief but almost overwhelming poignancy and often joy – in spite of the impassive and irresistible flow of time, and the final sense of brevity.

Resisting the Self-Censorship of Memory

We try to rewrite our memories to serve purposes often hidden from ourselves. The censorship of memory has long been recognised by writers. It preserves self-conceit: 'Vanity plays tricks with our memory.' We try to select what to remember and how to look at it as part of our efforts at self-justification, though some are less culpable than others. Or we discard, because, though a particular memory does not reflect to our discredit, it is too painful to be remembered – the appalling misbehaviour of someone we admire, for instance. Stevenson caught the general process nicely: 'I've a good memory for forgetting.' Shakespeare noted that it grows and distorts with age: 'Lord, Lord, how subject we old men are to this vice of lying'; to ourselves as to others, and in the memory as in the present, he might have added. Corneille, in a sentence similar to that of Montaigne quoted earlier, contributed his word: 'A good memory is needed after one has lied.' Yes, and again for lies to oneself even more than to another.

215

Memory as an Index to the Present and a Pointer to the Future

In a sense, as I agreed much earlier, all time is eternally present, or we carry it forever behind us, like a snail's silvery trail. More insistently, memory is in the end all and always about the present, about accommodating and assimilating ourselves to the time in which we are now living. Reconstituting the present, we are constantly recreating our own selves so as to go on living, obstinately and sometimes against the odds to keep on going 'forward'. Which brings us back, in spite of what was said in the preceding paragraph, to that overriding *power* of memory which was noted at the very beginning of this chapter. Montaigne again; he gave the power to memory itself, not to our control over it: 'The memory represents to us not what we choose but what it pleases.' Matthew Arnold remarked on what seems at first like the reverse but is actually the other side of the same coin: 'We forget because we must, not because we will.'

As we age and realise we are now older than we expected ever to be, the procession of the dead must lengthen also; and is painful to recite. At this point I originally wrote 'the chill foreboding mist momentarily mounts above the ankles'. I deleted it because I was there being led astray by a fancy and excessive image; it's not as bad as all that.

A reverse thought: of non-memories, memories we never made, unachieved recollections. As we pore over memories and, so far as we can, assess them, we realise some of the things we have never done and now will never do, and wish we had: expertly riding a horse, climbing a rock face, flying an aeroplane; freeing ourselves from ourselves, if only intermittently.

Any trawl through memory brings into clearer light, usually by unexpected recurrences, some generalised themes more important than we had expected. Before starting this book, I had not fully realised, as I hinted much earlier, the crucial importance of tolerance and the need to be suspicious of all gurus. That sounds simple and perhaps slightly pious. It acquires fresh force when one sees the increase of fanaticism across the world. Fanaticism,

I suggested much earlier, is a long, deep-rooted branch of self-love enhanced by fear; a cancer of the emotions which has rampaged through the healthy cells and poisoned them; a form of total self-righteousness which cannot put up with uncertainty, constant second thoughts, with all those open habits of mind which are intensely difficult to sustain but essential to a humane consciousness. In contrast, and essential also to a truly civil society as well as to the individual (the two are inextricably meshed), is a mind which doesn't rush but gives all things time to sort themselves out, is respectful of others by recognising differences, patient and moderate; but at the final, denying point is ready to make a stand.

And a mind which is active in the defence of language. Language is the surgical tool of thought, and so its cleanliness, its purity, has to be maintained; often against the odds nowadays, when so much language is sullied, interested rather than disinterested, the servant of one form or another of the obsessed or the corrupted mind, or of today's apparently untethered, but actually tethered by unvaluing, mind, which is as often academic as more widespread. Any attempt at recovering memory and its meanings must begin and end in the attempt to find a fair language for the record.

In spite of all the obvious practical achievements, indeed gains, at depressed times one feels like deciding that human beings hardly manage to advance one inch in the movement towards a better sense of the limits of self and the importance of communal feeling. At other times, one is delighted to see what looks like evidence of an advance. Many losses, but still a continuing and widespread sense of a duty to 'do better'. So, for instance and yet once again, in spite of all the cheating and cruelty which remain in Britain, much of the sense of neighbourliness, and that of voluntary public service, and of friendship, also remain.

About the individual self, cluster-realisations can be even sharper. I had not until now realised how much of my life was spent, almost unknowingly, in the service of unfashionable institutions and causes: such as in university extra-mural work, the Cinderella of the academies; in UNESCO, the cultural arm of the United Nations and so habitually little regarded or demoted as, once more, something which does not belong in 'the real world'; fighting for the merits of Goldsmiths' College in the University of London during the time it was wholly controlled by that often impercipient federal body, which took refuge in a convenient statutory anomaly to keep the college somewhat below the salt. Engaging also, on behalf of 'democracy', in the debate about populism versus élitism; I conceived almost a passion about the need for better argument on such causes, the assertion of their worth well beyond what the devaluing world thought. At times it has seemed like trying to hold together by main force the ends of two wires which needed to be connected, so that helpful power might flow through.

I also learned more than was ever expected about that peculiar type of belonging I have mentioned more than once earlier, of belonging to the land; which would seem almost against nature to an outsider contemplating the life of pre-war city streets. I love visiting America, but every visit, especially to the great open spaces with small scattered towns, impermanent and two-dimensional-seeming – Auden's 'raw towns that we believe and die in' – strengthens the sense of place and depth and history aroused when, on return, I walk down an English lane or up an old town or city street: the dirt, the damp, the smells, the whole lived-in-for-centuries feel under the feet. And the smallness, so that sitting in, say, Norwich you can feel, grasp, inhabit not only that place but its history and its position in a touchable, an embracing Britain, as a whole; and yourself within that entire and manageable fabric.

Above all, I hope that such explorings will reduce the sense of the importance of self, discourage pride and excessive self-involvement, encourage unpretentiousness and the ability to see and seize moments of happiness when they appear.

One can reduce incipient self-regard by remembering, as

always, the advice of many an author. From Shakespeare as from others before and after him: 'For there was never yet a philosopher that could endure the toothache patiently.' Thomas Fuller was less polite: 'The higher an ape mounts, the more he shows his breeches.' Straightest of all, Montaigne's: 'Kings and philosophers shit, and so do ladies.'

Great causes are to be fought for but not too solemnly; we have to retain the ability to laugh at ourselves, especially in our more serious moments. Ibsen advised against going out to fight for our ideals in our best trousers, and Thoreau of the need to be suspicious of 'all enterprises that require new clothes'.

9

The Sense of an Ending

THE TWO GREAT Victorian Poetic Masters were each at certain times preoccupied with ageing and death, but in different
ways. Browning was usually optimistic: 'Grow old along with
me/The best is yet to be'; or bold and hearty: 'Fear death/To
feel the fog in my throat?' Tennyson could be resignedly cheerful: 'Old age hath yet his honour and his toil;/Tho' much is
taken, much abides'; or horrified: 'And Time, a maniac scatter-
ing dust/And Life a fury slinging flame'. Those are all, yes, from
dramatic poems and may be said to represent no more than the
attitudes of the characters the poets created. Yet they are all in
some ways 'typical' of their authors and differ greatly in their
force. One could not switch the names and retain credibility.
Lawrence's point stands: 'Never trust the teller, trust the tale.'
Even in fiction, and no less in dramatic poetry, we write most
often and most strongly about what in ourselves we feel most
powerfully.

Traditional sayings tend to be more accepting, undramatic:
'You don't get a second time round' – which sounds like the park
boating lake again; and the conventional, phatic, street comment: 'They're falling like flies this winter, I've noticed.'
Shakespeare had his vividly ironic, social image: 'Time is like a
fashionable host/That slightly shakes his parting guest by the
hand,/And . . . grasps in the comer'.

Youth and its Uneasiness before Age

The world divides into those under thirty-five who are pleasant to those over sixty-five, and those who are not; there are a few in between, trying hard.

Some not yet thirty have difficulty in treating anyone over fifty as real. They associate them with hair poking from the nostrils and ears, a tendency to dribble, perhaps a slightly musty smell.

Those in the middle way, about forty-five, find this a tricky position, a time for sums and readjustments, the recording of the decades. Fifty is not far off and that surely is the threshold of old age, the entry gate to a different universe – which many more than we have been used to now pass through at this time – where one needs to make major adjustments, the ante-room to what may finally become senility. How can one face such a future? Or even more, contemplate sixty-five, seventy-five; anything further is unthinkable, not conceivably manageable. So, at forty-five, many are uneasy before anyone over sixty; their past is another world, their manners unpredictable.

Dr Johnson remarked that if a young man leaves his hat behind after a gathering, it is not commented on; but if an old man does so, people say: 'His memory's going.'

We treasure, or claim to treasure, old objects, buildings, literature, music, paintings, sculpture. That can be genuine or a form of culture snobbery, or nostalgia; but painless. We are less easy with the living, human, old. We invent a palliative, patronising, false phrase for them: 'Senior Citizens'; to which any crusty, self-respecting person will reply: 'No. Not Senior Citizen. Old Age Pensioner'; or simply: 'Old Man [or Woman].'

There are a few exceptions: composers, painters, actors – even writers – over eighty can become cherished images on special plinths; and so may 'a distinguished senior politician', if he or she retains some sparkiness. For the rest, a gulf. My brother was a very active headmaster until he was sixty-five and retired. The next day, at the post office where he was drawing his bus pass, the clerk, a former pupil from some years back who did not at first recognise him, looked at him as at a great awk and felt it necessary to shout since, it was kindly assumed, he was bound to be half-deaf.

During the war I did officer training at Llandrindod Wells. We were in a bulbous rococo/Edwardian/Art Nouveau hotel, the Gwalia, built to provide for the elderly taking the waters. For us, it was a lively place full of men in their twenties heading for artillery commissions. It had a circular atrium, looked down on from iron railings fronting the rounds of bedrooms. Passing through Llandrindod Wells a couple of years ago, I sought out the Gwalia, over fifty years on. It is now used as county offices, but its main features seem unchanged, except for a reception desk at the back of the atrium, or lobby as it is probably called. I stood in the middle, hearing voices from the past: of this witty one who went on to service in India and then to a successful acting career; of this gentle and sensitive boy from Bedales; of this one killed in Burma; of this other who was timid and gave a false sense of incompetence, but whom we helped through right to the passing-out ceremony; and of a kindly training sergeant with whom I am still in touch.

The receptionist, in her late thirties or early forties at a guess, eventually put down her phone and called out in the not-actually-unkind-but-certainly-disengaged voice which is usually and it seems almost paradoxically followed by a routine, as if recorded: 'Can I help you?' 'No, thank you. I just wanted to see the lobby again . . . I was billeted here during the war.'

'Oh, you're one of *those*, are you?'; said smilelessly, as though she had been required to add one more to her list of rather importunate applicants for some council hand-out, or a mildly irritating, bedraggled duck which had wandered in from the nearby park lake looking for grub, but which one had best ignore rather than attempt to shoo out; and she bent again to her desk. I felt as though I was wearing a dirty mackintosh. The sense of separation, of not belonging to the same branch of humanity, was strong. She may have been tired; she may very well have been a good wife and mother. Or perhaps nothing in her imagination had given her empathy, fellow-feeling, with the old, with what they had known and lived through before she was born; and to which she too would come.

Age and its Embarrassments

The reactions of 'the old' can be defensive, resigned and occasionally extremely tetchy; even with their contemporaries. Once retired, my brother and his wife went on some coach tours for the elderly. Only twice. They soon decided that old age pensioners as a group are more unpleasant to travel with than groups of teenagers; competing hard for the best seats, fussing about the food, the air-conditioning, the 'comfort' stops.

One old man will mention his age early in a conversation, perhaps in the hope of receiving a polite demurral, an expression of surprise; but more likely so as to forestall an insensitive reaction to the account of some difficulty he has met, one which could happen to any of us at any age but which for him produces the response: 'Of course, at your age you can't expect . . .'.

At another moment, there is relief that we are now out of that competition. It seems a long time since we read in George Moore, almost incredulously, of the sexual attractions of older women – women 'of a certain age', those who have passed *thirty*. Forty to fifty can now seem physically attractive; and later. We alter the rules as we go along; we deceive ourselves about ourselves as we go along. We seek to ignore what Edmund Burke called 'The silent touches of time'; and Seneca's resigned: 'Death takes us piecemeal, not at a gulp.' We only notice, and unwillingly, from the evidence of hair loss, lines on the face, thinning shanks, perhaps a dulling in the eyes and some loss of hearing, that we have entered another phase.

In spite of what I may have illustrated so far, literature has many passages on the benefits of old age, so much so that one begins to feel that some writers, such as Tennyson, are constantly having to cheer themselves up. Hardy is more bracing, out of his unexpectancy; he never expected much.

But, just as it is easier to pick holes than to mend fences, so memory causes us to dwell at least a little on the aches and pains, the slights, the discomforts. 'Age will not be defied', said Bacon with blinding matter-of-factness. Matthew Arnold claimed to be startlingly old before his time: 'I am past thirty and three parts iced over'; and that was said in his proper person, not by an invented dramatic character. Baudelaire wrote the resignedly cultivated epitaph for all book-lovers: '*La chair est triste, hélas at j'ai lu tous les livres.*'

At this point I realise that, of course and after all, I prefer people to books; well, their everyday sayings line up to be appreciated: 'Can't grumble. I've had a good run'; 'It's being so cheerful that keeps me going' (radio copying life); 'Ah well, you've got to laugh, haven't you? Otherwise . . .'. The old verbal work-horse: 'You're only as old as you feel' is not so silly a cheering-up chant as it may at first seem. The towel can be thrown in early, sometimes far too early.

There are many such moments in addition to the well-known rituals. I was once telephoned by a man newly retired from a high position in public service. He had his knighthood, but that did not compensate for the sense of Othello's occupation gone. His parish and his perspective had been worldwide; his very comfortable part of London was virtually less known to him than Whitehall or the first-class lounges at Heathrow; for years he had swished out of and back into Wimbledon in the institution's car. He faced a future for which he found himself quite unprepared. He did not wish for, and was not equipped to slide into, City directorships as do many former cabinet ministers. He did not wish to play golf or bowls with his contemporaries; he was lost in his own garden, which did not attract him. He could not find within himself what Richard Steele called 'good grace' in growing old. Did I know of any interesting, more than local, 'stretching' and useful voluntary work? He died not long after, of what I do not know; but wondered whether he had not had much wish to fight on.

At this time, fairly good physical health is a boon. Even the apparently healthiest, those not felled early by a stroke or a heart attack or the sudden discovery of cancer, soon begin to be conscious of the body in a way not felt in the first sixty years; in the first thirty of which, though you did not really expect eternal life, you found it quite hard to believe you would eventually die. Now you know and have known for some time; especially through the messages from particular parts; a friend says quizzically: 'I'm aware of my bum all the time these days.' You are grateful if your own lot is no worse than a few occasional aches and pains. You no longer expect 'animal good health'. More or less regular aches, even if mild, can now and then tend to 'pull you down'. It is harder to get out of bed, takes a little while to uncrank the joints, gear up for the day. You make at least intermittent acquaintance with hospital interiors.

Sometimes, as you finish another meal, you feel like the stoker of a rudimentary organic engine which needs attention every five or six hours. Ingestion, digestion, rejection. You have to pee at least two or three times a night. The parts are wearing out.

You may notice increasing fussiness, excessive attention to trivial detail, perhaps a tendency to irascibility and moroseness. You grow impatient and tend not to listen carefully, not to let others finish their sentences. So little time, so many minor annoyances. Successive hints of ageing occur, like the tapping of a deathwatch beetle behind the arras. Whilst outside the window – an ironic light chorus – the new young birds start singing.

Shopping in town on Saturday morning, you realise that that grey, bent figure is the sprightly, newly retired major who used to sell good shrubs at the corner of the high street; and that overweight, white-haired woman was, twenty years ago, an attractive forty year old.

The See-Saw of Cheerfulness and Unexpectancy

But the pages just above are far too low-spirited and untrue to the whole experience. Characteristically, I have allowed myself to be carried away by the taste for metaphors. In spite of all, hope, expectation, cheerfulness can awake at only a slight touch: a few days' total freedom from odd aches, a warm letter from a friend, good news from a member of the family or about something you've written; these shafts of sunlight can take twenty years off your age. For, and this is the most surprising reality: most days you do not 'feel anything like your age'. You feel alert and perky as ever; you can note no intellectual loss in your mind. Occasionally you wonder whether this is a self-induced error, whether people are saying of you as they said about Dr Johnson's man who left his hat behind: 'His mind's not what it was. There's a loss of grasp, and energy.'

Still, much of the time the mind refuses to recognise what the body knows; and the mind acts accordingly until, in late evening, the body nudges that time is up for that day. As you rise from the desk you are surprised that you can still sit there writing, believing yourself as sprightly as ever – or almost – for four or five hours at a time. 'Within, I do not find wrinkles and used heart', said Emerson. He did go on to say that he found 'unspent youth'.

About death itself, we all hover between an occasional fear, which Bacon captured with beautiful simplicity: 'Men fear death as children fear to go in the dark'; and a resigned stoical accept-ance, as in Falstaff's noble: 'We owe God a death', and Emily Dickinson's polite getting on board: 'Because I would not stop for Death,/He kindly stopped for me;/The carriage held but just ourselves/And immortality.'

Or we face death's approach with the universal regret: 'There would have been a time for such a word . . .'. Macbeth is, there, caught in that familiar 'between the stirrup and the ground' trap, which closes before we have time for what should have been said and done; to 'save' both of you. He is echoed in

Richard II and many another of Shakespeare's plays and sonnets. 'O! call back yesterday/Bid time return'. It does not, and there is always too little time, too much to do.

As to the failure to gain belief even when the end nears, it will be plain that I expect to remain one of the exceptions to the majority tartly noted by Clough: 'And almost everyone when age/Disease or sorrows strike him/Inclines to think there is a God/Or something very like him'. Not so; not all acquire, even tentatively, the 'comforts' of religion. Those friends who have that comfort are mistaken if they think us perverse, guilty of avoiding some existential duty. Nothing can reduce for believers, agnostics or atheists the initial recoil from Emily Brontë's 'Cold in the earth and the deep snow piled above thee'; or the even greater force of Shakespeare's 'Ay, but to die, and go we know not where;/To lie in cold obstruction and to rot;/This sensible warm notion to become/a kneaded clod'. The choice of cremation hardly lessens that; only the will.

Yet, for some of the time, it seems not later than early or late evening; just about time to close the shutters as the day shortens; no more. Certainly, the time in bed lengthens or, in reaction, we get up earlier and earlier and start work on the word processor. All the rest can coexist with a fundamental content, in general being fairly at ease with yourself, especially where there is reciprocal affection. For Yeats, age was often a time for regrets. There was folly in 'being comforted'. Yet he could also say: 'Time can but make her beauty over again', and, underneath, believe that, just as much as he believed anything less hopeful. Imaginative defiance can seem to conquer the ruins of Time.

Time itself can be a near-obsession; above all, the shortness of our stay here. All the phases and changes, marked out by, first, the stages in the children's lives, and second, by the deaths of friends. 'To view each loved one blotted from life's page/And be alone on earth, as I am now'; Byron, on a painfully characteristic note. It has all been so brief; all the elements, which once seemed lengthy and absorbing, even near permanent or at least immensely long, threaten to collapse into one compacted but convoluted memory. Blank unexpectancy has to be fought; that is an early form of mental death.

Luckily, the eager character of all those years ago does still, more often than you expected, peer from under the shadows. You need the time to finish the next book; which is always, nowadays, to be the last. But somehow you don't quite believe that. There is always another – one more – interesting job to attempt.

Behind all this you know that the next main phase must be the death of one of you; and then the last death. It is as if each tree in your, as in others', private woods has been marked and numbered, with its due date for felling, the number of its rings, including the tree that is you. Pascal was quite brutal here, or frank in a French rather than an English way, seeing us all under sentence of death, seeing friends butchered, and towards the end in grief and desperation waiting for our own call: 'The last act is bloody, however fine the rest of the play. They throw earth over your head and it is finished for ever.'

'We die as we live, alone.' Not quite; but we go into the dark alone, as those curtains close. 'You have played enough;/You have eaten and drunk enough. Now it is time for you to depart.' Many early writers, such as Horace there, were consistently stoical: 'Lament no more/These things are so.'

As the last of the aunts and uncles on both sides dies, we realise we are now within the near-final group of Time's cohorts. 'Next for shaving.' It is all so temporary, the possession of a bit of space and a fragment in time. A friend went to look at a house in Leicester in which he had lived as a child. A little boy stared at him curiously from the small garden. The stranger said: 'Hello. I used to live here too. This was my home once.' The boy was entirely uncomprehending. Who was this unknown old man making a claim on his family's earth, private enclosure? 'No', he answered, 'this is our house.' So it is. Until the next bus comes along.

The army of the dead increases weekly, monthly, falling around you like spent leaves. At the worst, you come back from holiday wondering who has 'gone' in your absence. Occasionally, you even feel left behind. The caravan must move on and pick up more and more passengers, more and more speed, leaving little mounds of memory – voices, presences – most of which will last no more than until the next generation. Yet for you, these people remain present; not simply not forgotten, but *there*. It is eventually a little crowded. You acquire the habit of looking first each day at the obituaries in the newspapers. The sense increases that the call may come on any day, in any way.

On some days you think of things still not done or done badly. In some translucently painful poems, Hardy looked back with remorse at his own misuse, abuse, of time. Yet still: 'Never, I own, expected I/That life would be all fair.'

On other days you are cheerful, as though you really will live for ever; or if not that, then you will 'go on regardless' until you drop. You do not share, or not yet, the 'boom, boom' which Forster's Mrs Moore hears, the final echo of meaninglessness. You respect her, though, for facing bravely the lack of any props of faith, any sense that she should be 'redeeming the time', that time can ever be redeemed.

Taking Stock; and Soldiering On

Past the time to sort out the Inner Last Will. Time to rid yourself of spare baggage, material and mental; time for stripping down and keeping only those worries, duties, hopes which are worth keeping. 'How much must be forgotten, even love/How much must be forgiven, even love'; Auden's haunting couplet is too hopeless, too bare, for me, even at this stage.

Stripping down is not indifferentism. You may be virtually certain that the years to come could be counted on two hands, if not one. But you have to go on; as if . . . . You must not allow yourself to say – except in the most practical way: 'This suit will see me out.' Be ready to be bored by the old one; go out and

229

buy another. Neither say: 'I won't see that' of a grandchild's wedding, or a cure for cancer, or the completion of a local bypass. Someone will enjoy or benefit from them afterwards. Remain neat and tidy and sunny. Worst of all is the unwillingness to welcome new experiences or even to make new friends. Die with your boots on.

Carlyle was Calvinistically harsh but bracing here: 'The foul sluggard's comfort – "It will last my time".' Less daunting, more reviving, is the down-to-earth injunction: 'Go on. Spend it. Enjoy it. Welcome it. You can't take it with you.' I remember with great pleasure a sign outside a Rotterdam 'porn' cinema: 'Old age pensioner couples half-price before 5 p.m.'.

Shakespeare's 'A good life brings a good death' sounds like a tenacious but hardly assimilated proverb. Yet Montaigne said much the same. It is a hard injunction; about being all the time ready, in the sense of trying never to do anything of which you might be, at the end, ashamed.

Parenthetically, stranger beliefs surround the habits of death itself. Such as that the best and young go first. 'Whom the Gods love dies young', Menander said, and an English proverb echoes it. 'Death devours lambs as well as sheep.' 'Oh Sir, the good die first . . .' opened the passage from Wordsworth quoted earlier. Those sentiments will survive as long as men go to war; and are probably even more deep-seated and lasting than those man-manufactured reapers.

On the manner of facing death when you know it is near, Browning in 'Prospice' was typically confident: 'I would hate that death bandaged my eyes, and forbore/And bade me creep past'. One might hope so, and hope that Kipling's less histrionic lines on a military execution, but histrionic in his way, would not be nearer our attitude: 'I would not look on Death, which being known/Men led me to him, blindfold and alone.'

Calm Acceptance; The Room at the Back of the Shop

When they are not caressing us with flatteries, today's mass media of communication bombard us with 'oo-ah's, with carefully tailored instances of the apparently irreducible cruelty, barbarism, wantonness of mankind; all of which is true, but in their hands becomes presentation rather than substance. As it does when they change tack and become callow, shallow cheerleaders. At such times we need, recalling Montaigne's homely image, to retire to our room at the back of the shop, where we can be ourselves and take stock. I would prefer then, so far as possible, the company of those I love, and of books, the comforts of language and so of mind and heart working at best stretch. Somewhere in there we may begin to at least half believe in the intensely slow movement towards civility, if not towards more.

There are special exceptions. Some who have contemplated or, more, attempted suicide, look thereafter not as though they would try again but rather as though they have passed through a certain gate, and come back; and that ever after they can face the thought of death with equanimity, whether it comes heralded or unheralded. They hold quietly firm but are ready when the time comes to let go without complaint.

'Time must have a stop', says Shakespeare's Henry. 'Good' say some. The idea of endless life cannot be borne. 'If there wasn't death I think you couldn't go on', Stevie Smith remarked equably, echoing Bacon's earlier 'I have often thought upon death, and I find it the least of all evils.' This is a different cast of mind from that of most.

Emily Dickinson, we saw, also mounted that chariot willingly and equably: 'You'll find it – when you try to die – / The Easier to let go – For recollecting such as went – / You could not spare – You know.' Even more assured is the condition of being 'absolute for death'; that is rare and, as in Shakespeare there, recommended most often by those not immediately threatened.

Swinburne, characteristically and whether the music fits or not, caught the tired-with-life mood lyrically:

231

We thank with brief thanksgiving
Whatever gods may be
That no man lives forever,
That dead men rise up never;
That even the weariest river
Winds somewhere safe to sea.

Music apart, the weight of the whole passage, its pivot, lies in that small, remarkably comfort-bearing word, 'safe'.

At other times, when their spirits are low, old people may be driven towards the end of hope. If death is not the end, what will the end be? Even for unbelievers it is hard sometimes to accept a total blankness. Somehow, as I said at the very beginning of this book, the sense persists that a sort of consciousness will remain, a sort of meeting. Not, perhaps, something the Christian might recognise. Yet that tenacious half-conviction may be itself a last remnant of Christian teaching. Meanwhile, and certainly for the Christian Auden in old age, though I like to think also for agnostics: 'After so many years the light is/Novel still and immensely ambitious.' When his time came, he added, he would like to 'Bugger off quietly'; as he did, in a Viennese hotel bedroom. Quickly is not a bad way to go so long as we have just time to tidy up a bit. Perhaps best to have our little going-away bag ready.

So: a bundle of similarly, on the whole, cheering comments. Goethe, nice and tart: 'It's not that age brings childhood back again. Age merely shows what children we remain.' Yeats boldly, histrionically or bluffingly facing the emptiness: 'Death and life were not/Till man made up the whole/Made lock, stock and barrel/Out of his bitter soul.' Forster the humanist, in *Abinger Harvest* quietly, wisely, accepting: 'Death destroys a man but the idea of death saves him.' I now think I can just about understand and agree with that. Emily Dickinson, again, at her gnomic best:

> Forever – is composed of Nows –
> Tis not a different time –
> Except for Infiniteness –
> And Latitude of Home –

And a light-hearted Aeschylus: 'Old men are always young enough to learn with profit'; and Eliot, grave as so often but still setting out: 'Old men should be explorers.'

A Little Night Music

Now, as I reach the end of this field trip, I wish I could sum up, briefly and however simply, my own journey from Potternewton and its grave all those years ago to today. I do not think I can manage that. My life has seen many and surprising changes; and – I think – I regret none of them. Shaw once remarked: 'Everywhere I went, I learned something.' I could not totally make that claim; but much of it, yes.

I want only to say or indicate a little about Englishness; not about chauvinism, that corrupt form of patriotism which so often makes one shy away even from claiming to be patriotic.

Of all the foreign places we have known, we were lucky enough to live in three for a moderately long time. From each we learned something about confronting life gaily, openly, expectantly, directly; none of those are lessons England *pre-eminently* offers. I could imagine being a proud citizen of any one of them.

But we almost all are pulled back to our native land, and find there an inwardness we can find nowhere else. We discover then, if not before, qualities we love. None of them is unique to England or to any other country; but their special mixture, their brew, is unique to each place and holds its native-born.

Irving Horowitz, in *Behemoth*, his recent massive survey of political sociology, has a generously humane and measured judgement. The English, he says, may not have equalled the achievements in high culture of the Germans or the French.

But they have, more than these others, 'a constitutional tradition of compassionate justice'. I hope that's right.

So here is a clutch of four sentiments I would greatly like to claim as typical of this culture at its best; something of the unique English mixture: down-to-earth; companionable; sometimes optimistic, humane, even mystical; sharing the sense of time and place and the neighbourly:

Shakespeare, illustrating simple rooted depth, the acceptance of mortality and a sharp marketing eye: 'Death, as the Psalmist saith, is certain to all; all shall die . . . How a good yoke of bullocks at Stamford Fair?'

Johnson's acquaintance Oliver Edwards: 'I have tried too in my time to be a philosopher; but, I don't know how, cheerfulness was always breaking in.'

The extreme but homely poignancy of being left on the shore when all friends are dead: 'Since Penelope Noakes of Duppas Hill is gone, no one will ever call me Nelly again.'*

And George Herbert, surfacing once more. We need not share his faith to appreciate his joy:

> And now in age I bud again,
> After so many deaths I live and write,
> I once more smell the dew and rain,
> And relish versing.

---

*I do not know where I first found this wonderful lament. I have since seen it in Auden and Kronenberg's *Faber Book of Aphorisms*, but even there it is attributed simply to 'An Old Lady'. I would be very glad to know its source.